ChristianDior

Christian Dior
THE MAN WHO MADE THE WORLD LOOK NEW

Marie-France Pochna

Translated from the French
by Joanna Savill

Foreword by
Stanley Marcus

ARCADE PUBLISHING
NEW YORK

FIRST ENGLISH-LANGUAGE EDITION

Library of Congress Cataloging-in-Publication Data

       Pochna, Marie-France, 1941–
         [Christian Dior. English]
         Christian Dior : the man who made the world look new / Marie-France Pochna ; translated from the French by Joanna Savill ; foreword by Stanley Marcus. —1st English language ed.
            p. cm.
         Includes bibliographical references and index.
         ISBN 1-55970-340-7 (hardcover)
         1. Dior, Christian. 2. Fashion designers—France—Paris—Biography. 3. Costume design—France—Paris—History—20th century. I. Title
        T T505.D5P6313 1996
        746.2'092—dc20   96-13219

Published in the United States by Arcade Publishing, Inc., New York

Distributed by Little, Brown and Company

10 9 8 7 6 5 4 3 2 1

BP

Designed by API

PRINTED IN THE UNITED STATES OF AMERICA

To all those who wake up late in life

and to the one who keeps me from sleeping

Fashion is an act of faith. And in an age where no secret is sacred, where fabrications and false confidences are the stuff of daily life, fashion has retained its mystery...and never has it been talked about so much — the best possible proof of its power to enchant.

—Dior, *Christian Dior and I*

Contents

Foreword

My first meeting with Christian Dior was on his initial trip to the United States in September of 1947 when he came to Dallas to be the recipient of the Neiman Marcus "Award for Distinguished Service in the Field of Fashion."

My brother Edward and his wife Betty were in New York on his arrival from France, and met him at the dock and escorted him to his hotel. That evening Edward telephoned me to say that they would put him on the plane the following day for the continuation of his journey to Dallas.

"You'll find him to be completely different from any of the French designers you've met," Eddie told me on the phone. "He is shy, he's more interested in learning how America lives than in the subject of fashion." He added, "Treat him gently."

After six years of a fashion blackout that prevailed during the war period, the debut of a new couturier was news in itself, but his initial collection in the spring of 1947 was explosive because of the radical silhouette he introduced, known as the New Look.

The revolutionary nature of his designs was reported so widely and enthusiastically by the fashion press that by the time copies and interpretations of the clothes reached the stores some months later, fashionable women were clamoring to see and buy them. Nothing as exciting had occurred since Coco Chanel startled the fashion world in 1925 with her La Garçonne style.

The name Dior achieved identity almost overnight: a new star had been born! The New Look, with its nineteenth-century ceintures and stiffened body construction, was a modernized rendition of the fashions of yesteryear.

For his audacity, Dior was labeled by the press as the new "fashion czar" and as "dictator of the silhouettes." Actually, this modest person was somewhat amazed by what he had wrought. For he had no more ambitions to wield power or pretensions to dictatorship than Charlie Chaplin had when, playing his role of the tramp, he was thrust into power in *The Great Dictator.*

Dior was a gentle, kind man who had concern about the aesthetics of the world in which he lived; his interests in art and music, flowers and costumes were his qualifications for his career as a creative fashion designer. He demonstrated the bon mot of Oscar Wilde, who commented, "I have the simplest of tastes; I am easily satisfied with the best."

This was the man who stepped off the plane in Dallas on a hot afternoon. To my relief, it was unnecessary for me to use my inadequate French, for he spoke and understood English.

As we drove away from the airport, I told him I was going to drive through a beautiful section of Dallas where the rich and famous lived. He quietly said, "Oh, no. I would much prefer to see where and how the working people live. The rich live the same all over the world."

So we altered our route to accommodate his desire. We talked about contemporary art, books and painting, cooking and wine — everything but fashion. He was so communicative that by the time we arrived at his hotel I felt as comfortable with him as though I had known him for years.

And so it continued as our acquaintanceship matured into friendship. In Paris, in the country, at theaters, in museums, at luncheons and dinners, rarely did we ever mention fashion. Never did he pressure me to buy, though his *vendeuses* were never shy in reminding our buying entourage to respect the *caution,* or minimal purchasing requirements, for the privilege of attending *les collections.*

In this biography I was pleased to note that Marie-France Pochna has acknowledged the able staff that Dior assembled for his *maison de couture,* a remarkable feat for a neophyte in the world of big business — which the House of Dior rapidly became.

Among them, I should like especially to mention the names of

Madame Bricard, who edited the collections, and Jacques Rouët, who became general manager and financial controller, and provided Dior with experienced business counsel without ever intruding into the artistic domain. His contribution to the success of Dior was brilliant. Yvonne Minassian and Elyette Roux were both superb couture salespeople. Roger Vivier, the great shoe designer who headed the shoe salon, and Ted Manteau, the director of Dior furs, brought immediate authority to two specialized fields of fashion. For a man who had never headed a large business enterprise, Dior, with the aid of Marcel Boussac, put together an extraordinary group of professionals, all of them stars in their own right.

Dior died in France on the eve of the opening of the first facsimile reproduction of the Dior boutique, created for the Neiman Marcus "Quinzaine Française" in Dallas.

Stanley Marcus
Dallas, Texas
April 1996

Preface

How did I come to write this book? The fact is, my entry into the Dior story was through the side door.

It was the spring of 1989. I had just published a biography of the Italian billionaire Gianni Agnelli, a book whose appearance had created considerable buzz. One day my publisher passed on a proposal unlike any I had ever received before: to act as a ghostwriter for an important French businessman. The idea tempted me. For one thing, the arrangement was to remain a secret and I love secrets. And the businessman in question was Bernard Arnault, a man everyone in Paris had heard of but no one really knew. Arnault had recently made the news by buying Christian Dior and also taking over the reins of the prestigious LVMH company (Louis Vuitton–Moët Hennessy) — at the tender age of forty. That had to mean he was brilliant. But as with most people whose rise to the top is meteoric, he was treated less than kindly by the critics. He had stepped on a number of toes, and popular opinion held him to be an unscrupulous corporate raider. Arnault had set out to write a book in the hope of clarifying the visionary strategies that had brought him to the economic pinnacle in the world of fashion and elegance. He also wanted to explain why he was drawn into the world of luxury and refinement. His two main companies, Christian Dior and Louis Vuitton–Moët Hennessy, consist of a cluster of businesses with interests in three areas: fashion, with Dior, Christian Lacroix, Givenchy, Kenzo, and Céline, and its perfumes; luggage, with Louis Vuitton; and finally, champagnes and spirits, with Möet Hennessy. The company's net value is in excess of $20 billion, making it the number one stock on the Paris exchange.

In early summer, I found myself face to face with the man and we began to work. It was fascinating to hear him talk, for he had that infallible lucidity one finds among people with a clear vision of the future. But at the end of the summer, Arnault suddenly announced that he had given up on the idea of a book. By then, however, I had gotten hooked by the project. Something told me not to let it go.

That "something" became clear several months later. One of the anecdotes Arnault had told me stayed with me. Why had he bought Dior rather than some other company? He had been handed the company's portfolio while living in the United States, having decided in 1981 to leave France, because the presence of Communists in the new government, he thought, boded ill for the business climate in his native country. He had set up house in New Rochelle, and one day, needing to buy a bathrobe, he went to a nearby Bloomingdales in White Plains. "The Dior display suddenly made me nostalgic for France. What was before me was so clearly more refined than the other displays. And it stood out in my memory. Later, when I was given the chance to buy Christian Dior, I remembered White Plains and Bloomingdales. I have no doubt that unconsciously it had an effect on me."

One evening, I went to a ball at the Château de Vaux-le-Vicomte, one of the most magical places in the world. The owners were renting it to Dior Perfumes, which was using it to celebrate the launch of their latest product, "Dune." The grounds seemed like paradise, and the chateau shimmered in the light. It was like a re-creation of those royal feasts at Versailles, reflected in the fountains and gardens seemingly inspired by André Le Nôtre himself. Arnault's story about the Dior display at Bloomingdale's came back to me. For me, this ball was rekindling the beauty and mystery and the unique tradition of French elegance. And Dior, to me, represented that tradition better than any other name. I began writing the next day. The door to Christian Dior was opening before me, and I went through it in search of that magic power Dior had used to create the New Look.

But how would I go about the task, since I had never met Christian Dior and was not a fashion specialist? In 1987 at Northeast Harbor I had the privilege of meeting the writer Marguerite Yourcenar. In the course of our conversation, she said something that has stayed with me and encouraged me. "Books," she told me, "are like a ladder; and other people's ideas are the steps." That is certainly true about this *Christian Dior*. It is the fruit of countless conversations (several hundred hours' worth), a host of stories, personal accounts, memories, and opinions that I have collected, pondered, and mulled over at length before finally attempting to recreate the person Dior was. But this re-creation has been a collective endeavor, made possible only by the fact that Christian Dior has remained so very alive in the minds and hearts of those who knew him that all I had to do was gather the fallen leaves to imagine how the tree must have been. There were days when a conversation with the actor Jean Marais, describing a Sunday in the country with Marlene Dietrich and Jean Cocteau, was all I needed to capture the lightness of being that was present in Dior. I spent a long afternoon with Denise Tual in the little apartment where she lives alone in almost Spartan simplicity, shriveled with age, but presiding with such radiance over photos, letters, and sketches done by friends — treasures amassed in the course of a life lived to the utmost. That one afternoon instantly gave me a sense of what it was like to live in the days when it was easy to strike out as an artist, a producer . . . a couturier, without ever really being concerned about money (certainly not in the way we are now, where everything revolves around it). I realized then too that even in the period when he could not afford a square meal, Dior would not have felt like a down-and-out. One interview that took me months to secure — as there are those who would prefer to keep "their" Dior for themselves — led me to the writer Edmonde Charles-Roux, in her *garçonnière* at the top of an elegant set of stairs in a house on the Left Bank, with a decor so alive with references to another era that one could easily imagine the Goncourts dropping in on a regular basis. Madame Charles-Roux gave a brilliant discourse on style, contrasting the overabundant, sensual world of Dior to Chanel's minimalistic approach, pointing up the right-wing approach of the former (the bourgeois) as opposed to the left-wing attitude of the latter (the orphan). I listened, fascinated, to this account of the way in which you can find politics lurking even in fashion. A drink at the Ritz bar with Art Buchwald with his omniscient pipe and gravelly voice was just like a blast from the Paris of the 1950s, and one of the best ways to find instant rejuvenation you could ever get for the price of two glasses of champagne. I could go on listing special moments like these — some of them amusing, others a jumbled mass of memories with a pearl buried somewhere in the middle — but each containing one precious scrap, unlocking new vistas like a newly turned-up card in a game of solitaire. In due course, I also met all those who had worked closely with Dior: Jacques Rouët with his infallible memory, who ran the business at Dior's side and continued to make it grow for thirty years, and Hervé du Périer, who was in charge of licensing. Their tales had the same flavor as those told to me by others who lived through the Dior years — all of whom saw that period as the greatest adventure of their lives. This book owes a lot, of course, to Dior's successors on the artistic side: Frédéric Castet, Marc Bohan, and Gianfranco Ferré, who creates the collections today. And of course, indeed, there is Dior himself. He must have known that, one day, others justifiably curious about his life and times would want to piece together the Dior puzzle and retrace his steps.

Careful man that he was, Dior could never have allowed posterity to make random assumptions about Christian Dior. It was for this reason that he provided some key pieces of evidence. His autobiography, *Christian Dior and I*, was written just a few months before his death, as if he knew what was about to happen. It has served as a guide for me throughout this book, revealing his love of riddles, astrology, and lucky charms — which even led him to give his dresses names like "Crossword," "Patience," "Guessing Game," or "Hide and Seek." I was not surprised to find a few pranks of this nature in his writing, nor to discover a series of clues that eventually helped me to unlock certain doors, including the most important one, leading to his childhood. That guiding thread was not always apparent as I wrote my book, but became crystal clear once I had finished it. After all, Dior himself had traveled back down that same path, one could say, forced by the circumstances of life to return to his youth in order to find the way forward. So it is that his creative calling, which he lost and eventually rediscovered, ended up providing the driving force, the suspense even, for this story.

The Christian Dior of this book is unlike the one who inhabits the pages of fashion magazines. It is the story of a man whose beginnings seemed to have so little to do with fashion design that he never dreamed of choosing it as his profession. Dior's extraordinary and sudden success led him to America, an America that would celebrate and consecrate his work and bring him international success. As in the world of art, fashion can be created in London or Paris, or Milan, but discovered and consecrated in New York. In essence, America did for the work of Christian Dior what France did for Woody Allen, Merce Cunningham, and Bob Wilson. As Cecil Beaton wrote in his beautiful book *A Century of Elegance and the Art of Living,* "We are all French." He was referring to the respect all of us have for beauty in all of its forms and particularly in our daily life. In that spirit, we can say that Christian Dior belongs to America as much as to his native land.

Marie-France Pochna

ChristianDior

1

Granville's Corner

Dior is that nimble genius unique to our
age with the magical name — combining God and gold [*dieu et or*].

— Jean Cocteau

*A*s September came and summer faded, one by one the chairs and
tables outside the casino disappeared, shutters were drawn over hotel
windows, and the resort town of Granville closed down for the season.
For the next nine months it would trade its light-opera gaiety and
dance-hall music for the more reserved air of a quiet English Sunday
afternoon. The locals resumed their sabbath promenades up and down
the Plat Gousset, the wide esplanade bordered by the sea on one side
and the cliffs on the other. The good burghers of Granville, their wives
on their arms, would raise their roll-brimmed hats to one another in
greeting as they strolled. High on the cliff tops you could see the old
shipping town to the left and to the right, glimpses of private homes
hidden amid the trees — like hesitant silhouettes floating across a
canvas by Eugène Boudin, masts dissolving in a sodden Pissarro sky, or

misty seascapes by local artist Léon Carré. . . . Once again the town became the domain of painters and solitary dreamers.

There was no time of the year little Christian Dior liked better than the stillness of the off-season. It was 1907 when his parents took up residence in a large house on the very edge of the cliff tops overlooking the plunging sea below. Its sparse vegetation only accentuated its desert-island feel, and Madame Dior quickly set about surrounding herself with a garden. A row of hastily planted pine trees became the small boy's first hiding place. Sitting among the tiny trees, he liked to imagine he was in some dense virgin forest. The little thicket, which grew as he did, would remain his private haven.

As dusk fell on stormy nights he would spend hours glued to the window of the linen room watching the gathering clouds darkening the horizon, while the chambermaids sewed by the light of the oil lamp. The ghost stories they told made his older brother Raymond chuckle but gave Christian goose flesh. So did the closet in the playroom next door. Raymond would sometimes push him into its black interior and play awful tricks on him. The linen room, on the other hand, was Christian's favorite. Lulled by the women's voices as they hummed popular ballads and lullabies, the anxieties of the twilight hours would dissolve into thistledown softness as he watched the flickering shadows cast by the lamplight. Outside, the three-master signaled her return to port, the fine Norman drizzle fell softly, funeral bells tolled. . . . Inside, the sounds of the night were muffled by distance and falling darkness.

Each Christmas the family would pay a visit to the Paris grandparents. The children would sit up on the long limousine seats in their sailor hats, surrounded by ladies in enormous feathered headgear with veils over their faces to keep off the dust. Parents, grandmother, governess, chambermaid, and mechanic would squeeze in too, with no thought for comfort, while a mountain of baggage teetered on the roof. But when the trip was finally over, after countless breakdowns and flat tires, there they would be in dazzling, wonderful Paris, the City of Light. This was the fairy-tale world of electricity, of the cinema, of Place de la Concorde, of the Châtelet Theater where you could see Jules Verne's adventure with Michel Strogoff large as life going around the world in eighty days or be frightened half out of your wits by Lucifer's real live horns in *Les Pilules du diable.*

This was a world a hundred times more marvelous than the pages of Christian's storybooks. At home in Granville he would pore over the pages of Charles Perrault's fairy tales or *Twenty Thousand Leagues under the Sea,* imagining the grand saloon of the *Nautilus* — to him, the height of splendor — and Captain Nemo's lair, where ghosts danced on trunks and sideboards. Equally fascinating were the Japanese screens and bamboo partitions decorating the hallway and staircase in the Granville house. He would clamber onto a stool to peer at them more closely, spending hours fingering the embroidered wings of a painted bird, clicking the beads of a blind, or reaching out to catch a butterfly. Time and again he would tumble to the floor as one of the leather seats toppled beneath him. He was Aladdin in a magic cave, with some glittering new treasure everywhere he looked. The glass cabinets in the drawing room thrilled him too: porcelain duchesses crammed against rococo pagodas and feathered fans, shepherds and shepherdesses embracing on the lids of china candy boxes, and bits of bright Murano glass. Best of all, though, were the giant plumes of pampas grass and satin flowers adorning the fireplace. Each night as he lay in bed staring at the colored-glass night light dangling from the sculptured ceiling-rose above his head, this jumble of mysterious objects would dance under his eyelids until he nodded off.

But nothing fired Christian's imagination more than Carnival. Celebrating the last days before Lent with a fancy-dress parade was a time-honored tradition in Granville and local children were initiated into its joys at a very early age. Christian was three when he first took part. Dressed in a sailor suit, complete with white hat and ribbon, he trotted along hand in hand with Raymond and a gaggle of other suitably chaperoned tots from good families. Such festivities! Flowers, colors, and decorations waved everywhere they looked, and when the King of Carnival passed by, their little eyes popped out on stalks. What guise was he in this year? His Exotic Majesty Abd al-Aziz VIII perhaps? Or the fisherman's protector, King of the Shores and Prince of Penguins? Why not the God of the Table, the Baron of Pancakes and Tarts?

Young Christian would stand for hours watching the floats go by. First came the Trumpeteers of the Farmyard, leading the Bibi-Tapins, veterans from the Thirty-second Regiment, and sounding a fanfare. Next came the gigantic, grotesque figures known as the Long-Days-Without-End, followed in stark contrast by the Lilliputians, no less grotesque with their explosion of bright colors and brazen gestures. Dior's childhood drawings were full of these fabulous images — marchionesses glowing against gigantic suns, mahouts in emerald bracelets astride white elephants. For four sleepless days and nights, an unforgettable cavalcade gamboled through flowered arches to the sound of waltzes, polkas, and fireworks.

The Carnival tradition in Granville dates back to the grand old days when it served as a point of departure for ships sailing to Newfoundland. Until the beginning of the century this town lying proudly atop a rocky outcrop overlooking the English Channel was most famous for cod fishing and shipbuilding (second only to its neighbor and rival, Saint-Malo). Voyages to Newfoundland would usually begin around Shrove Tuesday, but before weighing anchor and sailing off to face shipwreck, sickness, and cold, the departing voyagers would kick up their heels in an endless round of festivities. Although the seafaring activities gradually came to an end with the turn of the century, the Carnival tradition lived on. There was nothing to rival it, not even the spectacle of the fiercely contested races between the fishing boats of Granville and nearby Cancale, held in the bay between the Mont-Saint-Michel monastery and the Chausey Islands. The mood of general exhilaration that seized the people of Granville at Carnival was eventually extended right through into summer for quite a different audience. With the arrival of the railways and the new fashion for taking seaside holidays, the Granville of the Belle Epoque gradually shook off its past as a sober port city and became a fashionable resort.

This was the heyday of the bourgeoisie. They built new buildings, invented new pastimes, and indulged in them to the hilt. The original casino was replaced by a more luxurious establishment in 1911. The Tranchée des Anglais, the lane leading to the beach, was widened in a massive operation involving the removal of a whole section of the rock face. Behind this full-scale tourist development was the Société Hôtelière de Normandie, financed by the Goulds, a multimillionaire American family very much part of French society of the day. Their new Hôtel Normandie put an end to the reign of the Granville Palace and the Hôtel des Bains. With its fine sandy beach and full range of sporting and musical entertainment, Granville found itself rejoicing in the title of "the little Monaco of the North" and became the meeting place for the best society, who flocked there year in and year out, complete with a full entourage of trunks, children, and nannies.

Christian Dior was born on January 21, 1905, at one-thirty in the morning. He was the second child of Alexandre Louis Maurice Dior, aged thirty-two, and his wife, Marie-Madeleine Juliette Martin, aged twenty-six and born in the Loire Valley town of Angers. Physically there was a marked difference between Christian and his older brother. Raymond was solid, broad-backed, square-headed. Christian was fine-boned, with an almond-shaped face and quick, bright, slightly slanted eyes. The older brother was a true Norman while the younger had inherited the features of his Angevin mother.

In 1909, four years after Christian was born, he and Raymond were joined by Jacqueline, then by Bernard a year later. The second child continued to be the odd one out, resembling a delicate shaft of bamboo next to the solid forms of his brothers and sister. He would most resemble his youngest sister Ginette, born in 1917.

Maurice Dior's one goal was to make his family happy, especially his wife. It was chiefly to accommodate her that the Diors moved into the villa known as Les Rumbs (named for the rhombus-shaped points of the compass). These were new surroundings, far from the lower town with its shops and markets, its inn serving local cider, and its intrusive odors. In fact, whenever the wind blew in the wrong direction, sickening fumes from Maurice Dior's fertilizer factory in the outlying village of Dionville would waft through the streets. "It smells of Dior today," the townsfolk used to say wryly. High in their new abode by the sea, Maurice and his wife were now spared these irritations.

Madeleine Dior immediately set about the task that was to occupy her for years to come — surrounding herself with greenery. Her first alteration of the simple pink roughcast facade of the house was to add a verandah, as part of a conservatory she planned to put there. Little Christian soon became caught up in his mother's passion for plants. He learned their names and descriptions by heart from colorful mail-order seed catalogues and would rush to meet the postman each day in case another had arrived. He was the only one of the Dior children to inherit his mother's green thumb and followed her like a shadow, listening in on her conversations with the gardeners and sharing her concern in the ongoing battle with the winds that constantly threatened her botanical endeavors. Despite the windbreaks Madame Dior had built around the edge of their garden, her plants consistently failed to take root and she was finally forced to erect a greenhouse at the bottom of the vegetable garden where she could store her plants at the end of the season until the following spring.

In 1911 the family moved to Paris, relegating the Granville house to the status of vacation residence. The apartment was in the fashionable Sixteenth Arrondissement, in the neighborhood known as La Muette, near the Bois de Boulogne. Christian was six years old and initially found the change of scene most displeasing, uprooted as he was from his lazy, idyllic childhood cocooned in shrubbery and flowers. But he soon fell in love with the new home.

Madame Dior was bent on decorating her Parisian residence in the fashion of the day, ostensibly Louis XVI but adapted to the tastes, and interpretation, of the time. Her son became entranced with its lacquered moldings, glass-paneled doors, and damask wallpaper. It was the height of modernity, a complete change from the "haute époque" style of the 1880s or the heavy Napoleon III fashion predominant in upper-middle-class homes in those days. These were ordered, cozy childhood years, spent snugly happy in an attractive apartment in a fashionable neighborhood, between strolls in the Bois de Boulogne and schooling at the Lycée Gerson where he made his first friends.

Madeleine Dior was as methodical in bringing up her children as she was in the planning of her grand horticultural projects. This was the Victorian era, when open demonstrations of affection were considered likely to weaken the character, and strictness was the norm. Even the youngest, Ginette (who later took the name Catherine), recalls how her mother "was even stricter with us girls than with the boys." Christian was the only one who managed to bridge the gap between the two worlds. Considered "mother's pet" by his brothers and sisters, he found it nonetheless no easy task gaining entry to his mother's world. It was only after he had memorized the names of all her flowers and spent hours trailing her around the house, studying her at length in her chosen surroundings, that an unspoken complicity slowly grew between them, nurtured by the many rooms and gardens of his early years.

The telephone was barely in its infancy. So when Maurice Dior had one installed at Les Rumbs he was among the first in town to do so. Their number, in fact, was Granville 12. The ringing of the forbidden magical instrument never failed to excite the children, but no one "visited" the telephone without parental permission. Such rare treats entailed entering Maurice Dior's quarters, which were out of bounds to anyone but the master of the house. His study at the back of the building had its own separate entrance, allowing visitors to come and go without disturbing the rest of the household. Access was via a little enclosed porch with bay windows and a mosaic floor with the motif of a diamond-shaped compass needle (the rhombus) in the center. This was where the telephone was kept, locked away out of sight inside a wooden clock case to which Maurice Dior held the key.

His father's quarters made Christian stiff with awe. A Renaissance wall clock in a pewter case adorned with some particularly fearsome halberds, and a Negress mask that looked ready to devour him on the spot, filled him with unmitigated terror. The lithographs depicting swashbuckling, mustachioed musketeers were hardly more reassuring. Although he knew his father to be a good and gentle man, he always entered the study with a shiver of apprehension. This was also the scene of scoldings and punishments and, despite the fascination of the telephone, remained associated with less enjoyable activities — as did the dining room next door. The solid Henri II furniture was heavy with the stiffness of interminable meals under the stern and watchful eye of his father, who would preside over the gathering in his upright collar, every now and then uttering some incontestable pronouncement. Monsieur Dior exercised his fatherly authority with much the same directorial style he showed in his role as chairman of a number of companies.

Maurice Dior had, in fact, done very well for himself. Thanks to him and his cousin Lucien, his partner and a member of parliament (and future minister), the Dior family found itself elevated by several rungs on the social ladder — from the peasantry to the upper middle class. Originally from Savigny-le-Vieux, on the border between the Calvados and Manche *départements,* these farmers-turned-industrialists had built up one of the most flourishing manufacturing businesses in the French chemical industry, in just three generations.

The founder of the Dior fortune and of the amazing Dior success story was Maurice's grandfather Louis-Jean Dior (1812–1874), a tenant-farmer and mayor of the town of Savigny-le-Vieux. In 1832 he set up a fertilizer plant at Donville-les-Bains, just out of Granville. Initially he produced char from oxidized roots but then hit upon the idea of importing guano from Chile and Peru and using the local seaweed. His five sons subsequently expanded the business across the region. In the next generation the two cousins Lucien and Maurice Dior took charge. By 1905 the pair had increased the company's capital to 1.5 million francs, business was booming, and it was decided they would diversify into the manufacture of sulfuric acid for phosphate fertilizers, a concept unheard of at the time. In those days France was a leader in this field and Normandy, where Dior was the biggest producer, accounted for 15 percent of the nation's output. Dior also owned phosphate plants in the Meuse valley and the Ardennes Mountains on the Belgian border.

In 1912 Lucien and Maurice Dior converted the business to a limited partnership and named it Dior and Sons. They were the sole directors, sitting on a capital of 4 million francs. The business was at its peak and for the next twenty years would continue to grow. Subsidiaries were set up around Brittany, at Landerneau, Rennes, and Saint-Marc, near Brest, where the development of a line of detergents under the Saint-Marc name brought even further financial success. In 1923 the company's stock was floated and its capital increased several times over.

The boom years of his father's business were the years of Christian Dior's childhood. The move to the Paris apartment, on Rue Albéric-Magnard, coincided with the establishment of Maurice and Lucien's administrative headquarters in the French capital, at 9 Rue d'Athènes. Maurice's brother Henri was not so keen to leave his native Normandy, doctor of laws though he might have been, and so remained a silent partner, happy to live on the income the company provided while he indulged his love of letters and dabbled in poetry. And while their father Alexandre had moved to Paris only upon retiring, Maurice was still in his thirties when he decided to introduce his family to a life of grand Parisian style. Dinner at Rue Albéric-Magnard was served by maîtres d'hôtel in white gloves, and Madame Dior, whose flower arrangements were much celebrated, procured her blooms (often accompanied by young Christian) chez Orève, the most celebrated florist of the area. Money flowed like water. The astounding transformation of Les Rumbs, the Parisian high life, and this quest for magnificence at all costs was also linked to Madeleine's secret rivalry with her cousin-in-law Charlotte Dior, wife of Lucien the member of parliament. The partners' wives had fallen out but continued to monitor each other's doings from afar, and Charlotte Dior, who divided her time between a stately home in Normandy and her Paris apartment on Place Malesherbes, was never one to count her pennies.

Lucien was the leading light of the family. Born in 1867, he was a graduate of the prestigious Polytechnique and was elected to parliament in 1905 as the conservative Union Nationale candidate for Avranches, in the Manche *département* near Granville. He remained in parliament until he died in 1932. His father, Lucien senior, had been mayor of Granville, but young Lucien had greater ambitions. He held several posts at the local level, including chief judge of the Granville court (1903–1906), was codirector of the flourishing family business, and tirelessly promoted employment possibilities in Granville and environs, playing a significant role in developing the town's port facilities. When he became minister of trade in the Briand and Poincaré cabinets (1921–24) as part of the National Coalition, his particular interests in the area of foreign trade were in oil and silk products. To this day there is a Boulevard Lucien Dior in Granville, although he received merciless treatment from the local press at the time. The political climate of France's Third Republic was lively, to say the least. The Diors were Catholics and pro-Republic, which, in an era when the shadow of the Dreyfus affair still lingered, classified them as "enlightened Catholics" rather than anticlerical, and somewhat right-wing. Lucien Dior was elected primarily by the "reactionary" vote and, despite his constant assertions that he was a progressive, he was regularly lampooned in *Le Granvillais*, the local newspaper, which accused him of being a monarchist and other such things. As is the way in provincial towns, it was a reputation that extended to the rest of the family.

And who were the rest of the family? Five branches issued from Louis-Jean Dior, founder of the company. The eldest son, Louis (of the Dior-Bouttevillain line), left the factory to establish a brewery at Val-ès-Fleurs, a Granville suburb. One of his sons, Georges, set up a coal and cork treatment plant, taking advantage of access to the waters of the Val-ès-Fleurs river, well known to the people of Granville as the ideal spot for doing their laundry. His sister Marguerite was a doctor. The Dior-Perriers, descended from son Victor, were somewhat more original; they included Edmund, a postman by profession but a *chansonnier* by preference, who would sing while delivering the mail! His brothers were a bank clerk and a chiropodist. The line emanating from Armand Dior (the Dior-Lelièvres) was also in manufacturing — one son was a chemical engineer — but of all the Diors, it was clear that Lucien the cabinet minister and Maurice, Christian's father, were those who had done best for themselves. And what a meteoric rise it was! Their fathers, Lucien senior and Alexandre, had married two sisters, Anida and Ernestine Angé, daughters of a formidable mother who earned a living pushing a cart around her village and collecting rags. The rag trade was an integral part of the family's income, as the girls' father, though handsome, had little business acumen. A certain laissez-faire attitude is present in the Dior genes, especially in those blessed with good looks. Alexandre Dior, Christian's grandfather, was a jovial soul who kept open house of a Sunday and who loved baccarat and could often be seen at the casino. He would no doubt have been quite content to make a living at the gaming tables.

In the works of a French painter like Le Nain, there is no mistaking the nationality of the peasants. The origins of the characters in the Dior portrait gallery, tall, broad, rustic, slightly lazy characters, and all of sizable girth, appear similarly unmistakable. This was good Gallic stock, and had been for generations, well over a millennium indeed . . . or so, at least, it was believed. At one point the French origins of the Dior family had been contested — in the Chamber of Deputies, no less, during a parliamentary debate when the historian Salomon Reinach challenged Lucien Dior by insinuating that Dior was actually a Spanish name of Jewish origin. As a result, Lucien instigated a thorough genealogical search, which eventually dated the Dior presence in the region back to the seventeenth century. Once inspired, Lucien decided to take his ancestral quest further, along the ancient roads to the north and, ultimately, as far back as the Viking invasions. It transpired that Diors had come to France with the second wave of Norse colonization, at a time when the duke of Normandy had already consolidated his rule and a Norman state was formed, combining Scandinavian traditions with the Franco-Gaulish system. Prior to the establishment of its fortress by the British in 1493, Granville was a fiefdom encompassing the Lihou peninsula and ruled, it is believed, by a Norman chief by the name of Gran. Local historians, including the authority Charles de La Morandière, do not rule out the Viking connection. Lucien Dior's genealogical research in Denmark then traced the family's origins to Elsinore and their arrival in France back to a request by the duke of Normandy following the treaty of Saint-Clair-sur-Epte. Under this treaty King Charles the Simple ceded the region between Epte and the sea to Rollo, chief of the Normans. According to the invaluable documentation gathered by Lucien, "it is likely that the first Dior to settle in Normandy enjoyed certain rights over the abbey at Savigny-les-Vieux, which would explain the origin of certain title deeds held in the district archives."

Strange are the paths some follow in order to build themselves an identity. Christian Dior, for his part, felt no affinity for his father's world. The return of a ship from Newfoundland or the arrival of a three-master in port with a cargo of guano for the family warehouses failed to arouse his interest. His indifference descended at times to disgust — visits to his father's factories left him "terrified." As he was later to write, "this was certainly at the root of my intense dislike of machinery and my firm determination never to work in an office or anything of that nature." He was guided in all things by his mother. His senses were stimulated by the floral, ornamental opulence of her world.

Beyond a conventional desire to move up the social ladder, Madeleine Dior's passion for beautiful things might be interpreted as an unconscious attempt to make up for the rather less appealing nature of her husband's profession. Were her grand horticultural endeavors perhaps motivated deep down by a need to mask with the fragrance of flowers the unpleasant odors on which his fortune was based? Children are gifted with antennae for subtleties the rest of us remain unaware of and often home in on just the things we would rather remained hidden.

Fascinating too is the instinctive way in which Christian handled his relationship with his father, from a very early age. "Raymond, the eldest, became quite caustic and often clashed with his father," recalls one of the boys' cousins, Michel Dior, "whereas Christian was always very docile." It was as if Christian had already accepted which son should succeed the father, and had ruled himself out from the outset. He felt no need for a contest of wills but showed great respect for his father, with whom he had very little contact owing to an upbringing in which the generations remained quite aloof and a number of subjects were simply never discussed. In the best upper-middle-class circles it was customary not to talk about business or money in front of the children, and Madame Dior strongly adhered to that principle. As Christian Dior later wrote, "My early life was that of a very well behaved, well brought-up little boy, supervised by a series of fräuleins . . . in other words, totally incapable of finding my own way in life."

But such a closeted existence does not preclude the creation of an imaginary other world "between the lines," as it were. While Raymond, the eldest, took on his parents head-on, Christian sought refuge within his own little version of his family life, recasting it in a much rosier light. Obstacles like the lack of contact with his father and his difficulty in establishing a relationship with his mother (although in the latter he had some degree of success) became transformed in his imagination. Later on, in his memoirs *Christian Dior and I,* Dior himself gives us a key to interpretation. He takes his readers on a guided tour, room by room, through the house in Granville and the Paris apartment, from the conservatory to the linen room. Indirectly, through the atmosphere he describes and the places themselves, objects strewn here and there like pieces of his imagination and little havens for his emotions, we are able to re-create his childhood world. Whether intentionally or otherwise, Dior left all the clues to solve what is ultimately a very simple riddle. To young Christian, the Granville house, which he describes as an island in the midst of raging storms, is an allegory for his very first feelings of solitude.

*　　　*　　　*

Exceptional intelligence is inevitably stifled by a parental world that programs children like little automatons, surrounding them with governesses and judging them merely on their scholastic achievements, behavior in class, and aptitude for the piano. Christian, however, was fortunate in having a maternal grandmother who realized very early that this child was different from his brothers and sisters, if only physically. Raymond was a fighter, Jacqueline a tomboy, and Bernard, who was gentle as a lamb, had an introverted side that caused concern. Christian on the other hand was lively and affectionate, interested in everything — and with such an imagination! He epitomized the wonderment of childhood. Take Carnival, for example. Year after year he would await its arrival with mounting excitement, the eternal child. The music, the floats covered in flowers, and the masked balls would fill him with indescribable joy. His greatest delight was in dreaming up a new costume, a talent he displayed early on. He not only had the ideas, he was able to put them on paper. Each year it was Christian his brothers and sisters turned to for dressing up. He soon abandoned the predictable characters like Harlequin and Columbine, Hansel and Gretel, or duchesses in powdered wigs, coming up instead with the most amazing inventions. One year he transformed his sister into a King Neptune with a bodice made of shells and a raffia skirt. There was the time he needed a piece of tartan for a bagpiper's kilt; when none could be found, he painted the pattern directly onto the material. Never without a notebook, he scribbled down ideas as they occurred to him. While his school friends played at duels with wooden swords, he took such delight in fancy dress that he soon found himself sewing to order! He would spend days on end shut up in the linen room with Juliette, the seamstress, who was perfectly happy to indulge him. They set up a workroom on the third floor of the house, Juliette at the sewing machine and Christian at the drawing board. Grandmother Martin, who followed proceedings with great amusement, would be invited to inspect each finished outfit. And she was always there for the fitting sessions.

Christian Dior was very fond of his grandmother, who came to live not far from the family when she sold her home in Angers. She brought with her the handsome Napoleon III drawing-room suite with empire chairs that went to furnish Christian's favorite room, the parlor with the yellow moiré wallpaper where he had his piano lessons. Best of all, he could talk to his grandmother about anything. She knew the names of all the stars in the sky, she could hold forth on the Chinese, the Egyptians, or the Greeks, and even though she had never traveled, she always had something to say about the different countries of the world. She was no ordinary grandmother but believed in destiny, omens, fortune telling, and all sorts of fascinating things.

She would attend the traditional Sunday dinner every week, but when the economic crisis of 1918 took its toll on her modest income, she came to live with the family on a permanent basis. Her favorite grandson was delighted to have her even closer, although others seemed to consider her something of a chatterbox. She was a woman of decided opinions; the newspaper of her choice was the conservative *Echo de Paris*, and she never commented on the current political situation without adding some sort of prediction. The family liked to tease her about her predilection for soothsaying, in particular her son-in-law, who never failed to remind her of the times her forecasts had proved wrong. Though Maurice Dior had generously opened his doors to his mother-in-law, living at such close quarters occasionally led to family dramas — squabbles rather than mortal combat, but not without their share of harsh remarks from the head of the household.

"Like all other Anglo-Norman constructions at the turn of the century, my childhood home was perfectly hideous. And yet I have the fondest and most enchanted memories of it." As Christian was only too aware, Madame Dior blithely followed every cliché of the era, with all the certainty of unerring snobbery. And yet he glosses over her mistakes. What did it matter that his mother, "without the slightest regard for harmony, spoiled the lines of the facade with a protuberance, the conservatory in turn-of-the-century wrought iron"? Fake pagodas, glass cabinets filled with china figurines supposedly from Saxony, candy dishes of every description — any hint of excess or bad taste vanishes in Christian's tenderly lyrical vision of his childhood home. In his account of his childhood, the preciousness and gilt pretensions of the house take on a rococo charm and neo-romantic grace, and not only is his mother's fakery pardoned but her achievements are described as "an inexhaustible source of wonder."

He spent those early years basking in the charm and tranquillity of the Belle Epoque, a period regarded nowadays with increasing nostalgia. "I picture it now as a happy, jaunty, peaceful time when all we thought about was enjoying life. We were carefree in the belief that no harm threatened the wealth and lifestyle of the rich nor the simple, thrifty existence of the poor. To us the future would bring nothing but even greater benefits for all. Whatever life might have bestowed upon me since, nothing can rival my memories of those sweet years."

And so it was that the thunderbolt fell. This peaceful existence in Granville-on-Sea was shattered by the outbreak of war.

It was 1914. The announcement of general mobilization caught the Dior family right in the middle of their summer holidays, which they were spending as usual at Les Rumbs. They decided to stay in Granville, away from the German troops advancing along the Marne — as they had in the Franco-Prussian War of 1870 — and threatening to enter Paris. The enemy was checked just in time at Château-Thierry, east of Paris, but the subsequent flood of evacuees from the occupied areas and the situation in general were enough to persuade the Dior parents to stay in Normandy out of harm's way. Their life in Paris came to an end and Christian Dior spent his tenth through his fourteenth years in Granville. The cozy, sheltered years of the Belle Epoque were left abruptly behind.

Lying outside of the war zone, Granville rallied to the cause, taking delivery of convoys of wounded soldiers. The hospital was soon full to bursting and so the Hôtel Normandie, and later the casino too, provided beds for the seriously wounded. The *Granvillais* rose to the gravity of the occasion. These were sturdy folk, with chiseled features reminiscent of the brave seafaring faces of admirals, pirates, and fishermen venturing into far-off waters, proud of their glorious past.

There was to be no more embroidery or supervising of gardeners for Madame Dior and her friends. Instead they had more urgent tasks, sending parcels to prisoners of war and giving freely of their time to entertain the sick and the wounded.

Spared any part in these duties, the children rejoiced in the benefits of the new regime, left largely to their own devices with less parental supervision and more imaginative lessons. It is surprising, however, to read Christian's amused analysis of human, or rather female, behavior in a particularly observant description of his mother and the other ladies caught up in their new roles as charity workers: "They were suddenly rocked by the announcement in a fashion magazine which had come from the capital that Parisian women were now wearing short skirts and 'flying boots' with black, tartan, or bronze uppers, laced up to the knee. They were unanimous in their outrage and disapproval. But by the evening mail, each had hastened to place an order for boots and short skirts. Such was the unthinking frivolity of our era, with its genteel approach to a war that would ultimately destroy everything we had ever known."

It seems Dior too preferred to focus on the carefree aspect rather than the gloom of those years, like a dreamer covering his ears to block out the noise of the bombs, hoping in some way to banish this horrible thing. Why else is there no mention in his memoirs of the courage of his brother Raymond, who enlisted as a volunteer in 1917, aged eighteen? It was, after all, a heroic act, coming as it did during the terrible Somme offensive and on the heels of the defeat at Verdun, which had brought the death toll to one million. Raymond's unit was blown sky high and his whole platoon wiped out. The only one to escape, he was to remain traumatized by the experience all his life.

But Christian's silence on this subject may not have been the product of indifference, much less frivolity. Given the way his life subsequently developed, it is clear that his reaction actually demonstrated his incredible love of life and, with it, his fierce determination to avoid pain and suffering. One of the saving graces, surely, of an artist's calling is the ability to ignore the world as it really is and re-create it in a more beautiful form. Consider the famous *Piano Lesson* by Matisse, an idyllic depiction of his son Pierre seated at the piano next to a wide-open window. It was painted at one of the most heart-rending moments in the artist's life. It was 1916 and the young man at the piano was about to leave for the front.

2

Les Enfants terribles,
Les Parents terribles

Family! I hate you.

— André Gide

*P*eacetime is best taken as a clean slate, and to a teenage boy, the end of the war was as if nothing and no one had come before. A whole new world lay at his feet. The rest of the family had returned to a familiar Parisian existence after the four years of exile in Granville, but for Christian the capital was an endless voyage of discovery. He was in high school, studying for his *baccalauréat*, and while on the outside he gave the reassuring impression of a placid, polite, rather slow-moving boy, inside he was fired by impatience, feverishness — vertigo almost, at the prospect of Paris at his fingertips and the Great War now behind him. The streets of the capital teemed with people, the theaters were full, the cabarets open until dawn, and money flowed like water, as if the joys of victory had unleashed an unstoppable tide of festivities and celebrations. His childhood memories of the Châtelet Theater or the

17

lights of the Place de la Concorde were cast into oblivion in contrast with the strange, disturbing, uncharted territory before him. Women were short-haired, musicians were black, ballet companies were Russian, painters were abstract, and everyone was being psychoanalyzed. There was Montmartre, where bodies arched and wove to the sound of the saxophone; Montparnasse, the new meeting place for bohemian artists where Picasso, Derain, and Matisse now held court at Le Dôme and La Rotonde; and the Champs-Elysées, where music-hall audiences were swept up in the sensual gymnastics of high-kicking bare legs.

The rarefied atmosphere of the Dior household was carefully screened from these sorts of dangers, exuding instead the pure air of domestic bliss. Business had never been better for Maurice Dior. The family having expanded again with the birth of Ginette in 1917, the family moved to a larger apartment, this time at 9 Rue Louis-David, a dark little street between the Trocadéro and their old neighborhood of La Muette. Madame Dior, ever slender and elegant, at times a little distant, was assisted by Mademoiselle Marthe, the governess, whom the children adored. The decor was new too. While the dernier cri was all tangerine pouffes, lacquered screens in funereal black, marble vases instead of crystal chandeliers, and fake ebony furniture, Madame Dior considered this vulgar and opted instead for something more refined. She dispensed with the lacquered wood panels and pastel tints of the "Louis XVI circa 1910" look of which Christian was so fond and opted for "Louis XVI circa 1920" — color, damask upholstery, and paneling picked out in contrasting shades — altogether much closer to the authentic eighteenth century, it was felt. All the classics of the period were reproduced, with bronze brackets, pedestal tables, tapestried armchairs, and other dainty little finishing touches. On the advice of an antique-dealer friend, Monsieur Dior purchased some works of art, one by Lépicié and, for the definitive Louis XVI look, a Boucher. The total effect was a triumph of good, solid, conventional taste, perfectly in tune with children in uniform, chambermaids in white aprons, poetry recitals, family dinners, a stable economy, and a good life ahead.

Christian Dior was the type of boy who could pretend to be totally absorbed while secretly bored and distracted, a habit instilled in him by long hours of school and homework. His oval face, slightly receding chin, and thin hair gave him the air of a somewhat mournful clown. Scholastically he barely scraped by. School was the excellent Lycée Gerson, where he had been quick to work out which of his companions were in tune with the times, striking up a friendship with two of them — Jean Bertrand, who had grown up in an artistic environment thanks to his mother's friendship with the de Camondo family, who were renowned patrons of the arts, and a fellow Granvillais by the name of Hubert Sargenton. The trio shared a love of escapades into the seedier parts of town.

Christian's goal was to "explore every nook and cranny of this new, cosmopolitan, inventive and ingenious Paris with all the truly novel novelties it had to offer." That, at least, is how he described it later in his memoirs. After the isolation of Granville, Christian had found in postwar Paris a place to satisfy his all too precocious curiosity and assuage his heightened sensibilities. But his parents would have had difficulty recognizing this side of their son. They had no idea that, returning to Paris after four years in their Norman refuge, he would start keeping the wrong company and moving in circles far outside their ken. Our young hero's life was very similar to that of his older contemporary, the writer André Gide, whose way of rebelling against the constraints of work and study was to indulge his pursuit of pleasure to the hilt. Like Dior, Gide had a solitary, sheltered upbringing in comfortable surroundings free from the slightest material woe. An only child raised by his mother, Gide had been stifled by an excessive emphasis on religious and family morals. Dior, for his part, was burdened by the narrow-mindedness and petty prejudice of his home environment. Both felt the need to throw off the family yoke, yet neither felt moved to rebel overtly. Gide's account of his upbringing in the autobiographical *La Porte étroite (Strait Is the Gate)* mirrors Dior's experience right down to its setting in Normandy, symbolizing all that was bourgeois and repressive. And when Gide brought out his *Nourritures terrestres (Fruits of the Earth)* he became a key figure for his entire generation, living proof of the possibility of finding personal freedom while still living within the norms of society. Christian Dior did not resent his parents for being the perfect caricature of all the prejudices of their era, but he soon figured out how to comply with the demands of his family while satisfying his own needs for freedom. Reconciling the two required skillful juggling, however. His shyness was a useful decoy and an unshakable part of his image. "Dior is like a big adolescent with the old-fashioned shyness of a schoolboy," wrote the painter Michel Ciry, "and most charming in his childish awkwardness."

Why challenge his parents in their role, if this was how things were to be? There was his father, on the one hand, eminently worthy of respect, the classic bourgeois gentleman, as sure of himself as he was of the world around him, engrossed in his many company directorships and all the mysteries of the business world. Then there was his mother. Despite her austere manner, Christian had managed to carve a little niche for himself in her world, and had earned the jealousy of his siblings as a result. Madame Dior meanwhile continued her unflagging efforts to beautify the Granville home and garden, a lifetime endeavor. Christian still enjoyed assisting her and now began making his own contributions. At his suggestion, a little stone rotunda was erected on the pathway along the cliff top. It was the perfect spot for taking tea on fine afternoons, sheltered from the wind and looking out over the sea as far as the Chausey Islands. When in Paris he still went with his mother to the florist Orève to select blooms for her arrangements and, always interested in food, he enjoyed planning the day's menu. His biggest coup was securing an invitation to accompany his mother to her dressmaker, Rosine Perrault on Rue Royale, a privilege not even his sisters dared aspire to. Unlike Madame Dior, his eldest sister Jacqueline was not particularly interested in clothes, and her dress sense often shocked her brother, who found himself severely rebuked whenever he ventured to suggest an alternative. "Honestly, Christian! What would you know?!"

A loving and faithful son, he was nonetheless adept at making good his escape when the urge took him. The meeting place at the time was the bar Le Boeuf sur le Toit (The Ox on the Roof), which is now legendary for its seminal role in what the writer Maurice Sachs called the "education" of the youth of that period. Sachs gives a brilliant account of it in his autobiographical *Au temps du Boeuf-sur-le-Toit*. Its overnight success occurred when the irrepressible Jean Cocteau, already well known, turned up to hear the pianist Jean Wiener. Wiener sat down to play, Cocteau borrowed a complete set of drums from Stravinsky, and the show began. All their friends followed them and the next night it was full house. The Prince of Wales, passing through Paris, found himself there in the company of such luminaries as Artur Rubinstein, Princess Murat, and a hundred members of the Ballets Russes. It was not long before its original premises on Rue Duphot became too cramped and the "Boeuf" moved to Rue Boissy-d'Anglas.

Young men like Maurice Sachs, Christian Dior, and countless others sat perched on bar stools to gaze at the passing parade. As Sachs recalls, there were "Picasso, Radiguet, Cocteau, Milhaud, Fargue, Auric, Poulenc, Honegger, Sauguet, Satie, Jean Hugo, Breton, Aragon, Marie Laurencin, Léger, Lurçat, Derain and all the avant-garde of the day. . . . The society types came in tuxedos, the painters in pullovers. There were women in tailored suits and others dripping with pearls and diamonds."

Young Christian's other haunts were galleries, a loose description for tiny premises hung with primitives and naïfs. Was this, he wondered, the end of classical art? Cubism had come as quite a shock after centuries of figurative painting. Did it mean he would have to forsake painters like Pierre Bonnard and Edouard Vuillard or musicians like Ravel and Debussy for the likes of Picasso, Matisse, Braque, Stravinsky, and Schoenberg and follow the dadaists with their claim of "delivering language from the tyranny of precise meaning"? A gust of freedom was also blowing through the theater world. The simpering patter of variety had been supplanted by the bare boards of theaters like the Vieux-Colombier under director Jacques Copeau and his assistant Louis Jouvet. Evenings at L'Atelier on the slopes of Montmartre also became mandatory once the great actor-teacher Charles Dullin took up residence there in the fall of 1922. He too had shrugged off the conventions of the Academy of Dramatic Art. What heated discussions ensued on those bar stools following performances like these! With so much to distract him, one wonders how Christian managed to pass his *bachot*. Paris was a whirl of cocktails and surprise parties where the words "cubism" and "nervous breakdown" were as common as "bonjour" and where surrealism and cocaine were all the rage.

Despite such temptations, June 1923 saw young Dior, diploma in hand, contemplating the choice of a career. His natural inclination was toward the Académie des Beaux-Arts. With his love of homes and gardens, he dreamed of being an architect and was obsessed with art.

His prime concern at this stage of his life was to remain open to everything around him, free of any ties and determined to live for the moment. The concept of "*disponibilité*" or "being open to everything" was the leitmotiv for Dior and his generation. Here too the hand of the master André Gide was apparent. Gide preached throwing aside the shackles of an austere upbringing to embrace life without preconceptions, unhampered by ambition or any notions of achievement.

For all his eclectic wanderings, it seems Dior failed to anticipate his parents' reaction. Unaware of the artistic leanings their son had displayed in childhood, they had just as little idea of his ambitions. He had carefully hidden from them evidence of his solitary forays into the Paris that so fascinated and influenced him. His announcement was a bombshell. "There was an outcry," he relates. "Under no circumstances was I to join those Bohemians!"

Christian and his father could hardly have been further apart than at this moment. Maurice Dior intended to give his children a solid start in life, and from his vantage point as a company director and administrator, the Academy of Fine Arts was a sorry place. It could only lead his son to the tragic fate that awaited all artists, like poor van Gogh who perished before reaping the fruits of his labors. For Christian Dior to follow that course was quite out of the question.

What must have come as the toughest blow to Christian, however, was his mother's flat refusal to go along with his plans. With their common love of homes and gardens, he had counted on her support, even thinking perhaps that she had inspired him in his vocation. They got on famously; he was by far the most affectionate and attentive of her offspring. But Madeleine stood firm. The kinds of things one learned at the Académie des Beaux-Arts did not constitute a profession.

And so Christian gave in. "Families!" he cried with Gide. "I hate you." He would abandon any hope of the Beaux-Arts and bow to his father's determination to see him study something meaningful.

After initially digging in his heels, he was clever enough to realize that it was in his interest to find a compromise. "To gain time and in order to enjoy the greatest freedom possible," he wrote, "I enrolled at the Faculty of Political Science on Rue Saint-Guillaume, which entailed no commitments. It was a hypocritical way of allowing me to lead the life I liked." Everyone was happy and Madame Dior, with her old-fashioned ideas about suitable careers, breathed a sigh of relief: her son was destined for the diplomatic service.

The School of Political Science in those days was not the factory churning out high-ranking public servants that it has become today. André Ostier, who studied there in the same period as Dior and who graduated to become a photographer (proof of the school's eclecticism in those more liberal times), remembers going to the Rue Saint-Guillaume "chiefly to hear lectures by André Siegfried, a most elegant character with a lorgnette who spoke of the United States of America. He was fascinating. We had just discovered American movies and it was the birth of the idea of the States as the land of golden opportunity."

This was precisely how Christian envisaged spending his time there. He would resume his game of hide-and-seek with his parents, pursuing his own interests and hopping right back up onto his stool at Le Boeuf sur le Toit.

Christian Dior had the exhilarating feeling of being smack in the center of the action. Artistic convention was being challenged and reinvented, and he was right there in the crucible of discussion and public debate.

Back in 1921, Jean Cocteau was at the height of his career. A child prodigy at sixteen, the darling of *le tout Paris* was now thirty-two and had just staged his third ballet, *Les Mariés de la tour Eiffel (The Wedding on the Eiffel Tower)*. He was basking in glory, surrounded by an entourage of young people who flocked each morning to his home on Rue d'Anjou to see him rise from his bed as if he were the Sun King himself. Among the chosen few was Maurice Sachs, a charming, rather scheming young man, who followed every fashion launched by Cocteau, even to the extent of entering a seminary! The others, like Dior, were content to provide an admiring audience for the ballet extravaganzas in which Cocteau systematically overturned all conventions. The broader public, however, was scandalized, having only just reconciled itself to the Ballets Russes and the idea of Diaghilev as an infallible genius.

Cocteau's impertinence with *Les Mariés* went far beyond anything ever imagined. Like a magician delving into a prop box of childish pastimes, innocent artfulness, and harmless skits, he conceived a burlesque fantasia, a spoken ballet with a daringly witty score by a group of composers called Les Six — Darius Milhaud, Arthur Honegger,

Georges Auric, Francis Poulenc, Louis Durey, and Germaine Taille-ferre — of whom Erik Satie was to be the leading exponent. Costumes and comic masks were by Jean Hugo and sets in naive style by Irène Lagut. Christian Dior did not miss a single one of Cocteau's subsequent creations, more fascinated by his visual inventions than by his poetry or novels. Cocteau was the complete artist, the key figure in the avant-garde movement, at once the grand impresario and the thread that bound together painters, musicians, choreographers, dancers, sculptors, and poets.

As compensation for bowing to his father's commands, Dior was given permission to study musical composition. He had played the piano ever since his childhood in Granville and was mad about the new wave launched by Les Six, influenced as they were by Stravinsky and Satie. Dior was one of the students who were the main audience in the little auditorium at the Collège de France on June 11, 1923, when a group of young musicians created in 1921 and consisting of Henri Sauguet, Maxime Jacob, Henri Cliquet-Pleyel, and Roger Desormière made their striking Paris debut under the leadership of Sauguet. They would call themselves the Arcueil School, after the southern suburb of Paris where Satie took up residence. In the hope of joining them one day, Dior composed several pieces for the piano, which he entitled *Françaises,* like the pieces written by Henri Sauguet.

Shortly afterward Dior was introduced to Sauguet by a Dutch friend named Robert de Roos, who studied music with Darius Milhaud. Sauguet, from Bordeaux, had just arrived in Paris and Dior had organized a soirée in de Roos's honor. With the lights turned out, Sauguet and Dior took turns playing their *Françaises.*

These were the foundations of lifelong friendships. Henri Sauguet and Dior were later to recall that first evening in their respective memoirs. "That evening at Dior's," Sauguet wrote in *La Musique, ma vie,* "I met most of the people who were to become my best and closest friends." Dior was immediately captivated by the musician. "His lively gaze, sparkling with mischief from behind his spectacles, his incredibly mobile features, the wit and intelligence of his conversation . . . all that was so Latin and alive about this man from the Southwest quite dazzled the slow and taciturn Norman in me."

Other friends soon joined the group, which Sauguet christened the Club and which met every week at a bar on Rue Tronchet called the Tip Toes, run by a group of ladies with very British airs. The Club would gorge themselves on pastries and drink cocktails. Among their number were the painter Christian Bérard, the poet-painter Max Jacob, the actor Marcel Herrand, the writer René Crevel, and the historian Pierre Gaxotte. They discussed theater and literature and painting, gossiped, pondered, mimicked, and generally amused themselves.

Nine o'clock was time for a show. On Fridays this would be the Fratellini brothers or the trapeze artist Barbette at the Médrano circus, where the group always took the same box. On Saturdays it was the Bouffes du Nord where Solange Dumines and her theater troupe performed the grand repertoire — *Les Misérables, La Porteuse de pain, Chaste et Flétrie, Le Crime d'une sainte* — in period wigs and "very seriously." Wrote Sauget: "We found in those performances the scenic naïveté to inspire us in our attempts to escape literature, which we detested. It was sublime in its complete lack of sublime subterfuge."

And so in the space of three years was formed the group of friends to whom Christian Dior would remain faithful all his life. Except for Jacob, who was forty-odd, this little gang of gifted urchins were still in the throes of discovering their paths.

Bérard was a skinny chap with huge blue eyes who still lived with his parents. He had set up a studio in the smaller drawing room of their home in the Spontini Townhouse where, in the midst of chronic disarray, clad in an old pair of faded overalls, he would coat his canvases with a mixture of melted candle wax and paint. Christian Dior was transfixed by his inspired paintings and sketches and covered the walls of his room with them. He even managed to convince his father of Bérard's potential and persuade him to buy some of his work — which could be had in those days for a mere hundred francs!

"What fun we had," Sauguet continues, "what discussions, what ideas and plans. There was so much to tell, to experience, to voice an opinion on, . . . whether it be literature, art, or politics."

So much for formal studies. This little group nurtured their love of art and the bohemian existence with all the freshness and mischief of choirboys. Christian Bérard and Max Jacob wore kerchiefs and paint-spattered trousers à la Montmartre while the others tended toward bowler hats. Dior even opted for something of a British look in his wardrobe. A comparison with their elder counterparts in London's Bloomsbury set would no doubt have pleased them.

This was a bunch of good-natured dandies, passionate and exacting in their artistic quests, sensitive and fastidious in their opinions. Their meetings were lively, with a certain playful spirit but not without the inevitable jealousies. Besides Maurice Sachs's tendency to fall out with almost every member of the group, there was constant rivalry between Sauguet and Bérard whenever it came to staging a production. They also had a tendency to excess, and to rather mannered speech. The common bond for most of them, of course, was their homosexuality. Couples like Henri Sauguet and Jacques Dupont made the nature of their relationship perfectly clear. Christian Dior, on the other hand, suppressed his leanings or, at least, gave no sign of his preferences. André Gide may have been a liberating influence in this area, but the leap from thought to action was not one to be taken without some boldness.

One place the group particularly liked to frequent was a bookshop named Les Quatre Chemins, run by a man named Raoul Leven who would later become secretary to Jean Cocteau. "You could meet all the interesting young people there," recalls Maurice Sachs. Joyce's *Ulysses* was all the rage, as were Stock's translations of American novels. Proust was one of the chief French authors to have captured their imaginations, along with their guiding light, André Gide.

The publication of Gide's autobiographical *Si le grain ne meurt* prompted passionate debate. "It opened windows onto hidden secrets," André Ostier remembers. "It had an enormous influence on us, and we tried as a result to live as truthfully as possible." But imitating Gide's open indulgence in sensual pleasures without regard for established moral codes was a harder choice for most individual consciences, for whom the thought of conflict with their families was too much of a deterrent.

Jean Cocteau was one who did move out of his mother's apartment on Rue d'Anjou to pursue his homosexual amours and his taste for opium with greater freedom. Cocteau was at the summit of this Olympus. He and Max Jacob were the heroes, Cocteau with his clever turns of phrase, Jacob with his loud derision of all that was "genteel." While Jacob exercised considerable influence over their number, he was adolescent and playful in style, whereas Cocteau was more worldly and image-conscious. While Jean dabbled in every kind of literature, Max was permanently on vacation. He was affable and instantly familiar, and a dazzling conversationalist. From the famous Bateau-Lavoir — which was nothing but a ramshackle tenement where people camped out in extreme discomfort out of friendship for Picasso and Apollinaire — to his visions of Christ, Jacob was an expansive prankster with a knack for sparking incidents and stirring up intrigue. He was captivating in his vitality, prodigal and prodigious, a mystic, an astrologer, a gossip and a loner. He was the perfect example of the credo that life is the equal of art. In his company shy souls felt themselves open up and dreamers gave rein to their fantasies. Dior was the perfect candidate for falling prey to Jacob's charms. And fall he did.

Jacob lived mostly in a village in the Loire Valley called Saint-Benoît, but whenever he came to Paris he would stay at a little hotel in the Ninth Arrondissement. It was a modestly priced establishment called the Hôtel Nollet at number 55 on the street of the same name. This "sort of palace seen through the wrong end of a telescope," as Christian Dior described it, became the venue for madcap evenings and games made famous by Jacob's group of courtiers.

According to one account:

> Max Jacob's court, a lively and generally youthful crowd, would assemble late in the afternoon. Max would then come down from his room to join us. Music was the order of the day. Henri Sauguet and Cliquet-Pleyel would fight over the piano, improvising and singing, mixing bits of their own compositions with passages from their master, Satie. They were often accompanied by a very young, soft-featured man with a lazy gait. Christian Dior also had ambitions of becoming a musician.

>   *Tristement dort*
>   *Christian Dior*
>   *Au creux néant musicien,*
> Max would chant, parodying Mallarmé:
>   Sadly snores
>   Christian Dior
>   in the depths of a musical void.

Snore as he might, Christian was wide awake when it came to masquerades. One evening, for example, we were treated to the historical encounter between Madame Poincaré, the French president's wife, and Queen Mary, at the opening of the international runner bean festival at Arpajon. René Crevel, who was long and skinny, was the British monarch, Bébé Bérard was a plump president's wife. Christian's task was to dress them, and it was quite a sight to watch him turn the house upside down to find suitable apparel for these amazing characters.

That description comes from another member of the tribe, Jacques Bonjean. He and Maurice Sachs had set up a business publishing illustrated literary works, and while this was his first meeting with Christian Dior, their paths were soon to converge.

Dressing up was second nature to Dior. The adolescent in him had no intention just yet of relegating the Carnival of his Granville days to his childhood fancy-dress box. His love of brass bands, floral floats, and masked balls were all part of the sense of fantasy that drew him to Le Boeuf sur le Toit and the entrancing ambiance there, created by Jean Cocteau on jazz drums and Erik Satie with his perennial umbrella. It was also what attracted him to the improvisations and caricature that were part of the pantomime atmosphere surrounding Max Jacob. "To the music of a gramophone," Dior relates, "Max, who seemed to have remained the youngest of us all, would discard his slippers and dance in red stockings, miming an entire corps de ballet to Chopin's Preludes. And with a speed to rival Fregoli,* Sauguet and Bérard would transform themselves into a whole series of historical characters, with the aid of lampshades, bedcovers, and curtains."

It's easy to see why Dior loved these wild years with the somewhat surreal aura of a permanent party, so typical of Paris in that period. This was an era perhaps unique in the history of the French capital — a time when the night really did belong to the young. Thanks to patrons of the arts like Count Etienne de Beaumont or Viscount Charles and Vis-

---

* Leopoldo Fregoli was an Italian actor famous for his extraordinary ability to change costume sixty times during a performance.

countess Marie-Laure de Noailles, what might have merely been a casual utterance in a bar or an impromptu charade could be transformed into a ballet or a light opera in next to no time. The de Noailles would have their "baptism" when they backed Luis Buñuel's *L'Age d'or* and Cocteau's film *Le Sang d'un poète,* scandalizing establishment circles and bringing the de Noailles close to excommunication. Etienne de Beaumont was the first aristocrat to say that snobbish society should rank talent more highly than nobility. He was famous for his *soirées de Paris* — which Dior never missed — and balls inspired by his passion for masquerades. When the writer Raymond Radiguet described his character the Count d'Orgel preparing for a ball, it was in fact a pastiche of de Beaumont. "He ransacked the drawing room," Radiguet wrote, "placed a lampshade on his head and tried a thousand disguises, awakening in Anne the most abiding passion of his class over the course of the centuries — the love of dressing up." The theme for a ball would come at the drop of a hat, based on a word, a spontaneous flash of inspiration. . . . That, at least, was how it was meant to appear.

These parties and balls were not just an escape valve for bored society figures or young people trying to find themselves. The Paris into which Christian Dior dove headfirst was at the heart of "France's blissful orgy with the rest of the world," as Maurice Sachs put it. Foreigners flocked to experience things they could not have countenanced back home. They came for the dance halls, where mime, masquerade, and dressing up were as popular as they were in high society. The most exotic was the Bal Nègre on Rue Blomet, at which the painter Foujita was a huge success in the guise of a streetwalker. Gay Paree was for everyone, including lovers of every persuasion. Homosexuality was outlawed in Germany and England, but Paris, where it was not, became a mecca, welcoming them with open arms — and eyes closed. One celebrated institution, the Magic City dance hall, organized a huge party every year during Lent that attracted homosexuals from all over France and beyond. It also brought Paris out in force, a ribald and voyeuristic crowd who saw no harm in standing and staring. While rows of policemen stood outside pretending not to see, the throngs jostled at the entrance to revel in the spectacle of "sodomites" arriving in swan feathers, diadems, and multicolored makeup. After all, outrageousness was the theme of the night.*

Less frivolous than it might appear, the real story of this group of friends, who were first drawn to each other by a mutual rejection of sentimentalism in art and stylistic ornamentation in literature, was their joint voyage of discovery in the realm of art. They chorused their rapture at the freshness, spontaneity, and humor of the music of Les Six and applauded in unison when Cocteau uttered the phrase, "Satie has taught our age the greatest boldness of all: simplicity." They shivered with delight at Christian Bérard's characters on canvas. "He dares to be uninfluenced by Picasso," wrote Maurice Sachs. "That's the most interesting thing a young painter can do." Indeed, while their journey began under the auspices of the first shock of modernism, radicalism, and cubist abstraction, they allowed themselves to be guided by their sensibilities in their ongoing artistic quest, and in the choices they made. And while they came from very different backgrounds, the majority of them were the product of bourgeois families steeped in the classical traditions. No doubt that is why their taste, which developed in the middle ground between the two extremes of surrealism and cubism, would always resist any new artistic concept born of gratuitous frippery such as the dadaists or André Breton's attempts at indoctrination. This mutual love affair would ultimately bear fruit, as evidenced some years later with the neo-romantic movement in art.

It bore fruit too for Christian Dior — but even later still.

---

* For further reading see Gilles Barbedette and Michel Carasson, *Paris Gay 1925* (Paris: Presses de la Renaissance, 1981), 16–19. Willy (Henri Gauthier-Villars, Colette's first husband) and René Crevel also discuss it, Willy in *Le Troisième sexe* and René Crevel in *Mon corps et moi.*]

3

Passage to Freedom

> With his rotund ecclesiastical side, Dior
> was like a cathedral, a repository of
> countless secrets no one else had ac-
> cess to.
>
> — Geneviève Page

*M*adeleine Dior had never been happier. Her new pergola, with its climbing roses and lily pond, was the perfect place for lunching outdoors in the warmer months. On a clear day it offered an unparalleled view, right across the sea to the Chausey archipelago. This latest addition to Les Rumbs had been Christian's suggestion. He had drawn up the plans and lovingly assisted his mother in working out what to plant where. The surrounding garden was a mass of colors, fragrances, and nuances; the lawns and hedges were clipped and combed and manicured, with cacti and tropical plants adding an exotic note, and the trees looking suitably ancient. The greenhouse had doubled in size and the property had been enlarged with the purchase of a neighboring house as a place for guests to stay. But this spectacular result had meant years of hard work for Madame Dior; bringing a garden to maturity requires as much patience as raising children!

Raymond, the eldest, had just married. The match was everything his parents could have wished for: their new daughter-in-law was also called Madeleine, she brought with her a very handsome dowry, and she was pretty. Madeleine Dior could now turn her attention to her second offspring. She had a few hopes already, including a freckly English girl she liked very much who played an excellent game of golf and who she thought would appeal to Christian's love of things British. Peggy was her name and she was the daughter of a Colonel Evans who had retired from the British army to take up residence in Granville, where he was president of the club. But something about her second son worried Madeleine Dior. Her chief complaint, which she often voiced to her husband, was that Christian seemed incapable of applying himself to anything serious. She was not particularly keen on his interest in music. Admittedly, they had given their permission to study musical composition and, good parents that they were, they had — frequently, even — agreed to let him stage rehearsals in their Paris drawing room. These had proved to be rather unusual sessions. The young people would all sit on the floor with the lights off, leaving the Dior parents no alternative but to take refuge in their quarters and pray that one day such adolescent pastimes might cease. But how could she pin down this secretive son of hers, with his amazing ability to avoid confrontation of any kind?

Part of Christian Dior's skill in managing his life was his openness with his parents about his very different sorts of friends. Christian Bérard, Henri Sauguet, Jacques Bonjean, and many others, all from totally different circles from his parents', were often invited to Granville to discover its charms. Max Jacob even promised to make a detour to Normandy on a trip he was to take with his mother to Brittany. Dior had acquired a reputation for his generous hospitality at Les Rumbs, and one character trait that was no secret was Dior's sense of friendship.

He remained as faithful as ever to his old playmates and spent his summers in the usual manner, playing golf, tennis, charades, and croquet, swimming, going on picnics, attending charity fetes and costume balls. These were friendships that would last all his life. His circle included Serge Heftler-Louiche, the Diors' next-door neighbor, a magnificent young man from a very wealthy family; Nicole Riotteau, daughter of a ship owner and the most sought-after girl in town; Suzanne Lemoine and her sister Jeannette, sports-loving and full of fun, from a more modest background — their parents had a grocery store. He was particularly close to Suzanne, who was a champion at tennis and golf. Christian liked nothing better than the company of his friends, but he was never a leader. Given his natural indolence he was more inclined to stretch out on the sand while the others swam or fished. He was not especially fond of sports and, although he went to all the competitions, he usually confined his participation to presenting the prizes. In fact, one of the traditions of the golfing season at Granville was the Dior Cup.

Although Dior cut an elegant figure as he climbed out of his father's limousine in his summer suit and soft hat, he did not like his looks and considered himself physically unappealing. He was a great raconteur and fond of joking with his female friends, no doubt because he knew their relationships would never be anything but platonic. The girls' heads all turned whenever his handsome friend Serge Heftler-Louiche was around, but Dior also had a considerable female entourage. Referring to them as "my pets," he sketched ball gowns for them and sent them notes signed with the affectionate diminutive "tian." Some of his young lady friends still have those sketches. Suzanne Lemoine has a design he sent her for an "island negress" costume, with a note on the bottom of the page stressing that "the skirt should be longer at the back and so should the basque of the bodice. Gather the skirt up lightly with one hand."

Suzanne Lemoine was to become an inseparable friend and quickly realized the source of his reticence in some areas. She loved what she described as his contrasting sides, one "passionate," the other "shy." Dior had clearly decided to maintain all the appearances of a well-intentioned young man of good family, and would execute a mandatory fox-trot or two at society balls. He could not have allowed his parents to guess his secret. "He knew he would have upset his mother terribly," Suzanne explains.

The day came, though, when one aspect of his life could no longer remain hidden. His studies at the School of Political Science were leading nowhere and Madame Dior would soon have to accept the sad truth that she would never see her son an ambassador. Before breaking the news, however, Christian attempted to provide an alternative. Thinking a career in museums might prove a satisfactory compromise, he asked if he might enroll at the School of Paleography and Librarianship. But this option too was rejected.

Dior was well aware that he had no future in political science. Perhaps he might have continued his happy existence, moving to and fro between the two "families" that were his middle-class environment and his bohemian lifestyle. But he was twenty-two years old and had already repeated his third year at Rue Saint-Guillaume. He had managed to scrape through the course in public finance to reach the final year, but there seemed to be little hope of his obtaining his degree. He loathed examinations and had done everything he could to avoid sitting for the final session, fabricating one excuse after another. On May 15, 1926, he wrote to his professors pleading ill health — a bad case of flu, he said, had confined him to his bed. On April 27, 1927, he was "in London learning English." (His prime motive was actually to attend the London premier of *La Nuit,* a ballet with a score by Henri Sauguet and sets by Christian Bérard. It was also the cause of a major falling-out between his two best friends when Bérard tried to take all the credit for the production.) A third letter was one of protest. His professor had refused to allow him to enroll because he had turned up "in travel attire"! With the exception of André Siegfried's course "The Trade Policies of the Great Powers" in 1927, in which he obtained reasonably good marks, reports from his professors were variations on the usual theme: "He is a bright student but has not applied himself sufficiently." His oral presentations were lacking in assurance (Dior had a rather reedy voice) and his essays showed a somewhat spidery, sensitive, and occasionally undisciplined hand with a curious aversion to capital letters and an even more unusual signature, "tian dior," all in lowercase and minus the first syllable. In short, there seemed little point in his repeating the third year yet again. The records for July 1, 1927, show the entry "absent all semester" and for 1928, his signature preceded by the words "I withdraw." The only benefit of these wasted years was that they had served to delay his conscription into the army. But the facade behind which he had conducted a most enjoyable lifestyle was crumbling and once again the question of his future arose.

This time the circumstances were even more delicate than four years before. Maurice Dior had serious cause for disappointment: his two eldest sons refused to grow up. His firstborn was the source of greater concern. Raymond Dior had been employed at the Paris head-quarters of the family business for some years and, while he was not without intelligence, he clearly did not have the requisite abilities to succeed his father. He was sarcastic and provocative, and enjoyed putting forward subversive ideas. It had been thought his rebellious spirit might disappear as he grew older, but this was not to be.

For some time, Raymond Dior had been involved with the well-known satirical gazette *Crapouillot*. His views were unreservedly radical. He subscribed to the notion expounded in the Communist International that the only hope for the world was to wipe it out and start again. He was occasionally given some space in the journal, and his articles, according to Jacques Bonjean, were not without historical interest: "Raymond invented a catch phrase for his friends at *Crapouillot* that went on to gain a certain currency. 'Two hundred families,' he claimed, were responsible for all the ills of the land. He didn't specify whether his was one of them. So while his parents had no cause for genuine concern, they clearly lost any hope of one day seeing their eldest son ensconced behind a managing director's desk." It was dispiriting to Monsieur Dior to see his eldest a Bolshevik and the next a bohemian. The third son was another dramatic case. Bernard was eighteen years old, good looking enough but strange and antisocial in his behavior. Although he had passed his *baccalauréat*, he was decidedly unstable. Initially it was hoped that travel might set him straight. But there was even greater ignorance in those days about suitable treatment for the mentally ill, and three years later the unfortunate boy was permanently confined to an asylum.

How then did Christian Dior regard his future? Was this to be the end of his Socratic period or would he continue his life as a dilettante, a mere lover of the arts? It was certainly a most pleasant existence, this truant's life engaged in the pursuit of instant gratification, surrounded by a constellation of talented young souls dedicated to all that was frivolous. Why shouldn't life be a precious quest for beauty in the company of a few chosen companions?

Christian gave no sign of any great desire to persevere with music or painting, despite his obvious eye for the latter. The idea of creativity obsessed him but not to the point of renouncing his spectator status.

A factor here was his friendship with Christian Bérard. They were only three years apart in age and were the product of a similar upper-middle-class upbringing in the same part of Paris. Bérard had begun drawing as a child, reproducing countless scenes from the circuses and ballets his parents would take him to see, as well as sketches of gowns from his mother's fashion magazines. His characters all wore a certain enigmatic smile that quite entranced Dior. It was the start of a grand passion, the effect of which was to stifle his own artistic endeavors. As Dior wrote in his memoirs, the other Christian "had already realized that the human face and people's lives were worthy of far greater attention and honor than the simplified still lifes of the cubists or the geometrical figures of the abstract school. . . . Every one of his drawings was a lesson in seeing, in transforming daily life into a rich, nostalgic, fairy-tale world. I bought as many of his sketches and wonderful paintings as I could and covered the walls of my room with them." Dior was genuinely convinced he had met "one of the greatest painters of the day."

The same occurred with Henri Sauguet. The young musician had just embarked on his Parisian career when he and Dior met. But his great admiration for Sauguet's talent effectively quashed Dior's interest in his own. His memoirs reveal something of his feelings at the time: "He already had a certain reputation but to me he seemed tremendously famous. . . . His music united us all. It was what I would have dreamed of writing if heaven had granted me the gift of true musicianship. From his very first works it was clear that Henri Sauguet would bring spontaneity, romance, and a nonacademic approach back to modern music."

"All I required to be happy was friendship and people I could admire," he wrote. But perhaps it was not so simple. Admiring others can quickly translate into idleness, and an inability to act may be the sign of deeper problems, such as a lack of self-confidence or a certain pride that will not allow one to be anything but the best. It is clear too that Dior's comfortable financial situation provided a buffer (or perhaps a barrier) against the need to earn a living. He showed no desire for self-promotion, and was incapable of stooping to machinations like those employed by his friend Maurice Sachs, who was so consumed by his writing ambitions that he set about wooing the entire literary world. At one point secretary to Jean Cocteau, Sachs then took up a post with Max Jacob, incurring his fair share of their ire as a result of his fickleness.

Artists were much sought after by the grandes dames of the Paris salons. Women like Vicountess Marie-Laure de Noailles, Marie-Blanche de Polignac, Daisy Fellowes, Princess Dolly Radziwill, and Lili Pastré clamored over Cocteau. Bérard got his turn when he began designing sets for the theater. His greatest dream was to curl up at the feet of these beautiful madonnas, to be the star attraction at their soirées and a permanent guest in the homes of Dolly Radziwill or Daisy Fellowes. What more could he wish for than to be collected by Marie-Laure de Noailles's chauffeur outside his lodgings on Place Cambronne, where he lived with his companion Boris Kochno, and be driven to dine at her home on Place des Etats-Unis! Maurice Sachs, who charmed his way across Paris, set his sights on a wealthy patroness, Gabrielle "Coco" Chanel, managing to gain admission to the couturier's headquarters on the Faubourg Saint-Honoré by landing a dream assignment — setting up her library. He was paid a princely sum for his trouble but left Chanel's employ after a falling-out over some rather indiscreet behavior on his part.

Henri Sauguet was soon the toast of the salons and became particularly friendly with Charles and Marie-Laure de Noailles. He would subsequently spend summers with them at Hyères on the French Riviera, at their famous villa built by Robert Mallet-Stevens. Christian Dior did not venture into these circles, although he was invited to some of the balls and musical evenings at the home of Count Etienne de Beaumont on Rue Masseran. He enjoyed these events but his curiosity was often tempered by his shyness. For someone of his upbringing, the thought of angling for invitations was most unseemly, and his insecurity about his looks tended to paralyze him. He was most at ease in the company of close friends, where his warmth and intellect were shown to their best advantage. And never did he discriminate against people with lesser social credentials.

Having said this, one might ask whether Dior was content to play second fiddle in the midst of such exalted company. Keeping "in touch" in that situation required pretty finely tuned antennae, and Dior was remarkably intuitive when it came to spotting creative genius. He was no blind devotee of the avant-garde or slave to the latest fashion. His love of the new ballet and his admiration for Cocteau were proof of his innate feel for what would prove to be the most significant artistic developments of the 1920s. These were theatrical events of great strength and beauty, juxtaposing the rhythms of choreography and cinematography, the visual and the musical, poetry and gymnastics. It was an explosive mix. The great revolutions in twentieth-century art essentially occurred in the decade after 1910, but the 1920s saw the popularization of choreographic art and set the tone for Paris as a unique and exciting city. Perhaps Cocteau's greatest achievement was to make beauty accessible to the man in the street, a distinction not shared by the more esoteric works of Picasso, Stravinsky, Picabia, and the like.

While Dior was captivated by such creative genius, and in particular by the power of artistic expression, his approach was that of an onlooker, someone with no pretensions of his own. It was as if his parents' disapproval had stifled any desire in him to seek his own artistic path. But when you are twenty-two, you can put your courage on hold and no decision seems irreversible. For the time being, Dior held himself in check, using the force of his parents' opposition almost as an escape clause. Subsequent developments suggest that this delay was somehow intended, that he was meant to undergo a long testing period before finally achieving success.

Let us focus on one final image of Dior in this period, before accompanying him as he moves toward his chosen career. It comes courtesy of Henri Sauguet, from an interview given in 1984 in which Sauguet talks about the incredible state of excitement he and his friend Dior found themselves in at the opening of the Exposition Internationale des Arts Décoratifs in 1925. These young men had never seen anything like it. It had all the dazzle of a fireworks display, all the wizardry of a science laboratory. From Le Corbusier's *Esprit Nouveau* pavilion to the Lalique fountains, the Alexandre III bridge awash with cascades of light and the steel beacon of the Eiffel Tower, it represented the culmination of what had come to be known as Art Nouveau. Parisians flocked to the exhibition to gaze at the marvels of the world as they saw it, while to the foreign visitors Paris *was* the world. Dior, Sauguet, and their friends spent every evening there. Le Boeuf sur le Toit had transferred itself to a barge on the Seine for the duration. A little farther downriver floated another three barges, the most beautiful craft of all, with the names *Amours, Délices,* and *Orgues.* They belonged to the couturier Paul Poiret, nicknamed the Magnificent. He had converted one into a restaurant for the occasion and a lively crowd thronged from one to the next.

For Dior this was to be an encounter with the first couturier to see himself primarily as a creator and decorative artist. Poiret considered fashion a form of artistic expression. His prewar designs inspired by the Ballet Russes put women into harem pants and turbans in the style of the seraglio. While the Eastern or Oriental look eventually ran its course, Poiret's influence demonstrated something quite new and significant about the power of fashion. Suddenly, thanks to Poiret, couturiers could be more than just dress designers. Poiret was a sorcerer and a pioneer, collecting, dealing, encouraging and promoting ideas. His role as a catalyst in the trends and thinking of the day was similar to what Dior so admired about Cocteau, and what would later inspire Dior himself.

Not that Dior yet dreamed of such a career. It was unthinkable for a young man of his background. With the exception of Chanel, whose unique personality set her apart from the rest, couturiers were accorded the status of tradesmen. For all his flamboyance, Poiret was not a part of fashionable social circles, nor would society figures have attended his parties. This did not deter Christian Dior from making a place for himself in the creative world that so fascinated him. There are those who stay out of the limelight but who are crucial to the success of the show; where would artists be without dealers, without prophets and critics and patrons?

Christian Dior in the meantime had made up his mind. "I opted for the most sensible choice, that is, the one which must have seemed the greatest folly of all to my parents. I would become the director of an art gallery." The idea arose almost by itself. Jacques Bonjean, a former diamond merchant with whom Dior had struck up a friendship, was thinking of opening a gallery and needed a partner. Bonjean's greatest passion was for art. His first venture in the field had been a joint enterprise with Maurice Sachs, publishing original illustrated works, but Sachs had moved on to greener pastures as Chanel's librarian. Max Jacob, who liked to look after his protégés, fixed Bonjean up with one Gaspard Blu, who proved hopeless and left after only a few months. The opportunity then arose for Dior. All he had to do was put the plan to his parents. He was convinced they would reject it out of hand, but after much deliberation they concluded that it was not such a foolish idea.

Dior had been given a period of grace before facing them. He was conscripted in October 1927 and posted as a sapper, second class, to the Fifth Engineers Corps at Satory, near Versailles. His job was to carry railroad tracking, which gave him a sore shoulder. His sewing skills came in handy making a little cushion to stop the metal rubbing against his uniform! In the course of his time there, he heard his comrades in the barracks mention another conscript who knew Picasso. A few days later Dior met the fellow in question, Nicolas Bongard, an elegant young man who was to remain a faithful friend all his life. Nicolas's mother, the poet Germaine, was actually the sister of Paul Poiret, the couturier. During the war Germaine had staged exhibitions in her town house on Rue de Penthièvre to assist painters who had been called up. Artists like Picasso, Derain, Kisling, and Marcoussis and musicians like Erik Satie were regular visitors, and when Dior returned to civilian life, he was also invited.

The time then came to finalize his agreement with Jacques Bonjean. Maurice Dior had come around to his son's wishes and agreed to give him the capital he required, several hundred thousand francs, to set up in premises Bonjean had found at the bottom of a cul-de-sac at 34 Rue La Boétie. Dior was content despite his mother's stipulation that "I was never to let my name appear in the title of the business." To Madame Dior there was no difference between a gallery and a grocery store, and having one's name over a shop would have been a social disgrace. The gallery was therefore known simply as Galérie Jacques Bonjean.

After spending her life cultivating flowers in order to obliterate the aromas of the fertilizer that was the source of her husband's wealth, Madeleine was prepared to defend the Dior name tooth and nail. Like Madame Bovary, she confused the signs of social success and placed architects and artisans, couturiers and shopkeepers, gallery owners and grocers in the same basket. His mother's intransigence had a profound effect on her son, which was to reemerge with a vengeance twenty years hence, the night the New Look conquered Paris. Leaving the House of Dior on Avenue Montaigne late that February evening in 1947, his ears still ringing with applause, Christian Dior turned to look at his logo light up on the building's facade. "If my poor *maman* had still been alive," he cried, "I would never have dared."

Their ever witty friends quickly renamed the Galérie Jacques Bonjean, turning it into the Galérie Jambon-Dior in a punning transposition of Bonjean into *jambon*, "ham." And thus the adventure began. Friendship and entertainment were the prime objectives. Dior and Bonjean were both part of the Max Jacob stable and shared his sense of fun. The gallery therefore was merely an extension of the "family," a place to assist their artist friends, albeit with a certain degree of seriousness. Dior had also discovered a shared love of music in Jacques Bonjean's wife, Germaine, and they would meet once a week to play duets. When the Bonjeans' daughter Geneviève (the future actress Geneviève Page) was born, Dior was asked to be godfather.

After his experiences with two unreliable partners, Bonjean was delighted to have found a more responsible codirector. They were, however, in for an initial disappointment. In giving his blessing to the Bonjean-Dior union, Max Jacob had promised them his gouaches to sell. But once the contract was signed, they discovered that the hermit of Saint-Benoît-sur-Loire had been a little absentminded in his generosity and had already given the commission to someone else.

The pair now had to come to terms with the differences between real work and play. Their careless, heedless years were over, and business was business, even with friends. On this score, Dior and Bonjean divided their responsibilities. "I am not fond of society," Jacques Bonjean wrote, "and I find these things awkward. Why should I have to force myself? Christian spares me this task, one he finds no chore. I admire the way he seems so at ease. I know he can win people over quite effortlessly."

With the help of his "brother" Christian Bérard, Dior's gallery proudly presented its leading light. "Bébé" Bérard's launches were a guaranteed success. Jacques Bonjean describes one such occasion:

> The place was pulsating with the upper crust, Bébé dancing from one person to the next, all smiles and largesse. Then the artist Jacques-Emile Blanche arrived, the longtime sovereign of the painting world, well accustomed to wearing the crown of social success. Bébé broke away from Marie-Laure de Noailles to greet his illustrious predecessor, offering to show him around the exhibition. The pair proceeded around the room, one providing a commentary on his works, the other examining them in silence. They paused in front of one particular canvas. 'So who is this large lady?' inquired the master innocently, breaking his previous reserve. Bébé hesitated. The work in question was a self-portrait, of a clean-shaven Bérard between two beards. (The first was sacrificed for a passing fling with a police constable and the second hadn't quite grown back.)

This anecdote comes from Bonjean's unpublished diaries, in which he provides a lively account of the adventures of the two greenhorns and their ambition — like all young gallery owners of the day — of becoming the next Vollard or Kahnweiler. There were certainly times when they thought they might have been sitting on "the golden egg of the century," as Bonjean put it. In 1928–29 the years of radical change were behind them; artists, critics, and dealers had lost their taste for animated discussions on the bar stools of their youth. A new movement was forming and the gallery was one of its breeding grounds. One of its prime exponents was Christian Bérard, along with a strong Slavic contingent represented by Pavel Tchelitchev, who painted blue works and bodies with three heads, and the brothers Leonid and Eugene "Genia" Berman, and a number of foreign artists who added an extra touch of fantasy, such as the German Helmut Kolle and the Englishman Sir Francis Rose. They were linked by their emphasis on a return to the human element and the rediscovery of the body and face — a reaction against cubism, surrealism, and dadaism.

The movement had its mentors: Jean Cocteau, Max Jacob, and Gertrude Stein in France; in England, Edith Sitwell, who nurtured a platonic love for Tchelitchev. "Our novelty — " wrote Virgil Thomson, "and I am speaking of less than a dozen poets, painters, and musicians — consisted in the use of our personal sentiments as subject matter. . . . Neo-Romanticism is the journalistic term for it. Spontaneity of sentiment is the thing sought. Internationalism is the temper. Elegance is the real preoccupation." As could be expected, the movement was fiercely opposed by André Breton, who considered it a purely retrograde step. This poet-cum-dictator extolled the virtues of a more channeled spontaneity, a blend of technique and Freudian theory manifested in automatic writing. But battles like these are what get people to notice you, and the Bonjean-Dior gallery made the most out of being in the eye of the storm.

Part of the excitement surrounding the neo-romantics came from regular visits to the gallery by Gertrude Stein and her companion Alice B. Toklas, who used to talk about the little bell in her head that only tinkled when it encountered artistic genius. Armed with her reputation for having discovered (and purchased!) Picasso before anyone else, Stein played cat and mouse with the young painters. She would decide on a whim who would be the best that year, and then go on to reject them all, one by one.

But as fortune would have it, the gallery was not far from her veterinarian's rooms, and every time she took her dog Basket to be shampooed she would come to look at the paintings while he was drying off. One day she stopped dead in front of a picture of a young man sitting by a waterfall. "Who is this?" she asked. "It's by a young Englishman, Francis Rose," she was told. She paid three hundred francs for the painting and left. But she was soon back . . . and ended up buying thirty.

The gallery at the end of the cul-de-sac began to look like the place to be. "The supporters of our young artists made up an active little group that considered itself quite an elite," Dior's partner wrote in his journal. "As each one fancied he had come across 'the golden egg,' they were prepared to overcome every obstacle to see it 'hatch.' Never once did I hear them rail against our badly lit alleyway piled with sacks, either white with plaster for repair work or black with soot if they were delivering coal."

The art critic Waldemar George was a strong supporter of the neo-romantics through his review *Forme,* and his columns regularly made favorable mention of the young gallery. Of an exhibition of contemporary German painting in 1931, he wrote: "Messieurs Bonjean and Dior have once again put together an interesting collection of works by Klee, Campendonk, Max Ernst, and Otto Dix." Later in that same year it was, "This is the best selection ever brought together. It could provide the basis for a Paris Salon." The pair featured works by artists as varied as Dalí, Léon Zack, Filippo de Pisis, Giacometti, Bérard, Miró, and Tchelitchev. In 1927 Jacques Bonjean signed up the leading light of Italian painting, Giorgio De Chirico with his dreamlike landscapes. Bonjean and Dior bought up all the works by Raoul Dufy in the collection of the couturier Paul Poiret, including the huge wall hangings that had decorated the three barges at the exposition in 1925 — a reminder for Dior of the wonderful evenings spent there.

In the best gallery tradition, Dior and Bonjean would alternate hangings of young talents with retrospectives of more established artists like La Fresnaye, Utrillo, Braque, and Marcoussis. This proved successful, and the gallery was soon able to pride itself on what Bonjean described as "good relations on both a professional and a friendly level with the handful of other galleries like ours with a focus on new values." These were establishments like that of the great Pierre Loeb, who championed Miró; the Percier Gallery with its interest in naïfs, which inspired them to exhibit a selection of "American primitives" in conjunction with New York's Balzac Galleries; and Léonce Rosenberg, whose interest in works overshadowed by the fame of Picasso and Braque prompted the Bonjean-Dior exhibition "The Heroic Age of Cubism."

There was an active turnaround, and in the quieter months they would cover the walls with the occasional snapshot of contemporary society, like Count Etienne de Beaumont's collection of folding screens, collages of pretty-colored flowers taken from horticultural catalogues. These were more lighthearted affairs, with no serious pretensions, as

Jacques Bonjean makes perfectly clear: "This was not surrealism, simply excellent decoration. It was something for the pleasure of the eyes, not the mind." Bringing together Dior's love of architecture with a rather more calculated nod to society tastes, the Emilio Terry exhibition was the first to present designs for furniture and architectural motifs in a neoclassic style.

This was the essence of running a gallery in the best of all possible worlds. These were what Dior described as "the vintage years."

4

The Shattered Mirror

Misfortune did not make him a poor man. It also taught him a great deal.

— Henri Sauguet

*A*n end-of-season breeze was blowing across the beach at Granville, carrying with it a forgotten head scarf and the remains of some glorious summer picnic. It was too early yet for the full desolation of winter, but in the general air of abandonment and emptiness the landscape had regained its natural colors. All that was left of summer were the smooth walls of sand castles not yet worn away by the tide, deck chairs stacked in careful piles, and folded beach umbrellas, their gaudy stripes and summer-afternoon brightness now barely visible.

The summer vacation was over and fall had begun. At Les Rumbs the Diors had put away their bathing costumes and lemonade pitchers, had said farewell to the gardens and to long shady afternoon siestas. It was one more season to store away in the family album. The year was 1930.

Behind drawn shutters and dustcovers their Paris apartment had also been in hibernation. In the still silence even the clocks had slowly wound down and now waited patiently for their owners to set them moving again.

But nothing can guard against those freak gusts of wind that sweep an empty house, slamming doors in their wake. In the Diors' deserted apartment, a wayward breeze brought a mirror crashing to the floor. It was nothing serious. The faithful governess Mademoiselle Marthe hastily brushed up the splinters of sharp, silvery glass and the little domestic mishap was forgotten. All Christian could think of, however, on learning of the accident, was seven years' bad luck.

Somehow it seemed more than just a broken mirror. It was more like a mirror maze, where what appeared to be a simple everyday drama took on all the grotesqueness of real tragedy. That September night in 1930, when sleep finally overcame him, the young man in the apartment on Rue Louis-David was assailed by images of the future in the colors of ice and snow.

Europe was enjoying the calm before a storm of which it had no inkling. The cyclone that had hit the United States with the collapse of the stock exchange on that fateful Thursday in October 1929 had already brought America to the brink of ruin. Stocks, shares, savings, fortunes large and small — everything was gone. Some were driven to suicide. The aftershock had not yet crossed the Atlantic, however. A tidal wave may have broken on other, distant shores, but no one in France seemed concerned. Maurice Dior was unperturbed; business was booming, he had amassed a tidy fortune by honest means, and he felt no reason to fear anything the future might hold. Besides, he had more pressing things on his mind.

Bernard, his youngest son, with his "pleasant looks" and "pretty little angelic face," to quote Jacques Bonjean, seemed to be possessed by the devil. He was displaying increasing signs of instability, even genuine insanity. The family was worried. Eventually, the inevitable happened and it was decided that this "fine boy who had become dangerous" would have to be locked away. He was sent to the psychiatric institution at Pontorson in Normandy, where he would remain until his death in 1960. His mother, tough as she was, found it hard to get over the shock. She had never learned to weep in public and certainly did not intend to do so now. She fell ill — quite possibly her way of reacting to such a blow. She was diagnosed with a fibroma and, that spring, was admitted to a clinic on the outskirts of Paris to have it removed. A month later, she died of septicemia.

It was May 1931. Madeleine Dior was fifty-one years old, Christian twenty-six. In his own reserved, understated fashion Christian records the event in his memoirs: "My mother, whom I adored, secretly wasted away and died of grief . . . ; her death . . . marked me for life."

The interment took place in Granville, an intimate affair. Christian was hit hard. In his melancholy, his image of his mother became fixed forever in his mind. He saw her only as the woman he had venerated above all others, the woman he had followed like a shadow. Their disagreements over his artistic aspirations were forgotten. Wandering the garden, her domain, he imagined being at her side, instinctively naming each plant just as the young Christian had done in order to win her over. In every petal, in every frond waving in the wind, at every turn of the garden path, he could sense her presence, sometimes smiling, sometimes strict — "elegant and delicate, distant at times but always gracious," as Jacques Bonjean described her. Now more than ever, Madeleine became the model of Dior's perfect woman.

In the months following her death, Christian was aloof and subdued. That June he went to the Exposition Coloniale in Paris with his Swiss friend Fernand Gampert and his sister, but it hardly stirred his interest. He wandered from stand to stand without paying great attention and seemed to take in none of it.

That August, when the family reunited in Granville, the sunshine and the warmth seemed to have left their midst. Maurice Dior was broken, a man without spirit. Blinded by the loss of his beloved wife, the woman he considered the adornment, the jewel of his life, the finest of his treasures, he himself was lost. With her invaluable energy, her elegance and distinction, she had somehow embodied his prosperity, as if she exercised a secret hold over this essentially indolent man, forcing him to go on producing even greater material fortune, year after year after year.

Maurice, distraught, hardly spoke. Nor did he fully grasp the extent of the financial ruin that was about to engulf him. Good sense had prompted him to give notice to the family chauffeur, as he realized this was no time for extravagant expenditure. It was not long before he discovered that it was no time for any sort of expenditure at all.

One wonders whether Maurice Dior had still cherished the hope of one day seeing his middle son follow in his footsteps. For Christian, obedience would no longer be an issue. In 1931 Maurice Dior found himself ruined overnight.

With the spectacular success of his factories and the sizable income they generated, Maurice Dior had begun speculating. In 1923, the family business had gone public and he had acquired a share of its capital. That made him "the richest man in the family," according to Jean-Luc Dufresne, a relative of the Diors and now curator of the Granville museum. Preferring to look after his personal wealth and fearing that none of his sons would be able to step into his shoes, Maurice Dior had begun to distance himself from the daily operations of the company, leaving those responsibilities to his cousin Lucien, the future minister. Everything had worked out well up to that point. What could possibly go wrong now?

In 1916 he purchased 4,321 square meters of land in Neuilly, on the outskirts of Paris, for 190,000 francs. By 1929 this property was already worth two million francs and expected to keep climbing in value. The block was covered in trees and suburban dwellings, and Maurice Dior planned to preserve the former and knock down the latter to build four luxury apartment buildings. Good provider that he was, Dior figured this would generate a solid rental income and a secure financial future for his offspring.

In October 1929, in order to finance his project and establish the Parc de Neuilly Realty corporation, in which his three eldest would each take a share, Dior decided to sell his share portfolio. But following the Wall Street crash, the value of his stock fell by 20 percent in the space of a few days. Dior saw no cause for panic, the stock exchange was ever thus, and so he decided to wait. In the meantime he obtained a loan for the sum of nine and a half million francs from an insurance company called La Séquanaise. He was confident that his property development scheme would be completed within the next two years and start going into the black.

Nothing, of course, went according to plan, and in the course of those two years the wave of devastation that had swamped the United States began to wash over France. Not only had work been delayed on Dior's construction project, but the market had dropped — especially in real estate, where it had gone into free fall. La Séquanaise, anxious to save its own skin in the face of the impending crash, called in its loan and demanded instant repayment of both the capital and the accrued interest. Letters of demand flew and Christian's father, whose shares were now worthless, was left high and dry, unable to find the cash. To make matters worse, the builder he had chosen turned out to be less than honest and tried to swindle him by presenting him with a pile of falsified invoices.

His back to the wall, Maurice left town for a while to take refuge with his brother Henri. He was alone, without his dear wife at his side, relieved no doubt that she had not had to live through such a catastrophe but adrift without her, the one who always knew how to put a brave face on things, no matter what. Gradually he would be forced to sell everything — jewelry, furniture, property. . . . As he slowly came to that realization, his confusion grew and he became incapable of thinking, let alone of taking any sort of action; he even considered taking a caretaker's job on the very site that a short time ago had been the symbol of all he had achieved.

The reactions of those around him varied. Raymond, the eldest, had been taken in hand by his young wife Madeleine, who was as patient and good-natured as he was excessive, stubborn, and provocative. Raymond was certainly not a man of action. In fact it was only the strong presence of his wife that prevented him from going under. Raymond had a suicidal streak and this family tragedy took a huge toll on him. "His father's bankruptcy was the final blow," Madeleine would later admit. And it was left to her to keep his head above water for the rest of their lives.

Bernard, locked away in his asylum, was lost in his own world, one where stock exchanges, portfolios, shares, and bankruptcy had no meaning.

As for Christian, as always when confronted with too unpleasant a reality, he felt a desperate need to get away. It was not a matter of cowardice, rather an attempt to go on dreaming just a little longer, to gain time and distance and to "digest" what was going on.

Christian did, however, take the precaution of moving several items of furniture, paintings, and other objects of value from the Paris apartment before they were seized, storing them with the father of his friend and partner Jacques Bonjean. Jacques remembers being impressed at such "sangfroid and presence of mind in the face of adversity from a seemingly frivolous, and previously privileged, young man."

Learning of a study tour to the USSR organized by a group of architects, his next step was to scrape together the necessary funds and join them. There were several reasons why he was attracted to the then Soviet Union. Like all self-respecting young men of good family, he had flirted with Bolshevism in the 1920s. The Russian Revolution, the ideal of universal well-being and a desire for radical change, inevitably held a romantic pull for Dior, coupled with the impression, at least from a distance, that Russia offered freedom and a new start. This was quite in tune with the bohemian lifestyle and comfortable anarchy to which he had long been accustomed. It also seemed to come at the perfect time economically. With capitalism in crisis, maybe communism really *was* the answer. As he recalls in his memoirs, "I used to have frequent arguments with my father which ended in doors slamming and the ultimate expletive, 'Filthy bourgeois!' "

Another seductive aspect of the Soviet republics was their artistic wealth. In music and ballet there were Stravinsky, Scriabin, Shostakovich, Prokofiev, Diaghilev, and Nijinsky. In painting there were Chagall, Soutine, Rodchenko, Archipenko, Kandinsky, Kupka, Malevitch, Tchelitchev, Leonid and Genia Berman, and many others. A country capable of producing such an abundance of talent and genius, even if not all to Christian Dior's taste, could hardly fail to arouse his curiosity.

He was convinced, finally, by the prospect of traveling with a group of architects, a profession he had dreamed as an adolescent of entering. In those days a pilgrimage to Moscow was almost mandatory for any self-respecting French intellectual. The novelist Jules Romains, in particular, had written in glowing terms about the fall of the tsar and the fascinating, inspiring victory of proletarian democracy. That too aroused Christian's interest and he was keen to see it for himself.

He was in for quite a shock, however. Where were the spectacular scenery and revolutionary fervor he had been waiting for? What of the stuff of painters' visions and symphonic mastery? Instead he found a nation devoid of color, devoid of life, devoid even of liberty. He was struck by "the crumbling facades of the palaces, the shops with empty windows and the dreadful poverty." Long walks, images of grayness and filth, no excess, no opulence, unsmiling faces, streets and avenues memorable only for their emptiness — for Dior the Soviet Union was sadness itself.

His immediate response was to imagine better days and a brighter future, rummaging in the past and turning the experience into wonderment at what must once have been. "Nothing could alter my impression that Russia under the tsars had enjoyed a better way of life than this."

Despite his shattered illusions and the discovery of misery and apathy and resignation where he had expected enthusiasm and drive, Christian Dior was not disappointed. He was not the type to think in ideological terms.

If everyone was going to Russia, then so would he. And he would devour it with his eyes and, ultimately, learn things he would have preferred not to know.

Unconsciously, the more he found reality distasteful, the more he would lose himself in the glimmerings of dreams. He was captivated by the "unsurpassed beauty" he encountered on the long journey home. It took him to the ports of the Black Sea and on to Constantinople and, finally, back to the West, where he arrived relieved, "despite the overriding crisis, the bitter sorrow and anxiety awaiting me." He had marveled at the "bazaars of Trebizond, stuffed with worthless trinkets," which he likened to an Ali Baba's cave. It had been a brief trip back to childhood, the place where stories have happy endings and everywhere you are greeted by floods of sunshine, warm colors, and smiling faces. Conquered by the rich, lively beauty of these lands, he spared not one thought for the happiness or otherwise of the locals, as if their energy were guarantee enough that life was good. This was his brief moment of indulgence, knowing that Paris was waiting with all his family problems and that his return would be what he termed (borrowing from the author Céline) "a voyage to the end of night." He breathed in the fresh air and replenished his energies.

But his problems were to catch up with him even sooner than expected. At Marseilles, he found a telegram from Jacques Bonjean telling him that Jacques too was ruined. It was almost inevitable. The economic crisis had taken on the proportions of an epidemic. From now on, the two partners would be forced to go their separate ways.

Christian Dior arrived in Paris quite alone. His family had moved back to Granville and the remnants of their previous life, so near and now so far. The Paris apartment had been confiscated.

He was on his own and without a home, but he was surrounded by his many friends, both close and peripheral. Those to whom he had given so much of himself now proved unhesitating in showing their gratitude and sympathy in his new, straitened circumstances. Well-bred fellow that he was, Dior remained the very soul of discretion and made himself almost invisible, never letting on that he was hungry (although he often arrived without having dined) and never asking for anything, accepting simply what was offered. Jacques Bonjean recalls Dior's "generosity" when the time came to divide up the stock. Neither had any intention of abandoning their friendship and at least once a week Dior would have lunch with the family and play the usual duets with Germaine. In accordance with unshakable ritual, he would never forget a present or some sweets for his goddaughter.

What artworks remained were placed at Pierre Colle's gallery on Rue Cambacérès. A friend of Christian Bérard, Max Jacob, and Balthus, Colle was a devotee of the surrealists and someone Dior and Bonjean had known for a long time. They had even organized a joint exhibition in 1929. His kind gesture came at the right time and sealed a lifetime friendship.

It was September 1932. Dior spent his days in the new premises trying to sell his paintings. "We went from losses to goods seized by creditors, while continuing to organize surrealist or abstract exhibitions . . . which drove away the last of our buyers." Few had escaped the economic crisis, and gone were the days of straight deals and negotiations. It was more like a permanent clearance sale. "Within less than a year after the stock-market tumble began, virtually all the foreign spenders had gone home. The Argentines had turned in their diamonds, the British sold their yachts, the Americans packed up their furs and children, left mistresses behind," wrote the musician Virgil Thomson, a Parisian at heart, who sighed as he looked down at empty hotels and hopeful faces waiting in vain for a tip. Gone were the casual strollers and browsers who once might have been moved to open their wallets. There was no more money around and wallets were bare. "With the exception of the occasional patron or art lovers like the Vicomte and Vicomtesse de Noailles or Mr. David Weill," Christian Dior notes, "dealers were reduced to selling their paintings to each other at ever decreasing prices." There were days when not a soul came into the gallery.

Thus a three-year adventure came to a bargain-basement end, leaving only a pile of urgent bills to pay and paintings to be sold off at half, sometimes even a quarter, of their value. All told, however, this had not been a negative experience. There had been exhilarating moments that made up for the dashed hopes, disappointments, betrayals, and intractable rancor that afflict the art world as much as any field. There were artists who failed to keep promises, others who conveniently forgot their contracts.

Christian Dior now began adapting to his new lifestyle. For the first time ever, he had the freedom of someone who has nothing to lose, and in his own way, he enjoyed it. He was twenty-seven years old but only now really seemed to have come of age, deriving a certain pride from the novel experience of having to manage on his own. It was also a universal experience. "There seemed no way out, not only for me but for my whole generation." Others' misfortune does not automatically alleviate our own but it does prove reassuring, as a shared catastrophe is something quite different — an act of fate, for which no one is to blame, rather than an error of personal judgment.

Dior and his friends found themselves going back to their old ways. Together in good times and bad, they appeared bent on behaving like children ever on the lookout for amusement. As once they had laughed at the bourgeoisie, now they thumbed their noses at the economic crisis. "How many times, tired of waiting in my shop for the unlikely arrival of a client, would I take refuge for hours on end with Marcel Herrand at the Hôtel Rochambeau where, as at the Hôtel Vouillemont on Rue Boissy-d'Anglas run by the delightful Delle

Donne family, the credit was unlimited. It was essential, as some of us were quite determined never to pay for a thing, come what may. The new rules of life in the land of despair had been drawn up by Maurice Sachs, who was the first of us to become rich and the first to be ruined."

The greater the despair, the more enjoyable escaping it would have to be. The best traditions had to be upheld. Le Boeuf sur le Toit continued to be their meeting place. The owner, Louis Moysès, had not escaped disaster and had been forced to relocate to premises in Rue de Penthièvre that were due for demolition. He remained faithful to his clients, however, whom he considered part of the family, and was unfailingly generous toward all those who had contributed to the ambiance and reputation of his establishment. The "new tramps" like Dior and his friends were never refused supper here, and even in such dismal new surroundings Moysès managed to preserve something of the sparkle and buzz of Rue Boissy-d'Anglas, much to the satisfaction of those clients who *could* afford to pay.

Moysès even managed to find two attic rooms above the restaurant for Dior and Nicolas Bongard. It was nothing fancy, with a leaking roof and no electricity, but it was a roof over their heads. And so it was back to their old carefree lifestyle, making merry into the small hours of the morning. As soon as someone had a little windfall they would throw a party. All that was needed was a phonograph or a piano and something to drink and off they would go again. "Charades in fancy dress were elevated to an institution. I can still see us now, Bongard, his friend, and me, dressed up as God knows who, dashing from gateway to gateway to get to some masked ball on foot without being noticed."

But no matter how seriously you take your fun, it is never a complete substitute for real life, and it takes a lot of energy to keep laughing when things are grim. The morning after gets harder to face and the aftermath of the party seems steadily more depressing. After three years of living one day at a time and partying all night, stretching the reprieve to the last, Pierre Colle's gallery was also forced to close down and Christian Dior, who had spent months living on his reserves of strength, fell seriously ill — with tuberculosis. An immediate change of scene was called for. But he was flat broke and there was no such thing as National Health Service in 1934.

Always the one who went out of his way for his friends, and who never failed to applaud their talents, Dior now saw his loyalty acknowledged. A group of his friends chipped in to finance a cure, initially at a sanitarium in the Pyrenees and then on the Balearic island of Ibiza, where life was a lot cheaper than in France.

Completely alone for the first time in his life, Dior was forced to face himself. He could no longer escape by turning an admiring gaze on those around him, or avoid exploring his own gifts rather than those of others. "In this retreat, far from Paris . . . I discovered a new desire to create something of my own." To begin with, he turned to what was available among the local handicrafts and developed an interest, indeed a passion, for the art of tapestry weaving. It was hardly surprising, given his talent with a needle — all those fancy-dress costumes! He threw himself into his new hobby with prodigious enthusiasm and even drew his own designs, quite unheard of on the island. Never one for half measures, he made plans for opening a workshop there and was only dissuaded by a lack of funds and the general apathy of the locals.

The upshot of all this was Christian's realization that he needed to "do" things, and do them with his own hands. He returned to Paris after a year's convalescence in the sun in a whole new frame of mind.

While time had stood still for him, in Paris things had gotten worse, especially for his family. They were virtually penniless. Maurice Dior had long since resigned himself to his fate. Christian, on the other hand, had returned strengthened and mature. His forced retreat had made a responsible adult of him, and he was only too aware that he could not go back to the old life that had brought him close to death's door. He no longer had the ability or even the desire to lead a life of fun and not-always-fancy-free frivolity. The contrast between his easy existence in the lazy heat of Ibiza and the atmosphere of a city brought to its knees by financial woes opened his eyes. His first task was to attend to his hapless father and younger sister, now called Catherine. Their former governess, Mademoiselle Marthe, had remained loyal to her former employers and offered them a home with her in the little town of Callian, in Provence. Her house was really nothing more than a shack, but in pleasant green surroundings, and life in the South was simpler, less expensive, and more peaceful. Marthe saw to everything, and both father and daughter had become almost entirely dependent on her. The only one with any hopes of finding, or attempting to earn, any money was Christian, who was still in Paris.

And so he embarked on the harrowing quest for a job, dreading the thought of missing or being beaten to an opportunity, trudging dejectedly from door to door to hear the same humiliating response, "Sorry, nothing here." All he wanted was some clerical position in an office, an insurance company, or a bank. He combed Paris, the employment pages in his pocket, increasingly pessimistic but refusing to give up. He felt a certain sense of injustice — here he was offering himself for work he had no interest in doing and no one was interested in him! Most companies were firing rather than hiring, and Christian had no illusions about his chances. But thanks to his ever-present friends who entertained him and provided a bed at night and encouragement each morning, he kept his spirits up. They all admired him. As Henri Sauguet was to say later, "Misfortune did not make him a poor man and actually taught him a great deal." The dress-up parties continued but Christian's heart was no longer in them.

Early each morning he would go through the same process — racing to the newsstand, quickly running his eye down the "positions vacant" page, then racing once again from door to door. As time went on he widened his search, trying everywhere he could, knocking at random, even at the door of the couturier Lucien Lelong, who was seeking to fill some sort of office job. "You're not what we're after," came the familiar, cursed reply.

"I think I would actually be more suited to the couture side of the business!"

The words just slipped out as he was leaving Lelong's, finding himself yet again on the sidewalk and unable to contain his frustration. But there they were. He stopped and repeated the idea, once, then again. It stirred him somehow. "I think I would actually be more suited to the couture side of the business."

Couture? Well, why not? It was like something nagging at you that you can't quite pin down but which won't go away. And now it was out. Couture . . .

He continued walking, wandering from one street to the next, forgetting where he was headed. Suddenly he was lost in his childhood memories of brass bands, Carnival floats, and masked balls. Was it really all so absurd? Life itself is a carnival. Put on a mask to appear free of care and let chance take its course. Who knows where it might lead you?

A driver nearly ran him over and shouted abuse at this idiot who wasn't looking where he was going. "Oh, but yes, I am," said Christian, remembering the prettiest costume he had ever made. Couture . . . couture? And why not?

All those hours spent inventing the most amazing outfits, a ribbon here, a pin there, using every scrap of material in the attic. The laughter, the colors, the festivity of it all. "Christian has an idea for a clever way of wearing that, for a hat made of a few odds and ends or a gilt buttonhole. . . . Come on, Christian, give us a hand. Think of something!"

He had no idea where he was, he had never seen this part of town before, but he kept walking straight ahead. To let himself go, to forget the well-bred existence for an amusing one, to escape its rules and regulations and live by his own edicts, to be a child hero in an adult world and finally assert his own ideas. . . . Couture! What a thought! But actually . . .

He felt quite dizzy as he recalled those times. People had admired his talent for inventing new and amusing getups. The timid, reserved little boy had used his skills without fear of censure or laughter, without a care in fact, and no one had called him "sissy." He walked on a few paces, his head in the clouds — and suddenly came to a halt. That was it, no more "positions vacant" for today. Couture, couture, couture . . . Let the Carnival begin!

Just then a piece of good luck came his way. One of the few paintings he still had left was *Plan de Paris* by Raoul Dufy. It had been commissioned by the couturier Paul Poiret to add the final touch to the decor on his barges during the Exposition des Arts Décoratifs in 1925. Poiret had sold it to Dior a few years later when he fell on hard times, and now, all of a sudden, Dior himself found a buyer.

More than just a windfall, the money was a chance for some breathing space. Christian set to work at once. No more fruitless pursuit of jobs that had never interested him in the first place. While the money was hardly enough to live on over the long term, it meant that he could help his family, his prime concern, and give up an existence he found unbearable and to which he was totally unsuited.

The next bit of good fortune came in the form of an invitation from Jean Ozenne, Christian Bérard's cousin. Later to become an actor, Ozenne was a fashion illustrator at the time and lived on the Quai Henri-IV, with the "most beautiful view of the Seine, the park on the Ile Saint-Louis, and the Pantheon in the distance." He asked if Dior would like to move in with him.

This was the break Christian needed. Not only was this a part of Paris he loved, but living with Ozenne was to be the real turning point in his career. A talented draftsman, his host had no difficulty selling his sketches to a number of fashion houses. He was much sought after and constantly in work. Christian, on the other hand, had all the time in the world to watch and admire him. But ever since Ibiza, he knew that watching was no longer enough. He wanted to create things too. Jean Ozenne proved an ideal companion in this regard. He had seen Christian making marvelous costumes out of nothing and assured him that he was more than capable of following Ozenne's example. In fact, he would give Dior a few pointers.

Dior threw himself into this new venture with determination. It was as if this was all he had been waiting for, someone who would say to him, "Come on, do it. You're good and I believe in you." He pored over illustrations in magazines, working out perspective and proportions, spending every minute absorbed in his brand-new occupation. Jean Ozenne's American companion Max Kenna, also an illustrator, taught him how to hold a brush, discussed colors with him, and encouraged him in his endeavors. Christian went over everything a thousand times, littering the floor of his room with pieces of paper, some thrown in the wastebasket, others torn up in disgust or scrunched into a ball. Lover of painting though he was, he realized he had never really known how to hold a pencil. Still, he sensed that he had found his vocation and nothing would stop him now.

Finally, one evening, Ozenne returned to the apartment triumphant, having sold six of Christian's sketches for the princely sum of one hundred twenty francs. Christian was beside himself. "It was the first money I had ever really earned with my own hands! I was amazed. Those one hundred twenty francs, brought to me by a caring and faithful friend, were like the first rays of sunshine after a long, dark night. They were to decide my future. And I can still see them gleaming!"

Heartened by this initial success, he decided to leave Paris for the South, where he could be with his family and shut himself away to perfect his new craft. He was thirty years old and full of the excitement of someone who has finally found his focus.

Once in Callian he sat with his paper and pencils for hours at a time, drawing strokes and lines, inventing mock-ups, starting over again, finding his own form of expression. Regardless of whether the result pleased him or not, he kept going with an intensity his father and Marthe and Catherine had never seen before. For two months he sat at his desk, inspired by the hum of the crickets and the scent of lavender, time passing without his noticing. He became impatient to put himself to the test once again, and decided he needed others to see his work and to voice an opinion. So he returned to Paris with the fruits of his labor.

Among the first people he turned to were his friend Michel de Brunhoff, the chief editor of *Vogue*, and Georges Geffroy, a designer and interior decorator. While they were honest in their criticism, they were also constructive and encouraging, and Christian listened attentively. He had become a model pupil, as if striving for the best mark, thrilled not to be laughed at or condemned without reprieve. Back to the drawing board he went, to start all over, correcting this and adjusting that.

Soon he was ready to knock on doors again.

People liked his work. His hats were particularly successful, more so than his gowns. The milliner Claude Saint-Cyr, for example, was quick to snap them up "to be sure no one else would get them."

Step by step, with observation, time, and slowly accumulated experience, his dress designs began to take off too. Rose Valois, Nina Ricci, Schiaparelli, Molyneux, Paquin, Balenciaga, and Patou . . . all the big names, in one way or another, picked up some of his work and he suddenly found himself making a name in the fashion world. In fact, from September 1935 onward, Dior's diary records sales to some fifty clients, including garment manufacturers, furriers, milliners, and fashion magazines. While initially he earned barely enough to live, he gradually began doing better and better, owing no doubt to the expressiveness of his drawings and the volume, movement, and energy of his strokes. He also had the gift of creating a very lifelike image of the women who would wear his outfits.

His life was transformed. He had found meaning to his existence and, with it, the good sense to go at things gradually, one step at a time. Finally, however, thanks to the steady income generated by his new profession, he was able to think about finding his own apartment. Since 1936 he had been a resident of the Hôtel de Bourgogne on Place du Palais-Bourbon, where Georges Geffroy also lived. It was quite common in those days for artists and intellectuals to live in hotels as a way of avoiding taxes. (Only those with a permanent residence were liable for income tax.) One day when out for a walk he saw an apartment for rent at 10 Rue Royale. It was the perfect spot, despite the four flights of stairs you had to climb to reach it. It had five large rooms for eight thousand francs a year. Dior took it and moved in.

Next came the glorious task of decorating his new abode. Chintz and cretonne, little upholstered armchairs, opalescent vases, sofas covered in white Spanish shawls . . . with his faithful friend Christian Bérard in tow, he combed the secondhand stalls and bric-a-brac shops. It was a return to all the charms of the bourgeois life. "He recreated a miniature Granville in the midst of the *grande ville,*" the fashion editor Alice Chavane recalls. As with Proust's famous madeleine, memories of childhood came flooding back in his new surroundings, complete with a marvelous cook from Martinique and Dior's unique brand of hospitality, intimate and solicitous. Not only was he now master of his own house, he was also head of the family, continuing to send money to Callian and keeping in touch regularly with his father and sister.

Just prior to his departure from the Hôtel de Bourgogne he made another fortuitous acquaintance, one that would take him another step further in his career. His neighbor Georges Geffroy introduced him to Robert Piguet, one of the couturiers in vogue at the time.

Piguet bought several of his sketches, then, impressed with Dior's talent, asked him to design some dresses for his next collection. The difference between putting an idea on paper and creating it in real fabric was enormous. This was Dior's chance to see some of his sketches actually take shape as dresses. And the couturier's faith gave him a little more confidence in himself. Until then his taste had been influenced by those he most admired, like Mademoiselle Chanel, whose "elegance, even to a layman, was quite dazzling; with a pullover and ten strands of pearls, she revolutionized fashion," and Molyneux, "whose dresses were exactly what I would have liked to see on the women I stepped out with." But Piguet wanted "Dior" and "Dior" was what he would get. Going out on a limb, Dior discovered that he did indeed have ideas of his own — and successful ones at that. His first gowns for Piguet were a hit. Suddenly he was no longer an illustrator touting his wares but a designer others wanted to employ. He no longer had to wait to be seen but sometimes even made others wait to see him, if, for example, an earlier appointment at another fashion house had delayed him. His apprenticeship was over. He became a correspondent for both *Le Figaro* and *Vogue*, not content with simply reproducing designs from the top couturiers but quite unashamedly adding personal touches.

In June 1938, Robert Piguet offered him a full-time position as a *modéliste,* responsible for designing the couturier's creations. Piguet proved a tough master with a capriciousness that made life a little difficult at times, but the experience at his *maison* on the Champs-Elysées gave the future couturier just the grounding he needed. "I was to be a shy but most attentive initiate into the world of *premières vendeuses* and *ateliers,*" Dior relates. "I would apply myself to unraveling the secrets of biases and pocket reinforcements." Piguet was very pleased with his new recruit. For his very first collection Dior designed a dress called "Café Anglais," described as "a houndstooth dress with a petticoat edging, inspired by *Les Petites Filles modèles.*" *Les Petites Filles modèles* was a classic of children's literature, a series of novels by the Comtesse de Ségur in which the child heroines displayed the most perfect manners. As illustrated during the Belle Epoque period, they wore dresses with round collars, little cuffs, and full, rounded skirts in broderie anglaise. "Café Anglais" was an outright sensation and when Christian Bérard introduced Dior to Marie-Louise Bousquet, one of the big names in Paris society, it was as "the creator of 'Café Anglais.' " Bousquet in turn presented him to Carmel Snow, the grande dame of fashion journalism and editor in chief of *Harper's Bazaar,* as a promising new talent she had discovered. Christian Dior had just stepped over the threshold of the exclusive palace that was the world of couture.

There is nothing like the aura of success. It spreads like a subtle fragrance. Suddenly his friends in the art world, where Dior was hardly a stranger, began calling on his talents. In 1939 Marcel Herrand asked him to design the costumes for his production of Sheridan's *A School for Scandal.* Only those unaware of Dior's obsession with detail would have been surprised to see him so immediately at ease with a craft that had fascinated him since childhood. He gained an instant following. His actress friend Odette Joyeux, one of the cast in the Herrand production, recalls a dress with wide black and pink stripes worn in the second act by Yolande Laffont which made the audience burst into spontaneous applause.

The play was directed by Roland Tual, and his wife, Denise, who attended all the dress rehearsals, distinctly remembers Dior's contribution. "His designs were almost caricatures, his hats were exaggeratedly large with upturned brims, and his use of color was quite novel, bright as those acid drops the English are so famous for. . . . I was particularly struck by the interest and intense concentration with which this young designer went about his task. This fellow was maniacal in his detail, giving extremely precise instructions and leaving no room for interpretation." What Dior was doing was applying the same approach to theatrical costumes that he used for the outfits he designed for Piguet. In the theatrical world, where illusion is the order of the day, he could hardly fail to be noticed, and so taken was Denise Tual with Dior the perfectionist that she would call upon him a few years later to do the costumes for her husband's film *Le Lit à colonnes.*

While maintaining extreme, if not morbid, discretion about his private life, Dior had nevertheless become a little more emancipated.

He was now sharing his life with a friend by the name of Jacques Homberg. Homberg, who was a decade younger, considerably taller than Dior's five feet ten, and slender where Dior was decidedly round, was a well-bred young man who was to pursue a lifelong career in public service. With his return to a comfortable material existence, Dior began indulging his love of travel and together the pair visited the museums of Europe, hunted down turn-of-the-century antiques, and enthused over the beauties of the French countryside, Dior's particular love. Only Granville was out of bounds in that period. Life seemed to be good again, or maybe the Parisians were too reckless or blind to see what was around the corner. The economic crisis was somehow forgotten and no one seemed to sense the sinister portents of events in Munich.

In the spring of 1939 Paris society was a whirl of endless balls and crinolines — the Viennese look was all the rage in the salons. High society had actually never stopped dancing, crisis or no crisis, and now the artists were welcome to join them again, provided they would lend a hand with the decor — spectacular entrances by the choreographer Serge Lifar, who later staged the Marquis de Cuevas ballets in the United States, brilliant decorations and costumes by Christian Bérard, Jean Hugo, or Coco Chanel. Poulenc was commissioned to write the music for the "Bal des Matières" given by the de Noailles in 1929 and came up with a short instrumental work for an eighteen-piece orchestra, which he accompanied on the piano. Everyone admired the backdrop by Picasso from Satie's ballet *Mercure,* which was now a central feature at the Beaumonts' parties, but tried to forget his *Guernica* from the Spanish pavilion at the 1937 Exposition. In her regular columns on Parisian life, *New Yorker* correspondent Janet Flanner never ceased to voice her astonishment at the frivolities she witnessed in the hallowed halls of the Faubourg Saint-Honoré. "It has taken the threat of war," she wrote, "to make the French loosen up and have a really swell and civilized good time."

The most spectacular ball of the season before catastrophe hit was given by a young American who was the Paris editor of *Harper's Bazaar.* Louise "Louie" Macy got the idea from Prince Jean-Louis de Faucigny-Lucinge — why not reopen the Hôtel Salé, a long disused historic mansion in the Marais district, just for one night? All that was needed were countless chandeliers, a mobile kitchen with catering for five hundred guests by André Terrail of La Tour d'Argent, and mountains of roses and lily of the valley to decorate the tables. Dior was one of the guests at this fairy-tale event, which included everyone from the Duchess of Windsor to Bébé Bérard to the staff of *Harper's Bazaar.* "From princes [to] fellow workers," wrote Carmel Snow in her memoirs, "it combine[d] American enterprise with French passion for quality . . . the best combination I know."

Louie Macy was one American to whom Paris was home. While many of her compatriots had fled at the first signs of the 1929 crash, quite a number stayed on. Parisians had a certain style that seemed to rise above the circumstances, a flair so unaffected by a lack of finances that money almost seemed to be of secondary importance. Every time Carmel Snow went with Louie to visit their great friend Marie-Louise Bousquet, future French editor of *Harper's Bazaar* and widow of the playwright Jacques Bousquet, in her home on Place du Palais-Bourbon, she would be amazed at the way their hostess managed to bring together the greatest minds in Paris over nothing more than a few glasses of orangeade and some cookies. It was a mystery that never failed to fascinate the more materially minded Americans. "It was another era," says the actress Geneviève Page. "I spent my whole childhood surrounded by unique characters who, whatever misfortunes may have befallen them, would never have been failures. Godfather was the classic example of someone who could remain elegant in the throes of bankruptcy. In his darkest years, when he came to have lunch with us, we would know that he might not have eaten for three days and yet he never came without a little gift, a trifle, but always something to show us he had thought of us."

These same intangibles conquered the American composer and music critic Virgil Thomson, who had also made Paris his home. A friend of Henri Sauguet and Francis Poulenc, and part of the neo-romantic movement (the handful of poets, musicians, and painters including their leading light, Christian Bérard . . . and dealers like Christian Dior), Thomson sums it up this way: "I was happier in France than I had ever been anywhere, felt snugger there and calmer, working away at my music writing and cocooned by friendships, loves, and tasty cooking against the nervous anxieties of America, the despairs of England, the disasters that were surely on the march in Germany."

It was at this point that the Continent began to echo with the sounds of marching feet, pounding to the rhythms of a terrifying new regime. Europe was once again at war and Christian Dior was about to face another period of hardship and starvation.

5

War, Peace, and Revelation

> Shelley once said that we are all Greeks.
> It might equally be said, "We are all
> Frenchmen." . . . It is no accident that
> they are past masters at the art of living.
> A truly civilized people does not scorn
> the minor arts, for it knows how impor-
> tant the manifestations of living can be,
> even when embodied in a less perma-
> nent form of expression than marble or
> indelible ink.
>
> — Cecil Beaton

*T*he sun was shining on that first Sunday in September 1939.
Christian Dior had been invited to spend the weekend at the seaside
resort of Villerville with his friends the Bonjeans. They were down on
the beach tossing around a medicine ball after a swim when, all of a
sudden, everything came to a standstill at the sound of church bells
ringing. In Villerville as everywhere across the nation, the church bells

were tolling to announce the outbreak of war. Peaceful Sundays in the countryside were forgotten as people came running indoors to their radio sets. Life was about to be snatched from them — for how long?

A few days later Dior was in uniform, as were Henri Sauguet, Christian Bérard, Jean Ozenne, Sauguet's companion Jacques Dupont — and the artist Leonid Berman, who had just been granted French citizenship after a twenty-year wait. Only Max Jacob, who was too old for military service, was left to go on celebrating mass at his home in Saint-Benoît-sur-Loire.

Dior was sent to the Second Reserve in the nonoperational zone. For the first seven months of this "phony war," while the radio repeated "nothing to report," the two armies sat camped behind their lines and foolish soldiers sang "We'll Hang Out the Washing on the Siegfried Line." Dior, however, kept pretty busy. His military service was to be spent in overalls and wooden peasant's clogs tilling the soil in a little town in the Berry region called Mehun-sur-Yèvre. In a kind of recycling operation known as "farm duty," a certain quota of conscripts was assigned to help farmers' wives or elderly people needing a replacement for husbands, sons, or brothers fighting at the front. It was a very pleasant option, and sleeping in the barn, getting up at cockcrow, going to bed at sundown, and living to the rhythm of the seasons and the chores they entailed certainly gave Dior a newfound passion for farming. He instantly forgot everything else. Forty million French people were seething with impotent fury at the stupidity of a war that everyone, except those in power, had seen coming a mile off. But Dior's reaction was typically unusual. It was not the first time in his life he had created his own little island in the midst of a tempest. He may not have had a penny to his name, but life was good under the sweet skies of France, which, despite their fair share of clouds and storms, still managed to keep their glow. A menu drawn up by Dior for January 2, 1940, featuring oysters, salmon, and turkey, shows that at Mehun-sur-Yèvre there was no shortage of provisions to celebrate the New Year.

Then the fateful moment came, the catastrophe everyone had predicted. With the signing of the armistice with Germany in June 1940, France was split in two and one side was occupied by Hitler's forces. Dior was fortunate enough to have been on the unoccupied side at the time and was thus demobbed and allowed to go free. He had the choice of joining the flood of refugees converging on the highways, convoys of vehicles bursting at the seams, trains besieged in the general panic, roads and communications cut, people fleeing wherever they could. In Paris it was as if the end of the world had come, and the capital was soon deserted. But while some might find such chaos and tragedy vaguely exciting, Dior was one of those men you would find quietly going about their daily business when Judgment Day arrived.

With harvest time just a few weeks away, there was no question of leaving the farm, and so Dior stayed on at Mehun-sur-Yèvre. He was to spend a year in this charming village dominated by the imposing ruins of the magnificent castle built by Jean de Berry, where Charles VII died. This was the France Dior loved, the France of his childhood — spent in communion with nature and nurtured by a love of flowers and plants. This unexpected return to a life on the land seemed like a blessing from heaven. His memoirs describe his pleasure at "the slow, backbreaking work" as he waited for "the cycle of the seasons" and explored "the perpetual mysteries of germination." When moving around became less hazardous and he decided to join his family in the little southern village of Callian, he only had one thought, to pursue the peasant's life under the skies of Provence.

Callian is like a village from a picture postcard, a cluster of tumbledown cottages clinging to a hillside on a plateau between Draguignan and Grasse, in the hinterland of the French Riviera. The tiny cottage that the ever faithful Mademoiselle Marthe shared with her former employer and his daughter was surrounded by a little plot of land, and as the soil of the region was ideally suited to market gardening, Dior lost no time in enlisting his sister Catherine's help, pulling up the flowers and rosebushes and planting runner beans and green peas instead. Everything was in short supply, and this type of produce was greatly in demand, as the hinterland produced virtually nothing apart from tomatoes, olives, and grapes. This time there were no flower catalogues, like those the young Christian used to pore over in Granville, but patch after patch of vegetable seedlings to be transplanted. Until the harvest was ready, however, things were going to be tough — the eight hundred francs Dior had received on being discharged were hardly going to last.

The cottage had no electricity, and to save on candles the household was ruled by the solar clock. But life was good in the sunlit land of Jean de Florette and Manon des Sources. One particular ray of sunshine came in the form of a telegram that arrived to cries of "We're saved!" It was from Dior's friend Max Kenna in the United States. He had managed to sell the last few paintings from the old Bonjean-Dior gallery and the proceeds of the sale were on their way. The thousand-dollar windfall would see them right through to harvest time — the moment when Dior and his sister would load their cart with boxes of freshly picked peas and set off to ply their wares at produce markets around the countryside from Grasse down to Cannes.

One day a telephone call shook him out of his rustic reverie. The fashion world had remembered Dior. René Gruau, the illustrator, had mentioned Dior's name to Alice Chavane, the young editor of the women's pages of *Le Figaro* (which had relocated to the free zone after the occupation of Paris), who was looking for someone to do sketches for her. Several couture houses had outlets in places like Monte Carlo or Nice or Cannes, including Chanel, Paquin, Maggy Rouff, and Hermès, but there were no photographers (and no film for that matter) to take pictures of the dresses. So it was back to the drawingboard for Dior. A farmer by day, he became an illustrator by night, working by candlelight and then setting off to deliver his drawings to Alice Chavane in Cannes, almost a day's journey from Callian. As Dior could not ride a bicycle, he would walk the fifteen kilometers to Grasse, then take a bus to Cannes. Alice Chavane was thrilled with his efforts and amazed at Dior's modesty. "It was the equal of a real collection by a top couturier."

Cannes was a refuge for Parisians in exile, and Dior took advantage of his excursions there to visit friends. There was quite a little colony of French film stars in residence along the Croisette, including Michèle Morgan, Micheline Presle, Louis Jourdan, and Marcel Achard, all of whom had chosen Cannes in the hope that the Victorine studios in nearby Nice might develop into a second Hollywood. In the meantime they spent their days sunning themselves in deck chairs on the beach in front of the Grand Hôtel. But the restaurants were rationed and there was little in the way of entertainment, so Dior was immediately adopted by a group of friends who tried to forget their growling stomachs by organizing their own fun — charades, costume parties, and the like. It was a familiar routine — all that was needed were some old curtains, lampshades, the odd hair piece or false mustache, and a sound knowledge of history. The studio of the painter MacAvoy was converted to a "theater" for the occasion and an audience quickly gathered by word of mouth. Among the members of the troupe were Micheline Presle, René Gruau, the writer André Roussin, society figure Marc Doelnitz, Louis Ducreux, who directed the Gray Curtain company in Marseilles, the photographer André Ostier, and Victor Grand-pierre, son of a famous architect, who was to become one of Dior's best friends.

"It was absolutely hilarious," recalls Marc Doelnitz. "We picked some really thorny characters too, like Proust's mother, Madame Dieu-lafoi, Ninon de Lenclos* — nothing easy like the Three Musketeers or Snow White. It was as much fun guessing the characters as trying to hoodwink the others if they guessed too quickly, just to make the fun last as long as possible."

But in the narrow-minded world of Riviera society, tongues soon began wagging. The Vichy government of the collaborationist Marshal Pétain had banned parties and balls in both zones at a time when a million Frenchmen found themselves behind barbed wire in Silesia. A few malicious gossips reported the theatrical escapades as some sort of bacchanalian orgy and the police warned that they would take action if this scandalous behavior continued.

A strange atmosphere prevailed in Cannes at the time. There was plenty of activity but people did not seem quite themselves. Lectures and performances were held regularly at the Hôtel Miramar, featuring the likes of the couturier-turned-playwright Paul Poiret and the cele-brated doyenne of the Comédie Française, Cécile Sorel. And yet every social encounter had a darker side — there were old gentleman with the melancholy air of one who has lost everything, Jewish friends you might be seeing for the last time. . . . Ultimately, Dior was only too

---

* Madame Dieulafoi was an archaeologist who accompanied her husband on digs in Syria and always dressed in a man's suit; Ninon de Lenclos was a sensuous seventeenth-century courtesan and bluestocking — both perfect material for elaborate masquerades.

happy to return to his relatively charmed existence, tilling the soil, selling his peas, and sleeping peacefully in his little village hut. Simple though it might be, life in the almost storybook world of Provence conveniently blocked out the thud of jackboots and the horror of arrests, firing squads, collaboration, the black market, and all the other ugly sides of war.

As Paris slowly began coming back to life, albeit under the Occupation, the couture houses reopened their doors. In June 1941, Dior received a letter from Robert Piguet asking him if he would like his old position back. This reminder of the world he had left behind came a little too soon for Dior, who was up to his elbows in his market garden. He wavered. Once again, the approaching harvest provided a convenient excuse not to face up to a less pleasant reality. His sister Catherine could hardly pick all those peas by herself, and by all accounts life in Paris was unenticing, not least because of the daily battle just to find something to eat. His friends' stories filled him with horror; you could buy provisions only on the sly — butter in the back room at the dairy, coffee from the well-connected pharmacist, poultry from someone's aunt's farm. . . . The idea of the black market he found quite abhorrent. Life in Callian might be rough, but at least it offered some sort of sanctuary from all that.

He waited until the end of autumn before deciding to head back to Paris.

Parisians had rediscovered walking. Besides, getting around by car was essentially a privilege reserved for the German occupying forces. All that was left was public transport, and even taxis were rare unless you wanted to risk your spine in a velo-taxi, a fragile cabin on two wheels pulled along by a cyclist with powerful calves. Pedaling your own bicycle was preferable, if you were up to it, and in fact the boulevards were teeming with them. Your only other alternative was a cupboard full of sturdy walking shoes, the prewar British type, but they were certainly not available in wartime Paris save on the black market, and then at exorbitant prices.

One person who had the good fortune to possess such footwear was the gentleman at 10 Rue Royale. Stepping through his front door every morning in his elegant brogues, he would head off in the direction of the Faubourg Saint-Honoré, every inch the Englishman in his funny, domed, flat-brimmed hat trimmed with a jay feather and his gray flannel suit with a cornflower boutonnière. This was Dior's statement on the times.

Infuriated by rationing and enforced blackouts — windows blackened at night and shops in semi-darkness during the day — people staged their own little rebellions against the Occupation. Women took their revenge by wearing the most enormous hats, piled with fruit, birds, and all sorts of other bizarre decorations — all the things they could not find to put on their plates. Dior's contribution was to affect a little British bravado, at least in the choice of his headgear, so offended was he by the yellow signposts at every corner pointing the way to the closest Kommandantur or Lazaret or Oberkommando in ugly Gothic lettering. It was behavior worthy of Oscar Wilde, the man who declared that the perfect way to deal with ugliness was not to look at it.

But there are times when misfortune dogs one's every step, and when Dior abandoned his safe haven in Callian he certainly had no illusions about avoiding what destiny held in store for him.

In this case, it concerned his twenty-five-year-old sister Catherine. Shortly after his return to Paris she joined the Resistance. It is not clear whether he knew, but every time she came to Paris she stayed at 10 Rue Royale, in the apartment his friend Jacques Homberg had kept just as Dior left it. During one of her visits, in June 1944, Catherine used the apartment for her underground work. Christian was away, but Henri Sauguet and Jacques Dupont were staying there following a bombing alert for the Batignolles neighborhood where they lived (a cryptic message broadcast on Radio London saying "Baty will get a gutful tonight"). Sauguet and Dupont had asked if they might stay with Dior until the danger passed. They landed in the midst of a bizarre situation — Catherine and her underground contacts coming and going at all hours, and Dior's Martinican cook quite beside herself with irritation. It did not dawn on Sauguet just how dangerous the whole episode had been until he learned that Catherine had subsequently been arrested by the Gestapo. "It was a very close shave," he was to write in his memoirs. "How would we have explained to the Gestapo that we were just spending the night there, far from home, at Christian Dior's invitation?"

Worse was to come for the poor girl. Catherine was placed on one of the last trains out of Paris and deported. Dior left no stone unturned in his efforts to secure her release, finally calling on his ever reliable friend from Granville days, Suzanne Lemoine, the type of person you always turned to in a genuine crisis. Lemoine immediately put in a call to the Swedish Consul General in Paris, Raoul Nordling (who was later to play such a heroic role in the liberation of Paris). The best he could manage was to get the Germans to agree to hand her over to Sweden if her train was still on French soil. "It's a matter of timing," he told Lemoine. "If her train has not passed Bar-le-Duc by 2:45 this afternoon, she will be handed over. Otherwise it will be too late and there will be nothing we can do. . . ."

But it was just too late, and Catherine Dior was deported. For nearly a year Christian had no news of her at all and found his only comfort in the predictions of a clairvoyant who assured him his sister would return. She was right: during the night of May 27, 1945, he received a call from Metz on the German border to tell him that his sister would be among a trainload of deportees arriving in Paris the next morning. He went to the Gare de l'Est with some friends to meet her and brought her back to 10 Rue Royale amid tears of joy and sadness. Without realizing that starvation had so ruined her stomach that it would be months before she could begin eating normally again, he had prepared her favorite meal, a cheese soufflé.

Dior was also greatly saddened by another disappearance, which occurred just prior to his sister's deportation. In a huge raid across the whole Orléans region, his friend Max Jacob was arrested by the Gestapo coming out of the little church in Saint-Benoît-sur-Loire after saying his daily mass. He was taken to the holding camp at Drancy on the outskirts of Paris for deportation to Germany. Jean Cocteau, Pierre Colle, Henri Sauguet, and all his other friends did all they could to intercede on his behalf, and there were great hopes he would be freed. But while awaiting transfer from Orléans to Drancy, he had caught a chest infection, and he died soon afterward.

When Dior had returned to Paris at the end of 1941, he could not

Christian Dior's father, his mother, and Dior himself, aged six. His early years were those of a well-behaved, well-brought-up little boy. *(Photographs: Catherine Dior)*

The family in Granville: from left to right, Christian, Jacqueline, Bernard, and Raymond; the youngest, Catherine, is seated between Monsieur and Madame Dior. *(Photograph: Catherine Dior)*

His childhood home was to influence both his life and his style. The picture shows Christian Dior, aged two, with his mother and brother in front of the house known as Les Rumbs, in 1907. *(Fonds Villa des Rumbs; photograph: DR)*

Young Christian Dior was a dreamer, as shown by his solitary love of nature and gardening. His lifelong hobby of designing flower gardens came from his mother.

(Photographs: Catherine Dior)

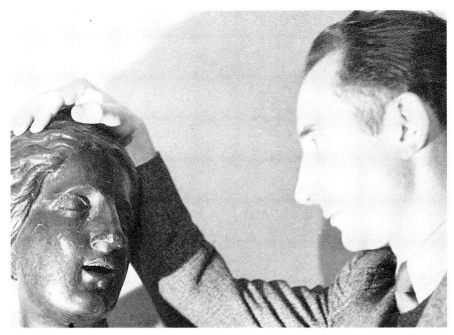

As an adolescent, Christian Dior cultivated his artistic talents despite his parents' disapproval. *(Photograph: Catherine Dior)*

Christian Dior as an art dealer, 1928.

(Portrait by Straker; photograph: DR)

The new gods of the arts: Max Jacob, Georges Auric, Igor Stravinsky, Jean Cocteau, Francis Poulenc, Darius Milhaud, and Pablo Picasso. For Dior, meeting them came just as he was discovering Paris for the first time. *(Sketch by Pruna; photograph: DR)*

Le Boeuf sur le Toit on Rue Boissy-d'Anglas, Jacques Doucet at the piano.
(Sketch by Foujita; photograph: DR)

At last, couture. Christian Dior made his debut at Robert Piguet in 1938.
(Photograph: Willy Maywald, ADAGP)

Dior was called up in 1939. He spent his military service harvesting at Mehun-sur-Yèvre, wearing wooden peasant's clogs. *(Photograph: Catherine Dior)*

The "two Christians," Bérard and Dior, considered inseparable, here pictured at the flea market. *(Photograph: Catherine Dior)*

The couturier-king on the Avenue Montaigne balcony in 1957.

(Photograph: Garofalo, Paris-Match)

At a trade fair with his childhood friend Serge Heftler-Louiche, who headed Christian Dior Perfumes.

(Photograph: Marie-Christine Wittgenstein).

Posing on the staircase at Avenue Montaigne, the couturier surrounded by his team: on his right, Madame Marguerite, "the queen of technique"; on his left, Mitzah Bricard, "the empress-muse"; in the second row, behind him, Suzanne Luling, in charge of the salons; on her right, Madame Raymonde, head of the studio, and then Jacques Rouët, the couturier's right-hand man, responsible for marketing the Dior label worldwide.

(Photograph: Brommet)

The couturier used a pointer with a gold-ringed knob to show where a design needed to be changed. Here he is checking the "charts."
(Photograph: Loomis Dean)

Chatting with one of his models. He called them all his *chéries*—"darlings."
(Photograph: Henri Cartier-Bresson, Magnum)

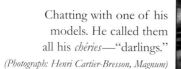

The workroom in full swing. Christian Dior liked to "allow each seamstress the freedom to express herself, out of respect for the happy outcomes of pure chance."
(Photograph: Bellini, Christian Dior archives)

The dress rehearsal on the day before the show-ings in the main salon was held in accordance with a strict ritual.

(Photograph: Bellini, Christian Dior archives)

The revolution of February 12, 1947, unleashed the fury of a handful of aggrieved housewives who attacked the first women to champion the New Look. . . . and tore their dresses to shreds.

(Photograph: Carone, Paris-Match)

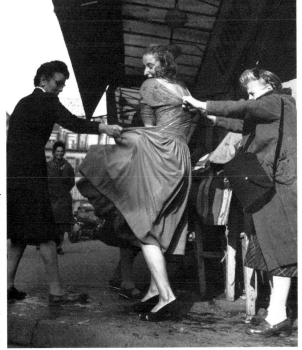

Marie-Laure de Noailles, beneath a Berman portrait of her. *(Photograph: Georgette Chadourne, DR)*

Top right: a client and a friend, Marlene Dietrich commissioned her screen wardrobe from Dior. *(Photograph: Horst)*

Above, from right to left: Carmel Snow, editor in chief of *Harper's Bazaar* and the first to use the term New Look, the photographer Richard Avedon, and Marie-Louise Bousquet.

February 12, 1947: in the center, Rita Hayworth, left, the Begum. *(Photographs: Willy Maywald, ADAGP)*

Dior had loved masquerades since he was a child. Here he is pictured dressed as a bistro keeper with his friend Francis Poulenc at the "Moon-over-Water-Ball" held by the Noailles in 1951.

(Collection of Francis Poulenc; photograph: DR)

Dressed as the King of the Beasts, in a costume designed by Pierre Cardin for the "Kings and Queens Ball" given by Count Etienne de Beaumont in March 1949.

(Collection of H. de Beaumont; photograph: DR)

As Barbey d'Aurevilly with his friend Georges Geffroy, as Alexandre Dumas, at the "Bal des Artistes" held by Charles and Marie-Laure de Noailles in 1956.

(Photograph: André Ostier)

The Moulin du Coudret at Milly-la-Forêt. It was a ruin in a swamp until Dior turned it into his hideaway. *(Photograph: Willy Maywald, ADAGP)*

Here he would indulge in his favorite pastimes, good food, music, cards . . . and the delightful task of creating his garden along with his gardener, Ivan. *(Photographs: Dahl Wolfe, Hearst/André Ostier)*

At La Colle Noire, his last residence, near Grasse in the south of France, Dior revived his architectural bent and engaged in some major renovations. He planned to retire here one day and live the life of the lord of the manor.

(Photograph: DR)

He made his own liqueur at the Moulin du Coudret, which he is seen bottling here.

(Photograph: Vic Vance, Paris-Match)

Dior turned fashion into news. Every new collection made the front page. In 1957, another first—the cover of *Time* magazine.

(Photographs: UFAC, Paris-Match, Christian Dior archives)

know what turns the war would take. Piguet had asked him to return, and he duly presented himself. But he was too late. The position had been given to a promising young Spaniard by the name of Antonio del Castillo. Dior did not seem overly perturbed: if anything, the lack of enthusiasm he had shown at Piguet's initial summons indicated his real feelings. In his years at Piguet he had learned all he could from the couturier. Piguet had taught him about fabric and the elegance of simplicity but had teased him — wrongly, Dior felt — about his predilection for *coupes savantes* or "fancy cuts." Dior found it particularly difficult to put up with the intrigue and office politics that his former employer so relished and which struck Dior as very negative aspects of the closed world of Parisian couture. Rather than getting upset at losing his position, he decided to wait and see what fate had in store for him.

What did disturb him greatly were the ghastly new Paris fashions. All the rage in wartime Paris was the *zazou* or zoot look, almost antifashion with its long, wide-shouldered jackets for men, reaching right down to the knees like sacks and worn over stovepipe trousers and thick-soled shoes. The finishing touches were long, slicked-back hair and an umbrella under the arm à la Chamberlain, no matter what the weather. He could understand that this was how these odd-looking fellows thumbed their noses at the arrogance of the Germans and the austerity of the Vichy government. But what he found most devastating, painful, even heartbreaking, were the women. In gray silence they sat astride their bicycles, their heads held high despite the gray of the smog and the gray of the sky. Everything about their attire spelled misery, suffering, and sham — clunky shoes with cork wedge-heels, a fake stocking seam drawn skillfully onto the leg, short skirts (there was no material to spare) with a split (to make for easier pedaling), and on top of it all a harsh square-cut jacket. Most curious, though, were their playful yet imposing hats — amazing concoctions in tulle and ribbon, cascading turbans in every material imaginable, like a joke or a touch of individuality and independence in contrast to the prevailing oppression. "Made up of remnants that could serve no other useful purpose, they looked like enormous pouffes, flying in the face of the all-pervading misery . . . and common sense," wrote Dior.

The war had certainly had a profound effect on women. Forced to adapt to the times, fashion had become increasingly down-to-earth, more vulgar and yet more subdued. But those hats were saying something quite moving. They stood for an ongoing belief in the power of the imagination, the need for a little fantasy in order to rise above poverty, to hold one's head high and escape the world around. . . .

As already shown, Dior had some good friends. Paul Caldaguès, an editor at *Le Figaro,* was one of them. Hearing about Dior's setback with Piguet, Caldaguès started asking around and was soon able to report that Lucien Lelong was looking for a *modéliste* and would be happy to meet him.

Lelong's was a top-drawer establishment, dressing the most elegant society women and the "big" foreign names. Lelong himself had been married to a princess, Natalie Paley, his favorite model, and his salons at 16 Avenue Matignon with their refined 1930s simplicity epitomized the good taste of their owner. He had the bearing of a very grand gentleman and presided over a little stable of designers who created outfits for the Lelong name. One of these was Pierre Balmain, with whom Dior immediately struck up a friendship, while the head of the design studio was a Madame Zehnacker, a remarkable professional whose blue-eyed gaze soon softened at the modesty, courtesy, and talent of the newcomer. . . . But more about Madame Zehnacker later.

Now that he had found his feet again in the world of couture, Dior began to sense the underlying turmoil wrought by the war, both economically and politically. Some of the biggest names had moved abroad — Coco Chanel to Switzerland, Schiaparelli to the United States, Molyneux and Worth to London. Others, like Mainbocher and Madeleine Vionnet, had closed down. But the Parisian fashion industry had no intention of going under. At stake here was a cultural heritage, the livelihood of twelve thousand workers, and an industry that used relatively few raw materials to bring in huge profits. (Prior to 1939, the export income from one single couture gown could buy six tons of coal.)

But saving it was no easy task. Haute couture, like every art form, needs freedom to exist. It also provides a means of rising above the conventions of the day. Such things were seen as provocations and acts of resistance by both Vichy and Berlin, and throughout the war years both regimes took repeated steps to suppress and stifle the fashion industry. They came very close to succeeding.

The slogan of Marshal Pétain's Vichy government was "Work, Family, Fatherland," and the slightest frivolity was not part of the formula. A return to traditional values was the order of the day: the French were expected to adopt a clean, healthy lifestyle both morally and physically and to reject anything that strayed from the straight and narrow. The prime targets, predictably, were certain films, literary works, theatrical productions . . . and fashion. Women were exhorted to dress like mothers, virtuously and sensibly. In a 1941 issue of the magazine *Votre beauté,* columnist Lucien François wrote: "We are going through the greatest revolution France has ever seen. Our military defeats have opened our eyes to the weakness our country has been reduced to as a result of many long years under a misguided regime devoid of moral values. If we wish to survive, everything must be changed, cleansed and purified."

Berlin, for its part, was envious of the influence and image of French fashion the world over, and irritated by its "free-thinking" ways. In July 1940 officers of the Reich ransacked the premises of the Chambre Syndicale de la Haute Couture and confiscated its archives, including files containing the names of its foreign customers. This Chamber of Couture had been founded in the late 1800s as a kind of trade union of dress designers, with the main aim of protecting their designs from piracy and plagiarism. Design houses must meet rigorous standards to join, and even today its members include only a handful of houses; these must maintain ateliers in Paris and their clothes must be entirely made to measure. The Germans' aim was to transfer the French fashion industry to Berlin and Vienna, which were to be the new cultural capitals of Europe. Seamstresses would be called upon to provide their inimitable skills and designers were promised "magnificent positions."

There was one man who had no qualms about voicing his undiluted opposition to this ridiculous totalitarian plan. "You can force us to do anything you like," said Lucien Lelong, who had been president of the Chamber of Couture since 1937, "but Paris haute couture will never move, neither as a whole nor bit by bit. Either it stays in Paris or it ceases to exist."

The government, in this instance, sided with Lelong, no doubt mindful that such a move would spell economic disaster. After all, the

ateliers of Paris employed a huge number of people. The Ministry of
Labor and Industry then asked Lelong to go to Berlin personally in
November 1940 in an attempt to convince the Germans. Adept at
winning time when needed, the couturier managed to explain to the
enemy that the couture industry was made up of a number of diverse
smaller industries like milliners, hosiers, shoemakers, and corsetiers,
not to mention embroiderers and textile manufacturers, which were
more than just individual crafts and trades but part of the country's
history and cultural heritage. . . . In short, this was not something that
could be broken up or "relocated." Observing that the Germans themselves were in the process of setting up their own highly subsidized
fashion industry, he stressed the need for each country to create its own
fashion and encouraged Germany to support local efforts rather than
usurp what belonged to France. The subtlety of his reasoning and the
force of his arguments soon won them over and the Germans abandoned their plans, allowing French couture to retain its independence.
But it lost the right to export and photograph its designs, which of
course considerably limited its reach. The fashion magazines were also
suffering from paper shortages and their operations were reduced
accordingly, in some cases brought to a standstill. French *Vogue,* for
example, ceased publication altogether upon the refusal of chief editor
Michel de Brunhoff to compromise with the Germans.

Such a high-minded reaction from his friend Brunhoff and the
forceful stance taken by his employer undoubtedly made an impression
on Dior. By placing him right in the middle of what was essentially a
resistance movement in its own right, the fates seemed already to be
setting out their pawns.

Everyone was waging an individual war, from the politicians
down. Every gown was the product of a battle to find raw materials.
Textiles became even scarcer and more sought after when winter tem-
peratures hit record lows. Designers tried new fabrics made from pine,
hemp, and gorse — without great success. The solution was to lift
hems, reduce the number of pockets and inlays, and get rid of lapels.
Every completed garment was a triumph over the rules and regulations
laid down by the Germans to stifle French couture.

During the Occupation, the Nazi regime tried fourteen times to
abolish the industry altogether. But Lucien Lelong stood his ground

and in March 1942 organized a group fashion show in Lyons in the unoccupied zone. He also tried to persuade the French authorities to make a particular effort to sustain this prestigious sector of the economy. It would be foolish, he argued again and again, not to back an area of production that employed a very large number of workers and used a minimal amount of primary resources. The powers that be were convinced and the "authorized" couture houses (of which there were eighty-five in 1941 and seventy-nine in 1944) were granted special concessions in fabric rationing. The collections were strictly regulated, however: they could not feature more than seventy-five outfits, and each category of apparel could only use a certain quantity of materials. The Germans still managed to close down Madame Grès and Balenciaga in 1944 on the pretext that they had exceeded their fabric quotas. The only one with reserves to last the distance was Jean Patou, who had been in the habit in the prewar years of buying up all his suppliers' stock, in order to retain exclusivity.

Almost miraculously, Dominique Veillon tells us in her book *Fashion under the Occupation,* couture not only survived all these restrictions but actually quintupled sales in the period between 1941 and 1943 — probably because the clients did not miss a single show.

In 1941 the Couture Création group sold twenty thousand "couture cards," indispensable pieces of paper available solely to the privileged and the only way of getting into fashion shows. A mere two hundred of these tickets were allocated to the wives of German officers. The clientele, therefore, was predominantly French, plus a few South Americans for whom the war was simply part of the ambiance. The Frenchwomen were either from the top echelons of society or part of a new breed known as the "B.O.F. wives." Their husbands, the *beurre-oeufs-fromage* (butter, eggs, and cheese) men, were the sharp operators who amassed incredible fortunes by selling farm produce at scandalously high prices. As Schiaparelli was later to point out, "This sort of profiteer appeared in a whole range of areas and really changed our clientele . . . and fashion too, as a result."

The effect of this was to give Dior a new understanding of his profession. Although he had entered the industry almost by fluke, he saw himself as continuing in the tradition of style and elegance established by the great names he so admired. As he said in his memoirs,

"We invent nothing, we always start from something that has come before." Molyneux, he added, had influenced him the most, but he also admired the "creative genius" of Balenciaga, Madame Grès, and Madeleine Vionnet, of whom he said, "never has the art of couture been taken to such lengths and heights." As for Chanel, she had "revolutionized fashion." A faithful follower of the grand old school, Dior was adamant that haute couture should always maintain its standards, convinced that nothing would impair those standards more than stooping to an inferior class of client. But it was hard to muster such a spirit in those difficult years. It was a touching sight, mind you — those Parisian ladies bent on remaining elegant come what may, never missing a couture collection, always perfectly made up. Even in the metro or the air-raid shelters they remained conscious of their appearance, despite the all-pervading atmosphere of oppression. If they were knitting for the prisoners of war, they would simply carry their needles and skeins from salon to salon. But what could a designer offer these women if not something essentially practical? From Nina Ricci came felt gaiters to protect the legs, from Lucille Manguin a short skirt they could lengthen with snaps, from Madeleine de Rauch outfits named after metro stations; there was even an outdoor fashion show called "Elegance on a Bicycle." The hairdressers had their problems too. At the Gervais hair salon, for example, it was not unusual to see two men on bicycles down in the cellar, pedaling away to keep the hair dryers running whenever electricity shortages hit.

But no matter how adept everyone became at making do, nothing could lift the gloom that hung over the couturiers' salons, by now slightly shabby places where clients came to while away the empty afternoons. Even Piguet's establishment, done up in full Napoleon III quilted pink satin, had a somber air about it. Christian Dior was never much taken with Piguet's "rather tarty" decor, to borrow a description from Marc Bohan, who followed Dior at Piguet. Dior had gone through some frustrating moments during his apprenticeship there, including being teased by Robert Piguet about his "fancy cuts." That remark had come on the heels of Dior's first success, his "Café Anglais" dress, which had left the novice designer feeling just that little bit more adventurous. Instead he found himself being sent back to the workroom time and again to "simplify, simplify!" Ego aside, Dior simply did not share Piguet's view and was later to state that Piguet "was wrong to criticize. It's only by developing technique that fashion can ever really change." But dresses had to sell. Both he and his friend and confidant Pierre Balmain underwent similar experiences at Lelong, forced to look on with disappointment, season after season, as Lucien Lelong presided over fitting sessions like a referee surrounded by a football team, changing this detail, sending back that gown, and rejecting suggestion after suggestion, generally for purely commercial reasons.

In the midst of the Occupation, a promising young director by the name of Jacques Becker made a film called *Falbalas* or *Paris Frills,* starring Micheline Presle and Raymond Rouleau, about the dream world created by fashion. But did that power still exist? There comes a time ultimately when a person with a real gift for creation, in any kind of field, is confronted by this dilemma: is one here to cater to the demands of the public or express one's deep feelings? Dior was too much an "artist" and far too responsible to elude the question. He matured a good deal in this period, forced to ponder not only his concerns as a dressmaker and craftsman but also the wider issues associated with fashion, its long tradition, and its influence way beyond the borders of its country of origin. In Lucien Lelong, Dior had the chance to observe a man of great talent, not so much as a designer but as a businessman. The Editions section set up by Lelong in 1934, for example, specialized in ready-made dresses requiring only a few alterations — the precursor of couture prêt-à-porter. Commercially, Lelong's was a very dynamic establishment, and of all the French designers, Lelong was undoubtedly the best known in the United States, thanks to a trip he made just before the war, at the behest of the French ministry of foreign affairs, to study the American garment industry. The war, however, with all its restrictions, had taken some of the sheen from French fashion internationally and suddenly it was no longer the benchmark it had once been.

In Rome, for example, the important clients from the upper middle class and the aristocracy who used to come to Paris for their wardrobes had changed their buying habits with the policies of Il Duce. Mussolini's plan was to promote Italian fashion and bring it in line with Italy's already well established reputation for fine footwear. In 1936 he passed a law declaring that at least 25 percent of every Italian couture collection had to be "Italian in inspiration." The princesses of Italy's royal family and the wives of other dignitaries were also seen to back the initiative.

Things were slightly different in Great Britain. When *Vogue* published photographs of elegantly dressed young women celebrating the liberation of Paris in the streets, Englishwomen were shocked. A certain amount of sartorial fantasy might have been a form of resistance in France, but in England true patriotism meant falling in with the constraints of rationing and general austerity, out of respect for the men at the front. British *Vogue* was still wildly popular but full of advice for young women on how to revamp, remodel, and transform their existing wardrobes and turn thrift into fashion. In one 1941 issue *Vogue* instructed its readers to see their wardrobes "no longer as a novel in three volumes but more like a simple short story in which every line counts." And photographer and fashion guru Cecil Beaton had no qualms about using bomb sites and other scenes of destruction as locations for a fashion spread. In London, a city better known for its gentlemen's apparel but also strong on women's wear with designers like Worth, Molyneux, and Charles Creed, the major couturiers pooled their talents to create a collection of unstintingly sumptuous gowns for export to South America. At the same time, they instantly agreed when the British government asked them to design a range of garments for mass production in keeping with the rules of national defense. In other words, the tactic on the other side of the Channel was solidarity, feeding the overseas market on one hand while attempting to "democratize" and fit in with the new reality of the mass market at home.

Those very same factors produced quite a different phenomenon in the United States. Before the war, America was French couture's biggest market. But with France cut off from the rest of the world by the Occupation, America was forced to go it alone. This was the decisive moment for the rag traders of Seventh Avenue and they were quick to seize their chance. With the arrival of a huge number of skilled garment makers fleeing Nazi Germany and thanks to a few American designers like Claire McCardell, fashion soon found the right tone and style for the local market. What Americans wanted and needed were comfortable, practical clothes that were easy to wear and easily affordable. They had a certain amount of style but were perfect for mass production, a concept still quite foreign to Europe. In 1942 the American garment manufacturers' union invested a million dollars in a campaign to promote American fashion, actively supporting the New York industry over French couture. Thus under attack, and in the face of such efficiency — streamlined manufacturing processes, assembly lines, a huge range of color and design combinations, standard sizing for every figure — not even the most optimistic members of the French fraternity held out much hope of their industry ever regaining its preeminence. As the war came to an end, anyone capable of serious analysis would have reached the same conclusion. The most worrying aspect of what was essentially the economic rationalist approach was its impact on the creative side of fashion. Without the support of its foreign clientele, Paris couture was destined to lose its spark, as the local market was too small to allow room for the hint of adventurousness Dior hankered for each time his designs were reined in by his employers. But Dior refused to believe this was the final word on the matter. Convinced instead that France must return to the tradition of perfection that had once made its couture stand apart from the rest, he rejected the free and easy attitudes that seemed to prevail around him. The more the world became "democratic," the greater the argument, as he saw it, for Paris fashion to maintain its raison d'être. In due course Dior would make a brilliant case for this point of view. But in 1945 he was just a designer with Lelong, who had no intention of consulting Dior!

Lucien Lelong was having to face those very same issues in his capacity as head of the Chamber of Couture. He and his colleagues were only too aware that the scales had tipped in favor of the New World. Amid the rejoicing of the Liberation, the couturiers forgot their quarrels and rivalries for a moment and decided to unite, aware that they would have to take joint action if they were to regain their reputation and international standing. In 1946 the Chamber of Couture, still headed by Lucien Lelong and his very active deputy Robert Ricci, brought together fifty-three couturiers to create the Theater of Fashion — some two thousand dolls dressed for every hour of the day and night, placed in settings designed by artists like Christian Bérard and Jean Cocteau.

It was a magnificent spectacle. Every detail, from the hairstyles right down to the tiniest accessories, gave evidence of a unique level of expertise. This was more than mere fashion. This was art. The concept was to tour the globe and prove once and for all that France was far ahead of the rest. No other country could have demonstrated such ingenuity and inventiveness, such luxury born out of such poverty.

Two of the dolls were particularly beautiful — one in a day dress in white and turquoise with a draped bodice and swirling skirt, the other wearing an evening dress in ivory tulle embroidered with flowers and leaves. Both minioutfits bore the signature Lelong and, although no one realized it at the time, they revealed the shape of things to come. They were designed by Christian Dior.

In order to show the rest of the world that the quality of French couture had remained unchanged despite a prolonged absence from the international scene, the Theater of Fashion traveled the length and breadth of Europe and then, in the spring of 1946, headed for the United States. It went on display in New York and then in San Francisco under the banner of the French patriotic charity Entraide Française. But it was to go no farther, as no other city was able to find the necessary capital to host the exhibition. The Theater of Fashion failed to make the grand splash hoped for by the French couture fraternity. In a world where life was still recovering from years of chaos, miniatures were no match for reality. Nor could any genuinely creative individual be satisfied with a collective initiative. What he needed was to find his own path.

6

Lucky Star

Dior? He was smart for a whole ten minutes of his life!

— Serge Heftler-Louiche

*R*umors always spread like wildfire, and in a fashion house, keeping secrets is harder than stopping an avalanche. The tiniest piece of news sets corridors and workrooms abuzz well before any official announcement, and for a week now, 16 Avenue Matignon had been humming with whispered conversations and discussions. The boss seemed to be the only one not to know, and under no circumstances was he to find out. All that was definite at this stage was that Madame Raymonde (Raymonde Zehnacker, that is, who ran the design studio) had told Monsieur Christian she would follow him wherever he went. Not that that was surprising. He was her little pet. From the day he started at Lelong she had eyes only for him. But there was more. It seemed that Monsieur Dior and Monsieur Balmain had decided to leave and set up in partnership together. No wonder everyone was so agitated. What would happen to Lelong without his two best designers? People might be laid off if they left. After forty years in the business, Monsieur Lelong might choose to retire rather than to keep such a big place.

Two weeks later, however, it was all off. The premises the future partners had set their sights on turned out at the last minute not to be available and Monsieur Dior withdrew from the venture. But imagine their cheek — the little town house they had hoped to call their own was right on Avenue Matignon, just a hundred meters down the street from their employer!

Despite this setback, Pierre Balmain was determined to go it alone. After five years with Molyneux and six at Lelong, he felt it was time to create his own label. On October 12, 1945, at 45 Rue François-Ier, the forty-five outfits in the first Balmain collection made a triumphant debut before the assembled press and a glittering array of royals and movie stars — including the Duchess of Kent, the Duchess of Windsor, Princess Radziwill, Josette Day, Simone Simon, and Maria Montez. As Bettina Ballard, the editor of American *Vogue*, wrote in her memoirs, "I particularly remember Gertrude Stein, with her familiar cropped head, and Alice B. Toklas, with her dark mustache, sitting in the seats of honor watching the pretty striped numbers go by, noting them meticulously on their cards with the same intensity of interest with which they had noted the Matisses and Picassos that had passed through their lives."

His friend's departure was a terrible blow for Dior and he had been unable to keep back his tears at the farewell party held for Balmain in the salon at Lelong. By the same token, however, he had prompted the move. He may have been the one left behind but he could hardly deny it was his own fault. When their first plan fell through, Balmain had persisted, Dior had not. Balmain's chance came with the help of his mother and two of his friends. They passed the hat, and in no time at all, there was Balmain with a 51 percent share in his own business. Dior was left behind with Lucien Lelong and work seemed even more miserable than before.

Was he destined to be the eternal onlooker, too timorous to take the plunge himself, while others around him achieved fame and success? But there comes a time in every life when one has to stand on one's own, and if Balmain had done it, why couldn't he? Why was he so timid in his dealings with others, yet perfectly capable of affirming his personality in his work? Life somehow contrives to make us repeat our mistakes, and here was Dior at forty just as reluctant to fight for his personal freedom as he had been at twenty in the face of his parents' opposition.

Instead of admonishing himself, Dior decided he had been lucky. He could go on living a peaceful existence without any of the worries his friend Balmain was having to deal with. Once Dior's work at Lelong was over for the day, he was free to do and think as he liked. He could go back to his pleasurable dilettante's existence and accept himself as he was, without striving for the impossible. After all, hadn't he always said that the secret of true happiness was to be surrounded by friends and enjoyable pastimes? And there were plenty of good times to be had. The only decisions he had to make were on how to spend the weekends — with the Bonjeans at Villerville by the sea or at Fleury-en-Bière in the forest of Fontainebleau with Pierre and Carmen Colle?

He was also a welcome guest at the home of Roland and Denise Tual in suburban Orsay and would almost always turn up with his friend Christian Bérard. As Denise Tual recalls, "They would invariably appear on the stroke of midnight. Polite, affable, and full of gossip . . ." The two Christians were eternal accomplices, with Bérard presiding over his younger friend's theatrical successes like a big brother. Thanks to his costumes for *A School for Scandal*, Dior had begun to make something of a name for himself in that domain, and had formed a friendship with Denise Tual, who described him as "a merry chap" and "a maniac for detail." She had also engaged him to design the costumes for *Le Lit à colonnes*, the film her husband produced in 1942 based on the novel by Louise de Vilmorin.

Neither of them would ever forget the epic expedition they undertook then to find fabric for Dior's dresses. Told of the existence of a hoard of material in an old mill in a little village on the banks of the Loire, they set off in a sputtering coal-gas-powered bomb of a vehicle to unearth this secret stockpile, laughing like two lunatics. The cache turned out to be surrounded by nettles and jealously guarded by an old man who looked like something out of the Brothers Grimm. Mission accomplished, during their return, "in a sea of tulle," Christian spent the entire journey fantasizing about all sorts of "fairy-tale outfits."

"I have never seen Christian's face light up the way it did the day we presented the ball gowns," Denise remembers. "He was like a child. That evening he hosted what he called a 'little dinner' in his apartment on Rue Royale . . . featuring a huge lobster some kind old soul had sent him from Granville." You were never in for a disappointment in that regard with Christian Dior.

And so he continued to act out the role in which his friends had cast him, that of a generous, imaginative bon vivant with a sometimes dry wit, given to perpetual clowning and a childlike passion for charades and fancy dress. He rented a little country cottage at Fleury near his friends Pierre and Carmen Colle and often on Saturday nights the whole gang would be found there — Christian Bérard, Henri Sauguet, Jacques Dupont, Marc Doelnitz, Carmen Colle, and Jean Cocteau, who also had a place nearby. Denise Tual remembers one such evening when "Bébé Bérard was in charge of the makeup" and Dior came up with a series of "amazing, whimsical creations. He picked one of those great dry plumed plants, the type you often find in suburban gardens, and turned it into a majestic aigrette which he pinned onto a turban in royal blue toweling." While they were outside, Jean Cocteau (who was going through a stage where he loved macabre pranks) stretched out on the sofa in the drawing room, his hands crossed on his stomach, playing dead. The scene was all the more hilarious because everyone fell for it. "Bérard gave an almighty scream. Everyone bent over the body, their elaborately made-up faces completely convulsed with shock. . . . In the face of such tragedy, those ridiculous costumes seemed both terrifying and pathetic, like something out of a Fellini film."

But beneath his outward insouciance Dior was undergoing a change of heart. It really was time to go it alone. Pierre Balmain's departure might have reinforced the idea, but the real motivation was artistic. He needed creative freedom. Dior was not ambitious, and if it had not been for his creative frustration, he might have been content to go on as he was.

It is hard to trace the various paths that led to his decision. Indeed, in his memoirs he appears to enjoy covering his tracks. His explanations for his actions are often quite fanciful, and if one were to believe his version of events, it would seem that the course of his life was altered by luck and luck alone. In the opening lines of his memoirs he pays almost solemn homage to the mysterious power of fate. "I would be both ungrateful and untruthful if I did not preface my story with the word 'LUCK' in large letters. And given its fortunate outcome, I must also pay due acknowledgment to my trust in fortune-tellers."

Right from his early years, fortune-tellers played quite a part in his life. His first encounter came in 1919, when he was fourteen. It was at a charity bazaar to raise money for the war relief and Christian had been enlisted to don a gypsy costume, hang a basket on ribbons around his neck, and sell lucky charms for a fortune-teller. At the end of the day, the woman offered to read his palm for him.

"You will be very poor," she said, "but women will be very lucky for you and bring you success. You will earn large sums of money from them and you will have to travel widely."

When he related her words to his family, everyone roared with laughter. The ambiguity of him "earning large sums of money" from women was enough to encourage the wildest of interpretations. But while he buried the prediction in the recesses of his memory for a long time to come, he remained instinctively drawn to things supernatural and the soothsayer's art. Whether this came from his grandmother, who used to have premonitions, or from his propensity for vivid dreams even as a child, or simply from an intuitive belief in the hidden meaning behind human behavior, the ups and downs of life would send him running to clairvoyants for reassurance and clarification. There were times like the long months between June 1944 and May 1945, when only fortune-tellers' reassurances kept his spirits up by continually predicting his sister's return from deportation.

Without wishing to undercut Christian Dior's superstitious interpretations, it is certainly tempting, in hindsight, to replace the word "luck" with "friendship." His friend Suzanne Lemoine puts a similar slant on it:

"To those of us who knew him inside out, it was quite obvious where Christian's success came from. Honestly, it was obvious. Why do I say that? . . . It is so rare to know someone all your life who has never let you down — never, as Christian would say, 'gone to water.' Well, that's what he was like, and the most surprising thing is that we always knew that about him, right from when we were children. Christian was a rare combination of two rare attributes — you could count on both his affection and his talent. . . . Once you realize that, everything else falls into place. And when Christian said to me, 'I have to go out on my own,' I swear I did not have the slightest doubt that he would succeed. Christian had a marvelous gift, that if he decided to do something it was bound to be quite brilliant."

Dior had barely breathed a word of his plan when rumors began to spread and a series of invisible forces came into play to guide him toward his goal. It set off something of a chain reaction along the extensive network of Dior's friends that stretched from Granville to Paris. "Luck" carried the idea along, and eventually it became reality.

Suzanne Lemoine had worked in advertising before the war, selling spots for the pioneering French adman Marcel Bleustein-Blanchet of Publicis. But the upheaval of the war years led to some unexpected career moves, one of which found Lemoine working in couture. A tall, sports-loving woman full of energy and humor, she had also sworn never to work with women. So it was quite a surprise to find her in 1946 assisting the milliner Maud Roser in setting up her own business, an enterprise she agreed to purely out of friendship. In a strange coincidence, Roser had happened to design the hats for Lelong's 1944 collection, which meant, of course, that they were worn with dresses by Dior. Suzanne Lemoine, who now went by her married name of Luling, was an enthusiastic type, to say the least, and immediately took matters in hand.

"Everyone was talking about this idea. . . . A whole series of factors made it inevitable. Personally, I know that it was just this constant thought of 'Christian wants to set up on his own' that did it. One day a childhood friend of ours called Georges Vigouroux came to Maud Roser's to inquire about some hats for a couture house called Philippe et Gaston. It was a solid, old-style sort of place, rather like something out of Maupassant. Georges Vigouroux was busy trying to modernize it a bit, repainting, decorating it with rows of box trees, that sort of thing. Fashion shows at Gaston were held in the evening and it was the sort of place where the gentlemen came in evening dress with carnations in their buttonholes. Vigouroux was trying his hardest to revive this Sleeping Beauty and he had an excellent backer who was quite prepared to spend whatever it took to revive Philippe et Gaston's fading name. The backer was Marcel Boussac.

"Everyone knew who Marcel Boussac was. He had won every

horse race held during the war years and his champion racehorse, Paris, which had been confiscated by the Germans, had just been returned to him . . . delivered to him personally by General Patton's army, in fact. He was pretty wealthy, some said the richest man in France, and he was nicknamed King Cotton.

" 'You've got the money and your renovations are very nice,' I said to Georges Vigouroux outright, 'but who's your designer?' And he said that, as a matter of fact, they were looking for one. 'Do you know someone?' he asked.

" 'Well, there's always Christian . . . he's with Lelong,' I answered.

" 'Yes, but he's with Lelong.'

" 'He wants to leave. Lelong knows. He wants to set up on his own.' "

This same story as told by Dior evolved into something of a legend. He put his own spin on it and skillfully wove in a whole series of magic numbers, coincidences, fortune-tellers, lucky charms, and other unmistakable omens — all to suggest the intervention of Divine Providence.

Take the chance meetings. The first occurs on April 18, 1946, at the corner of Rue Saint-Honoré and Rue Saint-Florentin, not far from where Dior lives. He bumps into a childhood friend who exclaims with delight at his good fortune — he happens to be looking for a designer for Philippe et Gaston. Does Dior know of anyone? No, Dior can't think of anyone. It doesn't even occur to him to suggest himself because, of course, that isn't quite what he is after. The second encounter takes place at the same spot just a few days later, and his friend still hasn't found this elusive designer. No, says Dior, he just cannot think who might be suitable for the position. But at their third meeting, when the question comes up again, Dior is ready and the deal is clinched.

Why this change of heart? Quite simply because right at that moment he stepped on a star — a gilt star that had fallen off the hubcap of a wheel. There was no doubt about it, this was a lucky omen, and Dior carefully pocketed his treasure. This time, when the question came, he found himself saying, "Why not me?" and was instantly overcome with his own daring.

And so here was Dior about to meet the famous Marcel Boussac, the man with the final say in choosing the new designer to take over his couture house. Christian's first meeting was with Boussac's right-hand man, Henri Fayol. Over the course of a "business lunch" with Fayol, Dior found his apprehensions vanishing. A Clark Gable lookalike, Fayol, the managing director of the Boussac companies, was one of those talented administrators who is also a man of the world. It was agreed that Dior would pay a visit to the premises of Philippe et Gaston. But the minute he set foot in the door, he suddenly felt doubtful he could save the business. So many others before him had done their utmost to restore the fortunes of prestigious establishments, without success. "The precarious existence of a couture house is even shorter than a human life span," he later wrote. "My heart sank at the thought of the risks involved, the cobwebs that would have to be swept away, and the difficulties of coping with the demands and problems of people who had been there for years . . . 'making something new out of something old' in a profession that is in itself a constant quest for something new. As I left Gaston, I decided I did not have what it takes to resurrect it."

Perhaps he was destined to spend the rest of his life at Lelong after all. Discouraged by his visit to Gaston, he felt the familiar disappointment at seeing another door close in his face. But he had not reckoned with Henri Fayol, who had no intention of letting things go at this preliminary stage. What made Marcel Boussac's right-hand man so "stuck on" someone he had only met once over lunch? He had taken a liking to him, which was quite justifiable, but there was another, more important reason. Henri Fayol's wife was a client of Lelong and could not praise Christian Dior highly enough. Nadine Fayol was a difficult woman to resist and her talents as a former actress plus her arguments in favor of Dior made a tough combination. She was convinced that her "little Christian" was the greatest genius in the world of couture and was literally "in seventh heaven" when she found out he was under serious consideration. Fayol had faced even greater challenges for the sake of his wife, who was Jewish, by daring to marry her at the height of the Occupation. So when Christian Dior called him, after his visit to Philippe et Gaston, to tell him he had decided to turn the offer down, Henri Fayol refused to let him go.

Clearly the two had very different ideas. Dior explained that he was not ready to leave Lelong unless it was to set up his own couture house. But Boussac's chief adviser, a master of diplomacy, suggested it wouldn't hurt to meet Boussac anyway, and organized a meeting between him and Dior. Well aware that the groundwork had to be properly laid for such an important encounter, Fayol skillfully planted the seeds on both sides. He had worked out how to deal with Dior, who was quite nervous at the prospect of coming face to face with the textile magnate. To relax him, Fayol told a story about his employer that served to illustrate the type of man he was.

It was a few days after the liberation of Paris and the roads of Normandy were swamped with Allied troops pouring into the country. Naturally the highways were out of bounds to civilian vehicles — except, it seemed, a gray Daimler with a Paris license plate. What's more, it was heading in quite the opposite direction from the victors. At every military checkpoint the car was waved down, and each time a chauffeur in peaked cap would roll down his window to explain, in English, that this was "Monsieur Boussac, the great owner of racing horses." What on earth had possessed Marcel Boussac to take his wife, Fanny Heldy, and his architect, and head off against the tide of jeeps and trucks? With the blissful unawareness of those with the world at their fingertips, Marcel Boussac had quite simply decided that now that Normandy had been liberated he would get renovations underway on his stud farm at Fresnay-le-Buffard, near Evreux. Eventually their progress was halted by a tank blocking the road. Undeterred, Boussac ordered his driver to head off across the fields, a move so bizarre that not a single officer was able to order him to turn back. Upon arrival at Fresnay, Boussac leaped out of the car and began reeling off a detailed list of the work to be done on the stud farm — enough to take the next ten years.

Fayol concluded this amazing and rather terrifying tale with the encouraging declaration that "when Marcel Boussac likes an idea, he takes it all the way!"

This was not the first time in Dior's life that he had encountered such a potentate, the type that sets the weak trembling and makes the powerful grovel. Fayol was careful not to elaborate any further on the personality of the man who both fascinated and worried him with his megalomania on the one hand and pure genius on the other. Henri

Fayol's father had been known for his theories on company management, called "Fayolism," and the son had been hired by the textile king to modernize the management of his companies, which had grown considerably as a consequence of the war. Fayol, still polishing his weaponry, as it were, found that his employer so far had more or less openly refused to give him the power to implement his plans, fearing no doubt that he would lose control in some way. Fayol had misgivings as to whether he would indeed be able to change the way in which the Boussac empire, modeled as it was on fairly outmoded and hierarchical lines, was run. The other question mark concerned the merits of continuing his career with CIC, the Comptoir de l'Industrie Cotonnière or Cotton Industry Trading Post, the flagship of the fleet. Perhaps this young designer would prove to be a test case. Would Boussac be prepared to risk his reputation on an unknown? The matter was shaping up to be most interesting.

The fellow in the gray suit with a touch of jovial stoutness who arrived that July morning in 1946 at 21 Rue du Faubourg-Poissonière showed none of Dior's usual trepidation. The headquarters of the CIC were housed in an imposing edifice built over three arcades, looking more like a bank and somewhat out of place amid the narrow streets and slightly crooked structures of Paris's Sentier neighborhood. As he entered the lobby, Dior was in a relaxed frame of mind. Relieved of the weight of the decision that had burdened him over the previous weeks, he felt confident in himself, fired with a touch of the pride one feels at refusing an offer from on high.

His first impressions of Boussac and the decor around him were positive. Behind the veneer of wealth and prestige, Dior could see the square, solid physique of Boussac's peasant stock. His office looked like a gentleman's smoking room, full of books and Empire furniture, bronze racehorses and etchings of Roman ruins. The two men soon found themselves chatting amiably by the fireplace. A businessman of Boussac's stature is often more easily interested by conversation in areas new to him than by the talk of colleagues affecting to know everything there is to know. And so Dior had no difficulty in communicating his desire not to revamp the house of Gaston as its new designer but to create his own house in a neighborhood of his choosing. Everything would have to be new, both in spirit and style. As he saw it, there was a general desire for change and renewal in the air that demanded something entirely new.

He then went on to describe the place of his dreams. It would be small and very exclusive, with only a few workrooms. It would carry on the traditions of the finest couture, for a clientele of truly elegant women.

"I would make gowns of apparent simplicity but using the most elaborate workmanship.

"After the long stagnation of fashion as a result of the war, there is a strong desire around for something entirely new. To meet this demand, French couture will have to return to its traditions of great luxury.

"My view is that, in the age of machines in which we live, such a couture house would have to be a craftsman's workshop rather than a clothing factory."

Being who he was, Marcel Boussac found nothing odd about this talk of returning to the great traditions of Paris fashion and restoring quality workmanship to its rightful place of honor. After the wartime extremes of the *zazou* look, he was happy to endorse the classic, serious-minded concept of returning to true couture, to well-cut, becoming clothes. Boussac was a man of conventional good taste and found nothing fatuous or decadent about this fellow. After all, Boussac had launched his own revolution some twenty-five years earlier with the introduction of brightly patterned cottons and poplins in checkered prints and gay stripes, which had brought color to the lives of millions of ordinary Frenchwomen, who promptly relegated their dark, monochrome dresses and black children's smocks to the rag cupboard. Boussac's store on the Champs-Elysées, A la Toile d'Avion, had become something of an icon. Never tiring of exploring the whims and mysteries of fashion, guessing the trends and anticipating their effects, King Cotton had now met someone with the same kind of mind. As he was later to tell the *Daily Express*, "In those ninety minutes we had the most fascinating conversation — an analysis of fashion over the last forty years. His comments, his knowledge, and his aesthetic judgments were absolutely flawless."

As Marcel Boussac saw his guest to the door, he said he found Dior's ideas most interesting, although they differed from his own, and asked for time to think it over. Two days later, he sent word that he agreed.

Such good news took Dior completely by surprise, and rekindled his anxieties — to put it mildly. He was seized by panic. His comfortable little world had just exploded in smithereens and he found himself in completely unfamiliar territory. He, an innocent and naive designer, had entered into negotiations with a great empire builder; worse, a ruthless businessman. The image of the "new woman" he had in his head brought him out in a cold sweat. Using the excuse of some disagreement over the wording of the proposed contract, he sent a telegram to Boussac calling the whole thing off. Then, completely at a loss, he raced to see his fortune-teller. He also confided in his friend the graphic artist René Gruau, who put himself on call day and night, trying as best he could to calm Dior down and stop him from doing anything rash. It is no understatement to say that Dior was racked by indecision. Was he ready to risk his independence and sign what might turn out to be a deal with the devil? Alice Chavane, another confidante, also remembers his fears about Boussac's wealth and his concern about the discrepancy between the image he planned to create, which he saw as the very epitome of elegance, and the Boussac name, which was synonymous with cheap fabric. How on earth was he to decide?

Denise Tual was another of Dior's friends to be used as a sounding board in that spring of 1946. It was during a dinner at the British embassy in honor of the writer Louise de Vilmorin, to be followed by a screening of the film based on her novel *Le Lit à colonnes,* for which Dior had designed the costumes. De Vilmorin was living in Hungary when the film came out, and to give her an opportunity of seeing it, her friend Lady Diana Cooper, wife of Ambassador Duff Cooper, had organized the dinner at which Louise also met Christian Dior for the first time. She congratulated him on the costumes, confessing that "she liked them so much she wanted us to give her the gowns worn by Valentine Tessier, the actress in the film!" But Denise Tual's chief memory of that evening was Christian's uncertainty regarding his future.

"Dior told me he had received two offers to set up his own couture house — at the time he was still with Lucien Lelong. His fortune-teller

Madame Delahaye had told him to accept one of the offers and that it would be a huge success. He had every faith in her and said she was never wrong. He told me to go and see her, which I did. She predicted that I would take a trip across the ocean, but that it would be postponed at the last minute. I didn't believe a word."

But it would be wrong to laugh at the part played by clairvoyants at this decisive moment in the history of French fashion. After all, they were the ones who finally induced this child of a man to seize the chance of a lifetime. Dior recounts the full details of this all-important episode in his memoirs.

"At this point I went to see Madame D., the fortune-teller who had consistently predicted that my sister would return from deportation. 'You must accept the offer,' she commanded. 'You must create the house of Christian Dior, whatever the conditions. Nothing anyone will ever offer you later will compare with the opportunity you have here today!' "

Henri Fayol was also doing his bit. He intercepted Dior's telegram and managed to turn him around. Here was Marcel Boussac offering Dior a small fortune to set up his own couture house, his chance to stand on his own two feet, and right at the last minute he was prepared to drop the whole thing. As if he were the only fish in the sea! Fayol displayed a knack for allaying his artistic fears and justifiable concerns about retaining his independence, while appealing to his more practical side by insinuating that there were many more designers where Dior came from.

There was another, hidden lesson in this story. Christian Dior might have appeared foolish, but his behavior, while totally genuine, was also quite cunning. Where shy people are particularly clever is in their tendency not to give things away. Unlike more ambitious souls, they are less concerned with the desire to shine than with avoiding the embarrassment of failure. This is where the weak end up being strong. They are also disinclined to get overly excited. "Being my own master," Dior wrote, "in my particular case has a lot less to do with enjoying the freedom to do as one wishes than with the urgent imperative of succeeding at all costs."

His tactics certainly paid off. In the ups and downs of the negotiating process, for all his equivocating, trepidation, and rash behavior,

Christian Dior had revealed an aspect of his character hitherto unseen — a streak of Norman stubbornness. The final contract was extremely generous. Dior would draw a salary plus a third of the profits before depreciation and tax. He was granted a record share in the company itself and, even more important, became its statutory head. He was entirely in charge of Christian Dior Ltd.

It was certainly no mean feat to get Marcel Boussac to give him exclusive power over the company. His coup inspired some cutting words from his childhood friend Serge Heftler-Louiche (soon to come back on the scene). "Dior?" he said. "He was smart for a whole ten minutes of his life!"

7

The Stage Door

> Dior was always in front. He never got it
> wrong. He always knew what was beau-
> tiful before everyone else.
>
> — Susan Train

The "New Look" had been waiting in the wings for many long months. Christian Dior's vacillations over his couture house had served only to delay it further. The flower women of his Corolla line (the name Dior had already coined for his vision of huge skirts spreading like petal cups from fitted bodices) had been ready to make their debut ever since early 1946. One of the first to sense their imminent grand entrance onto the fashion stage was Bettina Ballard of American *Vogue*, who came to Paris in February 1946 to cover the couture collections. "I was surprised by the sudden fashion interest to be found at Lucien Lelong's, a house not noted for the exciting personality of its clothes," she writes in her autobiography, *In My Fashion*. "I was curious as to whose hands behind the scene had given this fresh and tempting look to clothes in the lethargic postwar fashion atmosphere that pervaded Paris at the moment. The simplest way to find out was to ask Lucien Lelong.

" 'Let me introduce you, Bettina, to someone who I think has great talent,' he . . . replied proudly. . . . After asking all over, *'Où est Christian?'* there finally appeared a pink-cheeked man with an air of baby plumpness still about him and an almost desperate shyness augmented by a receding chin."

Still a virgin when it came to receiving compliments from the ladies of the press, Christian managed a smile that quite melted the heart of his American admirer. "The small mouth of the blushing man in front of me curled sideways in a disarmingly sweet but rather sad smile." Filled with enthusiasm, she instantly ordered an evening ensemble.

Two weeks later Bettina Ballard was in London, proudly sporting "a calf-length black satin skirt, a pale mauve chiffon off-the-shoulder bodice, and a covered-up jacket" — a totally new concept in evening wear. In her new finery she proceeded to one of the most fashionable nightspots of the time, the 400 Club, only to be turned away by an unrelenting doorman in a buttoned uniform for not being properly attired. "Englishwomen swept by me in their trailing prewar chiffons, shedding beads as they walked, but in my new Paris creation for the evening I was considered underdressed." Her escort, a young Guardsman, began protesting vigorously. How could England be so backward in fashion! It was scandalous to slam the door in the face of an editor of *Vogue;* in fact the whole affair was an outrage and ought to be brought up in Parliament! The affair became something of a cause célèbre when *Time* magazine took up the story and the controversy raged in newspapers on both sides of the Atlantic. While Britain mounted stiff opposition to any unconventional interpretations of fashion, public opinion in Paris was poised in waiting for something new to appear.

A similar event occurred a few months later — on December 13, 1945, to be precise. Jacques Bonjean's daughter, later to become the actress Geneviève Page, remembers it only too clearly. It was her eighteenth birthday. Her godfather Christian Dior had made her a dress for the occasion, black velvet with a wide, pleated calf-length skirt, a low neckline, and a black patent leather belt. It was pure New Look. Geneviève felt a little uncomfortable in a dress of such an odd length and tried to get her godfather to drop the hem by just a few centimeters. He was adamant, Geneviève recalls, "as if I had somehow attacked his authority as a designer. If I had insisted any further he would have gotten quite angry!" When she appeared in her new dress that evening, she felt all her friends' eyes on her, studying this outfit so different from their own. Her escort, Hubert d'Ornano, thought she looked quite ravishing and suggested they end the evening at the Club des Champs-Elysées. Here too, as they entered the room, she could not help noticing the way heads turned to look at her. Just as she was about to step onto the dance floor, she was approached by a gentleman she had never seen before. "My name is Marcel Rochas," he said, "Tell me, mademoiselle, who made that marvelous dress for you?"

There was every reason for Marcel Rochas to be intrigued. Influential designer that he was, he had anticipated this very idea himself, reintroducing the *guêpière* or waspie corset, with that same cinched waist and accentuated bustline, just prior to the war. A perceptive observer would have noticed a similar look in some of Jacques Fath's longer-line designs, and most unusual of all were the few dresses with bustier tops and cinched waists and sloping shoulders featured in the first collection by Dior's former colleague Pierre Balmain in 1945. Nothing is ever really new in fashion. Before she closed down in 1939, Chanel anticipated the new line in some of her suits. And Balenciaga did much the same in 1936. . . . As you go back in time you would gradually find the predecessors of every "new" look.

Bettina Ballard, meanwhile, had grown curious. She wanted to know more about this forty-year-old designer whom no one had ever mentioned before and who hid behind an unhealthy shyness yet produced such original ideas. She quizzed Michel de Brunhoff, head of French Vogue, who took great delight in telling her the story of his "little Christian." He knew it by heart. Dior was from a good family, had an interest in painting, but had suffered an enormous setback with his father's bankruptcy in 1929. He had a certain talent for drawing and had tried to get a bit of work doing fashion sketches. Brunhoff in fact had given him a leg up because he was someone everyone liked . . . and so on. It was music to Ballard's ears. Her journalist's antennae were twitching. Like every fashion editor worth her salt, she dreamed of "discovering" a new talent, of taking a promising young designer under her wing and turning him into a star.

"By the summer collections of 1946, Christian Dior was a much talked-about personality," she writes, "owing to the extraordinary news that Marcel Boussac, the cotton king of France and a great racing figure, was to back him in a couture house of his own that would open the next season. Lelong told me sadly that he could not help encouraging his star designer to branch out on his own with the talent that he had. Suddenly it was popular to claim Dior as an 'old friend.' "

There is nothing like money for encouraging people to take you seriously. Suddenly here was Dior being elevated from his spot among the rabble to a front-row seat — so much so that he actually eclipsed his friend Pierre Balmain, who had set up his own house the previous year with a capital of 600,000 francs. Balmain's story was the sort of lovely fairy tale that occasionally brightens the couture scene, but it was nothing compared to the miracle that was Marcel Boussac's bank account. Christian Dior Ltd. started out with a capital of 6 million francs, already a considerable sum, and with unlimited credit (Boussac ended up sinking 60 million francs into the enterprise!) Figures like these really turned heads in the little world of fashion, and the news spread like wildfire, starting with Paul Caldaguès at *Le Figaro*, followed by Michel de Brunhoff at *Vogue,* Alice Chavane, who had just gone on to *Elle*, her friend James de Coquet, still loyal to *Le Figaro,* and Simone Baron at *Jardin des modes*. People lined up to claim their part in their protégé's success, with the irrepressible Christian Bérard first in line. It was as if they had all backed a yearling that had suddenly won the sweepstakes. It was just what French couture needed to get back into the race.

In Bettina Ballard's view, fashion in the French capital had been reduced to a rather lifeless affair. Her account of postwar Paris couture is almost disdainful. "[It] was not at its most brilliant right after the war," she writes, "and none of the prewar stars were showing great leadership. Balenciaga was following his own good taste direction, paying no attention to what was going on around him, but he was not yet in his full stride. Robert Piguet, the Swiss, had come up greatly during the war and was now making pretty, young-looking clothes, strangely American in feeling. . . . Pierre Balmain . . . opened his own couture house with a small and charming collection that allowed the press to leap on him as a 'discovery' to add fuel to their reports. . . . Fath, whom I had known as a good-looking child prodigy, the little boy who had always been overdressed by his mother, made clothes for a few friends of his mother . . . and was now easing into couture. With an instinctive flair for publicity, he kept trying to enlist Carmel Snow's and my interest. Both of us, I am afraid, continued to think of him as a brash boy with slightly theatrical fashion ideas not worthy of the hallowed pages of *Vogue* or *Harper's Bazaar*. It wasn't until several seasons later, when Jacques had moved into important quarters on the Rue François-Ier . . . that he gained the respect of the top-fashion magazines."

Those American women were rapacious, there was no doubt about it! They needed constant stimulation and distraction. Deciding that the languishing state of affairs in Paris would not make particularly good copy, Bettina Ballard packed her bags after fifteen years in the French capital (not counting the war years, which she had spent working for the Red Cross). She returned to New York, where she landed the post of chief fashion editor, thanks to the head of *Vogue*, Edna Woolman Chase. It was a nice promotion for Ballard, who had learned her craft in the Paris office under the guidance of Michel de Brunhoff.

She would continue to make the trip back across the Atlantic twice a year for the collections, armed with all the authority of her new position but nonetheless entertaining the occasional regret, like the desire to polish up the "amateurism" of the Paris office. This was one of several episodes in the underlying ideological war that continued to surface between the tougher professionalism of New York and the less structured working atmosphere on the banks of the Seine.

Ballard's memories of the golden years in which Michel de Brunhoff was the Sun King of the fashion realm depict him enthroned in his office on the Champs-Elysées, which served both as the city's principal clearinghouse for artists and as the last of its salons. Her opinion, not so much of the man himself but of his editorial methods, shows a certain fond respect. In her memoirs she paints a humorous portrait of this masterful yet muddleheaded man presiding over piles of mock-ups, sketches, and photographs, incapable of working unless in the midst of a chaotic procession of people coming in and out of his office. He also derived great pride from the fact that a number of famous artists like Bérard, Dalí, and Cocteau had been persuaded to use their talents for the magazine. The creative atmosphere only really started bubbling around five in the afternoon. Bérard would be bent over his sketches, spilling cigarette ash and giving an account of the previous day's events, a dinner at Daisy Fellowes's, a ball at the Faucigny-Lucinges', the latest bon mot from Cocteau, or Chanel's most recent jibe. He always ended his visit with one of his favorite imitations of "Schiap" — Schiaparelli.

As a young trainee Bettina Ballard had plenty of opportunities to observe this little group, and was not always impressed. Among the beneficiaries of Brunhoff's own brand of charity was Georges Geffroy, later to become a decorator, whose fashion sketches left Ballard rather skeptical: "Georges Geffroy was another artist whom Michel de Brunhoff was doing his best to develop in order to save him from jumping into the Seine. He drew pale, distinguished figures but without much life in them, excusing himself for his dissatisfaction in a highly refined, Proustian manner."

Armed with her new stripes as chief fashion editor, Bettina Ballard, now Mrs. Wilson, made an important decision. The two annual editions of *Vogue* dedicated to the collections would come directly under her editorial control. This was a considerable slight to the Paris office. Previously it had been the arbiter of fashion, imposing its vision *urbi et orbi,* choosing everything on behalf of the New York office, from the designs to be featured down to the photographers. This little war did have its repercussions. Brunhoff was relegated to the offices of the less prestigious *Jardin des modes* with a smaller staff. This jovial arbiter of elegance, who looked like some old British major in his perennial attire of ancient tweed suits, complete with pipe, had lost his son in the war, and the blow made him look twenty years older.

Behind the swift and silent relocation of editorial control back to New York lay a radical shift in power. Fashion is a finely tuned gauge, all the more reliable as an indicator because its trends can never be determined in advance. For those who know how to read fashion, it is a turning page, a new era, a sign of things to come. Before the war,

America's fashion feelers depended first and foremost on Paris. One only has to look at the flourishing exchange between the two countries in the fields of literature, painting, music, social events, and the press, like Janet Flanner's "Letters from Paris" in the *New Yorker* and Ford Madox Ford's *Transatlantic Review*. Then there was the colony of extraordinary talents who chose to settle in Paris — people like Virgil Thomson and Gertrude Stein, Nancy Cunard and Natalie Barney. It was the taste and refinement of the Old Continent that nurtured the beginnings of *Vogue* when it was founded by Condé Nast early this century. *Harper's Bazaar*, its rival publication, used the same sources of inspiration. *Harper's* chief editor at the time was the petulant Carmel Snow, whose ambition was to make her readers into "elegant women with elegant minds." In line with this almost didactic view and the intention of producing a magazine based on "the top in everything," as Snow put it, Paris was a mandatory training ground. It was the era when young hopefuls like Bettina Ballard would spend at least two years in little rooms rented from countesses just to get "the Paris touch." Before the war, fashion journalism moved around the closed circuit of a handful of Parisian salons, including those of Marie-Louise Bousquet (which is still in existence), Daisy Fellowes, and Solange d'Ayen, the fashion editor of French *Vogue*. They were animated by the movements of a migratory species including Condé Nast's Alexander and Tatiana Liberman, the globetrotting jewelry designer and wit Fulco di Verdura, and the elegant blueblood Natalie Paley. But the geography of international fashion was in the process of change. Bettina Ballard, the new chief fashion editor of *Vogue,* had every intention of curbing the follies of Paris and drawing a whole new map.

Ballard, however, had not counted on the influence of her alter ego at *Harper's Bazaar,* Carmel Snow. Although not a pretty woman, Snow was vibrant, energetic, and full of fun. She wore little flat hats on a head of pale blue hair and carried herself with all the bearing of one of the Pope's Swiss Guard. Both Snow and Ballard had their own designated seats at the collections and no fashion show would ever start without them. The magazines operated in tandem but pretended to ignore each other, although the rather more mischievous Snow could never resist going up to Ballard after a show to tease her about their supposed rivalry, hoping all the while to pump her for her opinions on what they had just seen. The two could not have been more dissimilar, both in looks and personality: Bettina Ballard was tall and thin with a thoroughbred face, something of a puritan and very New England, while Carmel Snow was Irish, Catholic, and passionately loyal to Paris couture. The rivalry between the two publications was as futile as the Wars of the Roses, although there had been one traitorous act: Carmel Snow had once worked at *Vogue* but in 1932 allowed herself to be lured away without a second glance by William Randolph Hearst, who then put her in charge of *Vogue's* chief competition, one up on Bettina Ballard, who was merely fashion editor. From that moment Snow received star treatment in Paris. Her suite at the San Régis was inundated with flowers, cases of champagne, and a shower of invitations; she gleefully compared mornings in her hotel room, with their constant stream of telephone calls and visitors, to the king's bedside at the court of Versailles.

Carmel Snow adored Paris and France and was most distressed about the tribulations of French couture during the war years. She was quite shattered by the story of Lelong's fight against the Germans, and by 1944 she was agitating to get a visa and be one of the first to return to Paris. "During the war," she remarks in her memoirs, "there was a lot of loose talk to the effect that Paris was 'finished' as the center of fashion." But Carmel Snow refused to believe it. Her passion was as unwavering as ever. With her fiery temperament and her slightly chaotic nature, she embraced France wholeheartedly, warts and all. In the final months of the war she took great delight in her chauffeur's maneuverings to find gasoline for the car, restaurants that still served excellent meals courtesy of the black market, and the petty acts of heroism the average French person undertook just to make sure he or she had plenty to eat. Bettina Ballard, the puritan, meanwhile found the whole thing quite disgraceful.

They were opposites in everything. When Ballard returned to Paris with her new title, she was horrified at the adulation and special treatment she received as a result. She felt compromised in her independence and incorruptibility and refused steadfastly to fall in line with the dictates of Paris high society. That very concern was behind her move to wrest control of American *Vogue's* collection issues from the Paris bureau. Editors decide on fashion, she proclaimed, not duchesses. Gone were the days when Michel de Brunhoff would let himself be influenced by opinions heard around a society dinner table, or by the views of his fashion columnist, the Duchesse d'Ayen. Ballard was determined to put an end to the French modus operandi where staff were hard at it only after five in the evening, and there was to be no more confusion between business and pleasure when it came to the relationship between the editorial offices and the Paris salons. No more conversations in insider jargon, for that matter. Carmel Snow, on the other hand, seemed quite unruffled by the inevitable caprices of Daisy Fellowes, a prewar *Harper's* Paris editor and the same sort of fashion figurehead as Solange d'Ayen at *Vogue*. Daisy Fellowes, dressed from head to toe by "Schiap," was the perfect blend of wealth, chic, and modernity, with her swanlike elegance, fabulous jewels, and Neuilly town house complete with patio and flowering shrubs. No one could beat Carmel Snow when it came to vamping up a magazine with a host of flashy names — articles by Virginia Woolf, Jean Cocteau, Christopher Isherwood, and Truman Capote and impromptu mannequins like Lauren Bacall and Anita Colby — plus an editorial office buzzing with young assistants with all the right surnames. Bettina Ballard returned to New York after fifteen exciting years without, it seemed, a backward glance. On the contrary, she appeared almost pleased to leave behind her the romantic misfortunes of Marie-Laure de Noailles, the amorous intrigues of "Loulou" de Vilmorin, and the deceitful blue eyes of Christian Bérard. Carmel Snow, on the other hand, reveled in the racy atmosphere of the French capital. With her natural curiosity, humor, and enterprising spirit, she was the epitome of Parisian gaiety. Her private and professional lives tumbled on top of each other in this champagne-bubble existence (although she was equally and indiscriminately fond of sherry, gin, and bordeaux). While Bettina Ballard grimaced at the kind of Parisians who opted for the cerebral over the moral, Carmel Snow thought nothing of the fact that everyone seemed to feed from a number of troughs. Indeed she had no compunctions about snaffling Bérard from *Vogue*, to which he was contracted exclusively, and getting him to work for *Harper's* under the pseudonym Sam!

There was one point, however, on which the two defended themselves with the same tenacity: their uncontested prerogative as editors. "It is our role," said Carmel Snow, "to recognize fashions when they are still only seeds of the future. The designers create, but without magazines their creations would never be recognized and accepted." Despite their differing styles, the one cold and clinical, the other practically tropical, neither would give an inch when it came to her rank as chief arbiter and decision maker. At the collections, Carmel Snow took her place in the front row while her coworker and fashion editor Nancy White sat two rows back, leaving no doubt as to where the power lay to make or break the designer on parade. Bettina Ballard's insightful verdicts could be as lethal as the death sentence.

But behind such fearsome exteriors, soft motherly hearts were known to beat when it came to a particular favorite. Each in her own way lived out a perennial romance with Balenciaga, a simple, genuine, big adolescent of a man. Although he opened his house in Paris in 1937, fame eluded him until much later. (In fact Carmel Snow subsequently claimed to have "discovered" him.) The Spaniard had only two loves in his life, couture and his birthplace, a fishing village on the Basque Coast. He kept a house there called Igueldo, an almost spiritual blend of beeswaxed floors, silver objects, and Spanish spartanism, which aroused a good deal of mystical emotion in both women. They would go into seventh heaven at fitting sessions when Balenciaga got going with his scissors — blithely snipping away at a collar or sleeve that wasn't quite right.

It was customary for Carmel Snow to give an annual report on fashion trends to New York's Fashion Group — a body of industry professionals including buyers from the major department stores, advertisers, and editors. America was miles ahead of Europe in these sorts of things, with a level of teamwork and exchange of information that was unknown on the Continent. In February 1946, powerfully convincing with her small bright eyes and husky Irish-accented voice, she delivered what was essentially a dressing-down to the assembled group. "Very few buyers went over that February," she recalls in her memoirs, "and I urged them strongly to go over the next year, when conditions would surely be better. 'Lelong has a new designer,' I said, 'whose collection was sensational — full of ideas. His name is Christian Dior.' "

She had spotted Dior in 1937 when he first made waves at Robert Piguet with his "Café Anglais," a houndstooth dress with a tight-fitting black wool top that accentuated the bust. But in those days Dior was just one element in her overall commitment to "do all that was in my power to revive the fashion industry in France." Where Bettina Ballard was reserved — "I understood their reluctance to face reorganizing their lives and their politics. But I wanted to let them yawn, to stretch, to awake and feel the stimulation of activity again" — the editor of *Harper's* was far more dramatic: "I was no more willing to concede the permanent fall of Paris than was General de Gaulle. . . . Since fashion is the second largest industry in France, I felt that my personal contribution to the Allied cause could be to help the revival of that industry."

The question now was whether such Francophile fervor would have the desired effect, and whether Carmel Snow's hot-blooded assault would be enough to give new vigor to French fashion. Little did Dior realize just how much was riding on him.

It was July and Dior had other things on his mind. He was working on the winter collection, the last he would design for Lucien Lelong. He had already given his notice. At the same time he was preparing his own move. He felt like a producer who had suddenly been called upon to act as director, stage manager, entrepreneur, and artistic director all at once — not to mention the most essential role, that of *auteur,* creator. Not only did he have to create the look and decor of his *maison,* train a whole new team, oversee the actual making of the dresses, select the models, and devise the show, but he also had to keep his mind sufficiently unencumbered to design the collection! He had seven months to complete this Pirandellian feat . . . and for five of those he was still tied to Lelong. The winter collection that August was such a success that when it was over Lelong asked Dior to work on a half-season collection for fall (an additional, smaller presentation held between the main shows in winter and summer). His contract was to run officially until December 1. Christian Dior Ltd. was created on October 8. In the ensuing period he had to find eighty-five people ready to start work on December 15 at 30 Avenue Montaigne. So preoccupied was he with this race against the clock, and the general madness and exhaustion, that he did not have a minute to think about what might be going on in the rest of the world.

But there was one member of his entourage who had her finger firmly on the pulse. She knew well that the fate of a new fashion house rested in the hands of the American press.

Suzanne Luling was in Granville for the summer when she received a telegram from Christian Dior, announcing his impending move and urgently asking her to come to Paris for a meeting of the "group" on August 8. The "group" was Dior's way of referring to his financiers and he used the word "with a twinkle of mischievous wonderment," Suzanne Luling recalls. "To Christian, the 'group' represented a marvelous, terrifying, slightly mythical world — something out of a nightmare or a fairy tale. A 'group' could make a couture house spring up from nowhere, just like those paper flowers the Japanese make, which open into full bloom when placed in water."

The aim of the lunch was to ask Suzanne Luling to oversee shows and sales at the new Maison Christian Dior, which at that stage was still without premises. Suzanne was then working for the milliner Maud Roser but hoped to go back to her career in advertising with Marcel Bleustein-Blanchet. Dior knew she could not refuse him anything, even if it meant having to work with women, as she had sworn not to do. She was needed: as Dior himself put it, "to call her dynamic is an understatement. Even 'explosive' is barely adequate." She promptly gave her notice and by the end of the year was ready to embark on this new adventure.

One of Suzanne Luling's great merits was that she would stop at nothing when it came to doing her job. She knew she could not rely on the French press. It was not what it had been before the war, and certainly was not up to promoting someone on an international level. *Elle* magazine, promising as it was, had only just been started up by Hélène Lazareff. *Marie-Claire* had not yet reappeared. *Jardin des modes, Femina* and *L'Officiel* were the pillars of haute couture but with nothing like the circulation of *Vogue, Harper's Bazaar,* or *Women's Wear Daily.* Just why Suzanne Luling set her sights on *Women's Wear Daily* is not clear, especially as she did not even know the Paris correspondent, a

Mrs. Perkins, but she was well up on the habits of American journalists and their tendency to stay at the Hôtel Scribe. Parking her little Simca close by, she took up her position outside a fashion house where she knew Mrs. Perkins would be viewing the winter collection, paced up and down outside until the American journalist appeared, and then watched her try to flag down a taxi without success. "So I went up to her and asked whether she was going to the Scribe," Luling relates. "She was. Although I wasn't going that way at all I immediately said, 'So am I. Can I give you a lift?' "

On the way to the hotel, Suzanne Luling chattered innocently about her new job. She was with Maud Roser but was leaving to go to Christian Dior. You don't know who Christian Dior is? Well, it's a secret at the moment, but he is about to open a new *maison* in time for the next season. But for goodness' sake, don't tell a soul. It's highly confidential!

So it was that the oldest trick in the book, a seemingly inadvertent "leak," made headlines in *Women's Wear Daily* on November 17, 1946 — complete with a photo of Dior!

Well might Suzanne Luling "beam with pride" at her coup. *WWD* was considered the fashion bible and it was not long before *Life* took up the story. The aftermath of the *Life* article we shall come to in due course, but Christian Dior certainly was astonished at its impact. "I had no idea at the time how important an article in *Life* could be in launching my house," he wrote. "Like Fortune, the goddess of Publicity has been known to smile on those who court her least."

On December 1, 1946, Dior left Lelong for good and spent the next fortnight conceiving and designing his first collection. "It is in Paris that one breathes the air of couture," he later wrote, "but once I have spent several months inhaling it, I need the calm of the countryside to reflect and make my conclusions." He chose as his retreat the home of his friends Pierre and Carmen Colle at Fleury-en-Bière, where he was surprised by an unseasonable snowfall. On December 9, as he was filling his sketch pads with the first pencil strokes of what was to become the New Look, news reached him that his father had died. He immediately took the train to Callian, where he was reunited with his brother Raymond and sisters Jacqueline and Catherine. (His other brother, Bernard, was still in the mental asylum). The funeral service was held in the parish church, a little medieval building at nearby Montauroux, in the presence of their old governess Mademoiselle Marthe, who had watched over her former employer to the end. Apart from a few local parishioners, she and the family were the only people to stand by his coffin and accompany it on foot up the steep path to the cemetery above the village where he now lies buried.

Six months earlier, when Christian had told Maurice the news of his own couture house, his father had made no secret of his displeasure. Broken as he was through his own business failure, he had discouraged his son from leaving a stable position for a risky future. It was his mother's influence that had really left its mark on Christian, with her famous edict that the name Dior should never feature on a shop front. But, coming at such a difficult time, his father's death certainly had an effect on Dior, given his patently indecisive nature and his constant need for a sign before taking the slightest step. Both his parents were dead; just days before his new venture opened its doors, the last tie with the past was cast off and Dior stood on the threshold of the biggest adventure of his life. He was forty-one years old, "coming of age all over again." Finally free to be himself, at last he could become Christian Dior.

At nine A.M. on December 16, 1946, the little town house at 30 Avenue Montaigne became the Maison Dior. Five people entered its portals besides Dior himself. The first was Madame Raymonde Zehnacker, the one who had said to him when he joined Lelong, "I will follow you wherever you go." Dior put her in charge of the design studio. Then came Marguerite Carré, the *première* or technical director in charge of the workrooms. She had been with Patou for many years and brought with her thirty seamstresses. There were two men — the chief tailor, Pierre Cardin, aged twenty, and Jacques Rouët, the business manager allocated to Dior by Marcel Boussac to run the administrative side. Rouët was joined by his secretary, Olga. Gradually over the course of the morning a further eighty employees drifted into what was more like a building site than a couture house. The renovations were due to be finished in time . . . or so the tradesmen promised!

"Everywhere you looked there was someone painting, installing electric wires, filling holes or making them. They were pulling down partitions in one corner and setting them up in another. There was a smell of plaster and, already, a vague hint of perfume. There were eighty-five of us, mostly women, packed into this building site. It was like a circus, and we certainly felt like we were hammering in the tent pegs! In fact, we were quite a menagerie, running up and down stairs with notes in our hands or dress lengths on our arms, Christian's studio so small he was spilling out onto the landing. The dresses were hidden from view under meters of white cotton. White cotton covers were also used to protect the tables and growing piles of fabric pieces from gathering dust. The air was permanently laden with dust. And it wasn't as if we were the only people there with the masons and the painters."

This description of the early chaos comes from Suzanne Luling. But a new Dior was about to emerge, so organized in his plans that nothing could throw a monkey wrench into the works.

The first step had been to nail down a suitable location, preferably in the vicinity of a major hotel, given the emphasis on a foreign clientele. Suzanne Luling, whose task it was to comb Paris, remembers the process of elimination. "We immediately ruled out Place Vendôme — too old-fashioned. We liked the Ritz enormously but, as far as fashion went, it was no longer the address it used to be. The Prince de Galles and the George V did not match the type of clientele we were after, and besides, Avenue George-V was a one-way street, so out of the question. The Bristol would have been perfect but Faubourg Saint-Honoré is too narrow, the Lancaster had just the right clientele but the Rue de Berri was always jammed with cars. So all that was left was the Plaza, which in those days didn't cater quite so much to the 'nouveau riche' as it does now."

Only one place really fit the bill. For some time Dior had had Avenue Montaigne in mind, in particular a little town house at number 30. Unfortunately it had been taken by his friend Georges Vigouroux, for the couture house Philippe et Gaston with which he was still saddled. Other places were suggested: Place François-Ier, premises occupied nowadays by Pierre Cardin, or Avenue Matignon, in a pretty building the designer Jean Dessès was later to find to his liking. But nothing would dissuade Dior from his original choice. "It had to be 30 Avenue Montaigne," he wrote. "In all of Paris I knew exactly what I wanted. It was actually the house I had described to Boussac, although I hadn't realized it at the time. Many years before that decisive interview with him, I stopped short in front of two little adjoining houses in Avenue Montaigne, numbers 28 and 30. I pointed out their neat, compact proportions and discreet elegance to my companion, Pierre Colle (my dear friend who died, sadly, at a very young age). Pierre had done extremely well with his art gallery and was the first to suggest financing a couture house under my name. Standing in front of those twin facades that day, I said to him jokingly, 'Pierre, if your idea ever comes off, I will set myself up here and nowhere else!' "

Vigouroux was determined to hold on to his lease. He had battled for it with the previous tenant, the milliner Coralie. Why should he let it go for Dior's sake? Besides, there had never been so many town houses to let in Paris as in that period immediately after the war, and several were going begging. But mere details rarely deter an artist. Dior's request soon found its way up to the top of the "group." This delicate conflict between the future star and the ailing couture house was soon resolved and Christian Dior found himself holding the lease to 30 Avenue Montaigne.

It is hard to imagine the usually timid Dior behaving like such a prima donna. He had never ridden roughshod over someone before, not even on a professional level. No one likes to remember his lesser moments and in fact Dior uses a little literary license when recounting the episode in his memoirs. These were exceptional circumstances, after all!

The reasons for his choice were outlined during his meeting with Marcel Boussac, in which he laid out a set of precise, very pragmatic goals. To meet them he would have to follow his plans to the letter and choose wisely, both artistically and financially. That particular town house was perfectly in keeping with "the modest scale of [his] ambition," to create "a very small, very exclusive house . . . going back to the great traditions of luxury in French couture." Whatever the state of the economy, aside from periods of deep crisis, there is always a market for *grand luxe,* albeit restricted to the very privileged few. He had carefully thought over the commercial challenge when presenting his plans to Boussac and denied the general feeling that Paris couture was going downhill, despite the fact that the salons "were being invaded by a rather undiscriminating clientele, who bought big with money made on the black market."

Dior had decided instead to draw his clients from both "in and out." Suzanne Luling, who assisted him in targeting the right figures from the upper echelons of couture society, explains the process.

"The choice was simple. We could produce only so many dresses per season, and indeed that is all we wanted to do. So we drew up the list of what we needed — ten Americans, ten Englishwomen, ten Italians, and about the same number of South Americans. We wanted to be a little more careful when it came to Frenchwomen. Whatever some might say, clients do remain faithful and we did not want to steal people from other couture houses. Paris has to be taken as a whole. Balenciaga had a very loyal clientele. We liked Jacques Fath very much and we wanted Marcel Rochas to do well. We had no intention of trying to be the only ones."

This concept of making couture once again the domain of the chosen few required a couple of Very, Very Important People. One such person was the Duchess of Windsor. In order to attract her, Suzanne Luling began a bit of detective work to track down the Duchess's former saleslady, a certain Suzanne Beguin, who used to dress her at Mainbocher. Mainbocher was now in the United States, so Mlle Beguin had to be somewhere . . . but where?

The biggest hurdle in getting a new couture house off the ground is working out a way of bending the conventional etiquette regarding clients from other establishments. Obviously there was a known circle of elegant women who already made up the clientele of existing houses. Any new venture would inevitably acquire its own share of loyal customers from within that group. But throughout the terribly delicate exercise of winning their loyalty, no reference was ever made to the idea of "poaching." The whole operation was conducted behind the scenes, as it were, via the salesladies who had a good measure of influence over their clients. The sort of secret deal making that was required to navigate the labyrinth of the couture world was an art in itself and based on a subterranean network of information. The idea was to discover who was feeling dissatisfied, underpaid, or in some way unhappy in her current position and then approach her in such a way as not to arouse suspicion. She then had to be lured by a more generous offer, but so discreetly that the day she began work with her new employer it would appear quite aboveboard. Once the bait was hooked, the clients would follow as a matter of course. If there were a hitch, however, the Chamber of Couture would be called in, most reluctantly, to adjudicate. By then it was generally too late to mend the rift and two rival fashion houses would be in open dispute, which is why everyone preferred to turn a blind eye rather than suffer the infamy of an open violation.

Fortunately this case turned out to be a piece of cake. Mainbocher was no longer in Paris and Suzanne Beguin had been picked up by Hermès. When it came to judging the crime of disloyalty, there was an unwritten law that distinguished between poaching within the same field and moving from one branch of the fashion industry to another. As Hermès was a saddlery and Dior a couturier, disloyalty was less of an issue, making it all the easier to acquire Suzanne Beguin. She was delighted to be going back to couture, and the House of Hermès proved most understanding. In fact, her employer, Jean Guerrand, subsequently became firm friends with Christian Dior.

This glimpse behind the net curtains of the Paris fashion world with all its subtleties and complexities shows just how discreet the relationships woven by a new fashion house had to be. The type of diplomatic embroidery, the subterfuge and intrigue needed to ensure the success of a new venture was reminiscent of the court of Versailles. Advertising was out of the question. The emphasis was on word of mouth, which could work wonders in a way publicity, considered offensive, even vulgar, could not. "Too many people thought that the house of Christian Dior spent huge amounts of money on publicity when it started off," wrote Dior. "In our first, modest budget not a cent was allocated to it. I relied on the quality of my dresses to spread the word."

The main element in the initial outlay was on the creative side. Dior was uncharacteristically extravagant when it came to setting up his studio. He had three personal assistants, all women, each with a well-defined role — Madame Raymonde, Madame Marguerite, and Madame Bricard.

Raymonde Zehnacker, a strong woman with a gentle manner and enigmatic blue eyes, was the head of his atelier. She was responsible for every practical, organizational detail. Everything came under her supervision, essentially, and Dior considered her "my second self."

Marguerite Carré, formerly the workroom head at Patou, was Dior's technical director. She was the intermediary who took Dior's studio sketches to be brought alive in the workrooms. Carré came to Dior with a full workroom team; in the best couture tradition, she was followed by the thirty seamstresses who had worked under her at Patou. Dior had made inquiries all over Paris before choosing this woman of incomparable ability, and "poaching" her had been one of the most delicate operations undertaken in setting up his house. She was initially approached and wooed in a series of unofficial negotiations conducted by Jacques Rouët, the young administrative and financial manager. The final agreement, however, was worked out under the supervision of the Chamber of Couture after Patou lodged an official complaint. It was no easy task to enlist the services of this pink-complexioned woman who looked like a diminutive version of a Renoir painting. While Dior could not be seen to be involved directly, he stage-managed every step of the negotiations, as correspondence with Jacques Rouët has since revealed, and stood firm on a number of conditions.

The third figure in this formidable general staff was a muse in the full poetic sense. These days she might be called an artistic adviser. With her Nefertiti profile and relaxed yet inimitable elegance, Mitzah Bricard was one of a kind — which was precisely why Dior had chosen her. "Inflexible in her standards, her instinctive choice was always the most acute expression of that indefinable, perhaps slightly neglected thing called chic."

A trio of this stature came at a price, but although Dior had carte blanche when it came to spending Marcel Boussac's money, he was no squanderer. He was fundamentally cautious in setting up the business: three very full workrooms, one tiny design studio, the *salon* or showroom, a dressing room, an office, and six little fitting rooms, with a staff of sixty. When Dior presented his team to Marcel Boussac, he "did not hide the fact that it was relatively extravagant for a small business aimed at a fairly restricted clientele. But the quality I was aiming for required technical perfection and we required first-class ammunition to reach our target. Fortunately, Marcel Boussac realized he was dealing with a conscientious craftsman, not a megalomaniac."

Dior's silent partner was quietly surprised at Christian Dior's parsimonious attitude. "I always allowed Dior a completely free rein creatively," he later said. "And I was happy to go along with anything that would guarantee perfection. He was actually the one who kept tight control on expenditure when we were refurbishing the town house on Avenue Montaigne. He didn't want it to cost too much." As Suzanne Luling stresses, it was Dior's desire for autonomy that made him so anxious to run a profitable ship. "I had no idea whether it would be a financial triumph in the immediate term but even at that level it was structured as a viable financial venture."

All the provisions had been laid in for the winter. With the coming of spring, Suzanne Luling would need a few extra swallows to fly off in various directions. Dior turned to the wife of Pierre Colle, his friend and fellow gallery owner in the Bonjean-Dior period, and asked her to take care of the boutique he was planning. Carmen Colle was quick to rustle up her faithful troops. She was an exotic character of aristocratic descent, originally a Cormera — an old Mexican family of European origins. Christian Bérard had already done her portrait. She was something of a Creole queen among the artists and literati of bohemian Paris and was well known for intimate Sunday evening dinners in her kitchen on Rue de Varennes with such luminaries as the Hugos, the Kessels, Marie-Laure de Noailles, Balthus. All the talk at the time was of Christian Dior. Another childhood friend, Nicole Riotteau, also joined the team. Then there was Yvonne Minassian, who would figure importantly later, and Madame de Laba, who came with a wealth of experience from Chanel and Alix. None of them lost any time in getting out their little black books and reviving all sorts of lost friendships, so that by opening day, as if by magic, the front rows in Dior's showroom were studded with stars like Lady Diana Cooper, Baroness Just née Stern, Margot Fonteyn, Edwige Feuillère, the wife of the director René Clair, Mrs. Alec Weisweiller, Mrs. Lopez-Willshaw, the Countess de Boisgelin, and the wealthy Argentinean Madame Larivière. They may well have already had their own preferred couturiers but here they all were, much to the surprise of some, but not others. As to how they were "enticed" . . . silence is golden.

To head his publicity department, Dior hired a young American chosen more for his attractive personality and youth than his experience. "Come and see this wonderful boy I've found to do the publicity," he said in an excited call to Suzanne Luling. "Come and see him now."

"The 'wonderful boy,' " says Luling, "was Harrisson Elliot and he was just as Christian described him. He was American and dying to stay in France. Christian Dior (and there was no better PR man than Dior himself) gave Harrisson clear instructions: his brief was to avoid excessive publicity rather than stir it up."

"I specifically didn't want to advertise," Dior later wrote, "preferring to rely on the kindness of a few dependable friends to make sure the word got around." As his supply of friends was plentiful, and as success attracts success, news traveled fast. Bettina Ballard watched his popularity grow from day to day, recalling how "Bébé Bérard, the artist, and Georges Geffroy, the decorator, proclaimed themselves his personal advisers and hovered around him. The smell of fame was strong, attracting not only friends but workers who felt the stir of something happening in couture and who were willing to take a chance on this lucky man." His supporters could be found all over the city; from the Left Bank and Marie-Louise Bousquet with her famous Thursdays at her home on Place du Palais-Bourbon, to the Right Bank and the British embassy, the hub of social life since Louise de Vilmorin took up residence there in a celebrated ménage à trois with the Duff Coopers. The Mitford sisters were already on the list of future clients: That "charming Dior" had made such pretty costumes for "Loulou's" film, *Le Lit à colonnes!* Denise Tual, who coproduced the film with her husband, engaged Dior again in the fall of 1946 to create costumes for *Jeanne d'Arc*, Roland Tual's next film, starring Michèle Morgan. Dior's design for the Maid of Orleans's heresy trial was most unusual — "no streamers or armor, simply a tunic and a grotesque hat, humiliating but beautiful." (Sadly the project fell through when David O. Selznick created a full Hollywood *Joan of Arc* with Ingrid Bergman.) Dior continued to spend regular Sundays in the country with Denise and Roland Tual at Orsay, along with publisher Gaston Gallimard, the director Marcel Achard, Henri Lartigue, the poet Paul Eluard and his wife Nush, the composer Francis Poulenc, and all sorts of new faces attracted by the Tuals' artistic vitality. Their gatherings provided the first breath of fresh air in the period following the Liberation, sparking a renewed interest in American cinema and a desire to see some of the wartime productions revived. Denise Tual was almost certainly the first woman to mention the name Dior in America, which she did on a visit there in the spring of 1946. At a luncheon given by Natalie Paley (who had married Jack Wilson after divorcing Lelong), Denise talked endlessly about Paris and the launch of a new couture house by a designer called Christian Dior. Also present were the couturier Mainbocher, who had migrated to America because of the war but was very homesick, and some American friends of Marie-Louise Bousquet, including Diana Vreeland. Denise Tual's prediction that Dior would revolutionize fashion was met with some skepticism. "I'm sure I went on about him because he was my friend. They had all heard of him, even if only as a designer with Lelong." When she returned the following year, however, wearing her first New Look dress, things were very different. "They looked at me with a certain respect," Tual wrote. "I was the first one to tell them about the man they were now all in raptures over. Americans remember these things."

Other friends of Dior did not simply talk about him but dropped in at 30 Avenue Montaigne, like Count Etienne de Beaumont, who got into the habit of coming by to look on from behind his monocle and comment on the progress of the renovations. Christian Bérard was even more assiduous, "pacing around, with his beard and his dog, inspecting every corner of the site," said Dior. "We awaited his verdict with beating hearts. Fortunately he gave it his approval and even suggested a few improvements." There was a narrow space on the left side of the corridor that Dior wanted to convert into a boutique selling accessories and other luxurious trifles. "Bérard was the one who advised us to drape it with cretonne and scatter hatboxes with our name on them here and there, on the cupboards and in empty corners. The seeming casualness of it all really brought the place to life."

It was hardly surprising to see Bérard turn up to give his advice. He was "the oracle for every festivity and the arbiter of style, [our] dear Bébé with his infallible taste . . . escorted by his dog Jacinthe." Bérard had left his mark on "Schiap's" boutique, on the pages of fashion magazines, on theater sets, and in the elaborate decorations for a number of balls. There would not be one couturier he had not influenced in some way. He had a hand in creative endeavors all over Paris but, great painter that he was, he bestowed his talents on his friends and important acquaintances so magnanimously, so momentously, that it was like being awarded the Légion d'Honneur.

Dior could have done without the flood of advice pouring in on him from all sides, but he knew well how useful offers of patronage can be. He was also somewhat amused at finding himself suddenly the center of attention, a phenomenon he had witnessed many times before, but as an observer, not a recipient.

Nothing would distract him from the task at hand, however, particularly when it came to the decor for his new establishment. He had more detailed and precise ideas in this area of the enterprise than any other, and rather than enlist the services of one of his seasoned decorator friends, he employed a newcomer to the profession, although certainly no novice. Victor Grandpierre was the son of a great turn-of-the-century architect who had died at an early age. Aware that he was eager to follow in his father's footsteps, Dior's offer was a kind and thoughtful one. It took the form of an urgent letter that found Grandpierre on vacation at Cannes. He leaped at the chance and proved to be most adept at interpreting Dior's wishes, "giving the charming town house on Avenue Montaigne a decorated, rather than decorative, air," wrote Dior, adding that it "coincided perfectly with my tastes and my ideas. . . . We both shared that desire to recapture the magic years of our childhood." It was perfectly in keeping with Dior's commercial and artistic goals — a select clientele and the elegance of times past. Grandpierre's brief was to reproduce the neo–Louis XVI look "circa 1900" of his parents' first Paris apartment, with the woodwork and furniture painted white, gray curtains, glass doors with bevel-edged paneling, and bronze table lamps. "That kind of invisible elegance," he wrote, "is still to be found in the drawing rooms of the Ritz and the Plaza. . . . Sober, simple, but without austerity, classic in the extreme and very Parisian, it was a style that would not distract the eye from my collections. I wanted a couture house, not a theater, a place to show off my dresses, not the decor."

With the confidence of a man who knows exactly what he is

doing, Dior happily ignored the entreaties of those around him. His assured manner made the two short months before the appearance of the New Look seem like one big game.

The first, naturally, to be co-opted into the "Christian Dior" adventure were his friends and most intimate companions. He needed to trust his coworkers. In no time half of Granville was installed at 30 Avenue Montaigne, and a handful of other Normans for good measure, from Jacques Rouët, the financial manager, down to the doorman. With opening day fast approaching, no suitable doorman had been found. As Suzanne Luling explains, "he had to be tall, at ease with himself, friendly to a certain degree and speaking only when appropriate. Our ideal doorman was the one at Molyneux." But no one fitting that description had materialized. One day Dior was told about a certain Ferdinand from the Norman town of Saint-Lô who was interested in the position. He was then employed in the building industry and had no prior experience as a doorman, but the mention of Saint-Lô was enough for Dior. "Normandy, eh? That's a good sign. Get him to come and see me."

"The following Saturday," Suzanne Luling relates, "there he was, in his workman's overalls. We liked the look of him and so we decided to break him in. I pretended to be a chauffeur, sitting at the wheel of my car with Mr. Rouët at my side pretending to be a client. Still in his overalls but with white gloves, Ferdinand hastened to open the door, closed it again, and hastened a little more calmly to open the front door to allow Mr. Rouët to enter. Then we did it all over again." The lessons continued until Ferdinand was considered ready to greet clients, this time in a frock coat and with a new, rather British air about him.

Dior's old seaside playmates Suzanne Luling and Nicole Riotteau were soon joined by the handsome, elegant Serge Heftler-Louiche. Even before the business opened, he approached his friend Christian to suggest branching out into perfumes. It was a cold Sunday afternoon in December and Dior was sitting in the Pâtisserie Penny on Place de la Madeleine with his little godson Jean-Marc Heftler, aged six, and Jean-Marc's older sister Marie-Christine. This was a regular outing, the purpose being to devour Penny's deliciously sticky coconut cakes (still made today). On that particular day their father decided to join them.

Heftler-Louiche had been manager of Coty perfumes for twenty-five years and also owned and ran SFD, a perfume distribution company based in Rue Jean-Mermoz. He had already formulated his plan, and in the time it took for the children to plaster themselves with coconut cream from ear to ear, the deal was done. Contractually Marcel Boussac had no rights over any spin-offs like perfumes, but he could be asked to put up the capital.* Christian put his love of things British to good commercial use and came up with a name, "Miss Dior." The houndstooth design for the box came a few days later, at Victor Grandpierre's suggestion, inspired by one of the fabrics in the collection.

This improvising had more in common with the game called Consequences the surrealist poets loved to play, each taking a turn to add his own touch, than with the launch of a new perfume. It was all very lighthearted in comparison with today's costly process of market research, sales trials, and marketing campaigns, in which millions are spent without any guarantee of success. These were the good old days where Dior could call his illustrator friend René Gruau, ask him to do a poster to advertise his new perfume, and never dream of giving him a "concept" to work from. Gruau came up with an image of a white swan gliding across an orange page with a pearl necklace and black velvet bow around its neck, one which was subsequently used all around the world and for many years to come. Henri Sauguet composed an impromptu waltz in honor of "Miss Dior," and "there we all were together again," wrote Dior, "just as in our youth, in the days of picnics, fishing expeditions, and croquet matches. This time, however, another contest awaited us."

Like every good fairy tale, the story only works if the hero triumphs over adversity. The fragrance was an *alcydée* with *rose de chêne* created by the Vacher perfumery, a far stronger scent than others of the time. Dior held it under the noses of every woman he knew, from workroom heads to sales assistants and society ladies. Their verdict was

---

* Christian Dior Perfumes Ltd. was launched on March 4, 1948, with a capital of 2 million francs. Christian Dior held 25 percent of the shares, Heftler-Louiche 35 percent, and Marcel Boussac 40 percent.

unanimous. They hated it. But Dior paid them no heed and, convinced of its quality, gave it the go-ahead.

It is hardly surprising that the eighty-five members of his team had the impression of embarking on an extraordinary adventure. "We might have been on tenterhooks, counting the days until our first press showing," recounts Suzanne Luling, "but we weren't worried. Throughout the preparations we somehow knew that we were heading for an event the whole world would talk about."

When he first entered his atelier on Avenue Montaigne, Dior took a small gold star out of his pocket and put it on his desk. It was his lucky star, the one he stepped on in the Rue Saint-Honoré just when destiny brought him face to face with his old friend from Granville, the one who would lead him to Marcel Boussac. It was the star of victory. In the course of the eight weeks before opening day, another side to Dior emerged, almost imperceptibly. Behind his slightly fleshy features, smooth voice, and soft, plump body in its dapper gray suit lay a little French general with a sharp nose, abrupt gestures, and commanding tones. When he officiated in the midst of models and workroom heads or corrected the lines of a dress from the collection, he would wave a pointer with a gold-ringed knob — hardly the chosen accessory of a couturier. His language was full of military expressions — references to "a first-class general staff," "mobilizing my thoughts, and all my strength," being "on guard," "standing firm," and "the vital recapture." But this was a game, not a battlefield, and for this introverted, naturally indolent Norman to unleash his creative forces, he needed the type of playful inspiration found in the Carnival images of his childhood and the charades and pantomimes of those evenings with his friend Max Jacob.

For those about to launch it, the legend of the New Look was already reality. "It was a bizarre period of back-breaking work, hasty improvisation, racing against the clock, and putting things in place at a hellish rate," writes Suzanne Luling. Those rare occasions when she had a chance to stop for an instant to greet someone in passing on the stairs, she felt as though she had never known a better time in her life. Later on, when the staff found time to talk at leisure about it all, they remembered how every day, every hour, almost every minute brought something unexpected, a problem to be solved, some little incident or a burst of great hilarity. If only they had recorded it! Fortunately Suzanne Luling's account has preserved some lovely snippets from that wonderful odyssey during which good fortune somehow seemed to rain down on them.

A month and a half before the opening, for example, Dior was showered with dollars. An American stocking manufacturer turned up on the doorstep, having read about the impending launch in the November 17, 1946, edition of *Women's Wear Daily*. He asked Dior if he would be interested in a range of his colored stockings (the company was Prestige) for use in the collections . . . and a fee of $5,000. He also undertook to run advertisements in the American fashion magazines. Dior was then paid a visit by some New York silk merchants, Lida and Zika Ascher, who had heard about Dior and wondered if he would be interested in their series of silk head scarves printed with designs by Henry Moore, Graham Sutherland, and other contemporary artists, to sell in the Dior boutique.

There were some particularly colorful visitors too. A quirk of fate certainly livened up the recruiting of the first Dior models. A new law had just closed the city's brothels, and as a result Avenue Montaigne found itself swamped with unemployed prostitutes in outrageous makeup looking for modeling jobs. This batch of hopefuls proved more adept at taking their gowns off than showing them to best advantage, and their catwalk technique was more suited to street corners than the elegant beige carpets of the Maison Dior. News of this surprise invasion spread like wildfire through the building, prompting great bursts of laughter and bringing Dior out of his studio to see what the fuss was about. Not wanting to miss out on the pleasure of inspecting this interesting lot in person, his expert eye did manage to spot one suitable candidate lost in the throng, a pretty young girl by the name of Marie-Thérèse, a former secretary who was later to become one of his star models.

"It really was an incredible existence," admits Suzanne Luling. She shared with Harrisson Elliot a tiny office lit by the small round window in the entry hall. Cramped and dusty, it was an interesting observation post but plagued by a persistent draft. The enterprising Luling got used to creative problem solving, like taking the models back to her place on Quai Malaquais for photographic sessions, in the porter's lodge, of all places. "There was a lovely round window there too," she writes. "The girls would stand in front of it and we'd capture them like that, with their noses at the window and their mouths open with just the faintest expression of surprise." At ten o'clock at night when work was finally over, everyone would let off steam and go dancing into the small hours. "It was the start of something new. We were all people who liked and trusted each other, and who suddenly began talking the same language. Parisian in taste but provincial in our dedication, we were essentially outsiders. And the whole place buzzed with an air of hard work and success."

Rehearsals had begun and Dior too was working under extraordinary pressure. His studio was in what used to be the bedroom, and with no room to step back, fitting sessions would overflow onto the landing and even onto the stairs. They were an endless process of trying on dresses, then making changes and fixing problems as they occurred. One difficulty arose after another, and things reached fever pitch. To start with, the quality of the fabrics was not up to scratch, although one day a Chinese gentleman appeared with some shantung silk that ended up as the famous "Bar" suit. The chief problem was that the seamstresses had to relearn a whole series of forgotten techniques. "I wanted to 'construct' my dresses," said Dior, "molding them on the curves of the female body and stylizing its contours, emphasizing the waist and the width of the hips, highlighting the bust. To give my dresses greater body, I lined virtually everything with cambric or taffeta, harking back to a tradition of couture that had long since been abandoned." One workroom head had a nervous breakdown as a result of the pressure of work and had to be replaced on the spot. To everyone's relief, her replacement, a seamstress named Monique, rose to the task. "She and Christian were the ones who completed the collection," Dior wrote, "They even had to make the suits because the expert I engaged for that purpose proved incapable of doing it."

The lengths to which Dior would go in fine-tuning each garment occasionally verged on the comical. There was the day he was so irritated at the stiff way one particular dress hung and the lack of movement at its waist that he called for a hammer. "And with great blows of the hammer," Suzanne Luling laughs, "he banged away trying to get the shape he needed for his type of look." She hastens to add that no model was wearing the dress at the time. The troublesome component he was banging away at was a wooden dressmaker's dummy, the manufacturers of which later produced a prototype with perfect New Look proportions.

But not only wooden dummies suffered. One day a beautiful English model fainted dead away in Dior's arms. "I thought I had a firm hold on her," he relates, "but she kept sliding onto the floor, and I found myself holding . . . her bust! I had forgotten that, in my desire to highlight that particular part of the female anatomy, I had ordered all those less endowed by nature to get themselves what we prudishly described as 'an artificial bosom.'"

All this was minor compared with what was to develop just four days before the collection was due for presentation. The workrooms of Paris were called out on strike! Dior's seamstresses stayed loyally at their posts but a group of underlings from a nearby *maison* managed to force their way into 30 Avenue Montaigne, climb the stairs, and invade the workrooms, insisting that the women lay down their work out of solidarity. "To Christian, it was as if this blow of fate were personally aimed at him. He felt as though he were being struck down just at the moment when he was delivering up a major part of his life."

Suzanne Luling's account of this catastrophe provides a further illustration, if one is needed, of the unstoppable force behind the New Look and how it rose above every obstacle in its path. After an initial moment of complete paralysis, production resumed with those left "fidgeting with impatience, grumbling for all we were worth, and offering all sorts of good-hearted solutions as if we were trying to save a rustic fete at Granville from impending rain." Friends like Marie-Louise Bousquet, Christian Bérard, René Gruau, and Denise Tual came racing to the rescue, grabbing needles and thread and taking the place of the seamstresses in the workrooms to sew on tulle ruffs or take up hems. Two days later, when the fuss had died down a little, some of the workers tiptoed back in to resume their tasks.

Despite the dreadful anxiety caused by the strike and the moments of exhaustion when all Dior could do was collapse onto piles of material (the only place left to him), Christian Dior seemed remarkably serene. "Of all my collections, the first was the one that cost me the least effort and worry. I had nothing to lose, really. The public could hardly be disappointed, they didn't know me, they had no expectations and demanded nothing from me. Of course I had to please them, but more for my own sake than anything else." But was he surprised by his success? "My ideal was to be seen as a 'good craftsman,' a precocious aim indeed, since it implies both integrity and high quality." But as for the idea of launching a revolution — "I do admit that if I had been asked about my work and what I hoped to achieve on the eve of my first collection, the one that launched the New Look, I certainly would not have talked about a revolution. I could never have foreseen the reception it was about to receive. I had so little inkling of it but had simply tried to do my best."

Those around him, however, had a very strong sense of his upcoming success, and eventually Dior found it impossible to extricate himself from curious friends dying to view his creations. While once he had been spared such things, one of the prices of fame is the way others try to claim their share. With Bérard's fraternal solicitations, Marie-Louise Bousquet's overwhelming maternal interest, his closest friends constantly buzzing around him, best wishes from "supporters," and requests from insistent members of the press . . . Dior found himself under pressure to stage a special preview for the "insiders." On the eve of the collection, Bérard, who sensed what was about to occur, gave him this advice: Be happy, tonight, and enjoy it; after tomorrow you will always be trying to outdo yourself and things will never be peaceful again.

Confronted with such an initiation from a friend like Bérard who had known nothing but success, Dior felt quite giddy. "Perhaps they all expected too much of me. Perhaps they had too much faith in me." As his other friend Suzanne Luling remembers, what worried him was "not what he had achieved, not at all, but . . . the prospect of having to show it to other people. He was terrified at the thought of being so bold. It was almost as if someone had told the young Dior that he would have to take the costumes and playacting from those charades he indulged in so willingly with Max Jacob, Christian Bérard, Jean Ozenne, or André Fraigneau, and perform on a real stage in front of a thousand people."

It was with great reluctance that Christian Dior agreed to stage a kind of dress rehearsal for his closest friends in the salon, scene of several final chaotic days of hasty rehearsals amid workmen and ladders. When it was over Christian Bérard waxed lyrical, only to be outdone by Marie-Louise Bousquet, while Etienne de Beaumont applauded fit to burst. It all just made Dior the more anxious. Superstitious type that he was, he searched desperately for a piece of wood to touch. If only he could delay that dreaded moment, and put off facing the public just a little longer. Even his saleswomen were barred from the preview showing. "They too, like the press, would have to wait until the curtain went up on the appointed day," he decided. But Christian Bérard could not contain his enthusiasm and soon spread the word across Paris. Sitting at dinner he sketched the outlines of Dior's new look on the tablecloth and announced to all and sundry the revolution that was about to take place. Among the dinner companions of this St. John the Baptist of fashion was Bettina Ballard, who devoured every detail of the sketches with her eyes.

As Suzanne Luling explains, "Christian Dior was about to turn everything on its head. In one fell swoop he had gone back to long dresses, narrow waists, and wide skirts — everything the war had deprived us of. But there was nothing to fear from Christian. He was anything but a revolutionary. He never did anything to make a big statement, he loathed shocking people gratuitously and had the greatest respect for tradition. What he wanted was to revive tradition but with a contemporary slant. While some were absurd enough to suggest that he was 'wasting' material, he did it not to please his backers but simply because he felt that was the fashion of the day. Very few people are gifted with his sense of *l'air du temps*, the mood of the times. He could also detect the changes underway in society and the way things were heading, what the next rage would be. He was the type who could hear an apple ripen on the tree. Why do I say that? Perhaps because Christian liked to stay silent and just listen, never trying to shine in company, always looking out for the needs and desires of others, of those he loved. He was all affection, curiosity, and discretion. And of course, a genuine artist. . . . I may be disappointing those who can only see such a sudden revelation as some sort of miracle, but that first collection, I swear it, was no fluke. Of course we were impatient to see how it would be received but, above all, we were happy.

"At midnight when we finally stepped out into the night, onto the sidewalk outside the town house on Avenue Montaigne, he turned back to look at the building. The air was mild and we were all in the kind of stupor that comes after you have really exerted yourself and just prior to sitting for an exam. Christian smiled and made a little gesture with his hand toward the name over the door. 'If Mama were still alive,' he said, 'I never would have dared.' "

The next day was to be his moment of triumph.

8

Happy Days

By being natural and sincere, one often can create revolutions without having sought them.

— Christian Dior

February 12, 1947, was one of those days that never quite seem to dawn. The streets were empty save for a few passersby and the occasional motorcar, a rare sight in Paris these days. Gas was short, coal was short, everything was short. The radio that morning had announced a drop in the daily bread ration from 350 to 200 grams. The temperature, like the morale, had plummeted to below freezing — minus-six to be precise, only a slight improvement on the previous week, when it had been thirteen below. It was just ten o'clock but the cold had not stopped one particular huddle of people from venturing forth. They were an unusual sight as they stamped their feet for warmth under the gray canvas awning over the entrance to number 30, Avenue Montaigne — about a hundred of them, the women in mink coats and the gentleman all elegantly attired. From the way they stood on the pavement chatting loudly among themselves it was clear they all knew each other. They seemed almost to be marking time, barely inching forward despite the paste invitation cards they were waving at a doorman in a large gray frock coat. "Only three at a time, if you please," he intoned. Some of the women were becoming irritable. As members of the press, they weren't used to being made to wait, and their time was precious. All this for a few dresses! They had just sat through a *fortnight* of dresses, show after show.

In the midst of such confusion no one noticed a group of workmen slipping out into the street against the flow of the crowd. The carpet fitters had worked through the night to get everything ready, with a team of florists hard on their heels since the early hours. The most magnificent bouquets now adorned the entrance hall and the staircase leading to the huge pearl gray and white salon. It was a staggering sight — quite indecent really in a city of food queues and people dying of cold. After all, last week some workers had actually died of pneumonia, and with the canals frozen over, there wasn't a scrap of coal in the city.

Standing on the stairs inside was Christian Dior, who had dragged himself away from supervising the placement of some giant quincia palms in the entrance hall to inspect the immense oval wreaths frothing up over the mantel mirrors. The effect was quite enchanting and he pronounced himself duly spellbound. Around him, nervous chaos reigned. Harrisson Elliott, seating plan in hand, was examining the place cards pinned to the chairs. "Hélène Lazareff . . . yes. Susan Train? Haven't I got a spot for her on the *Vogue* sofa?" Oblivious to the young American's dilemma, Dior was lost in contemplation of the flush of tall blue delphiniums, pink sweet peas, and lily of the valley, his lucky flower. He plucked a perfumed sprig for his buttonhole. His favorite florists, Lachaume, had also delivered a floral arrangement to his partner, Marcel Boussac, the previous evening, courtesy of Dior. Boussac had been kept completely in the dark throughout the preparations of the previous months, and this long-awaited sign from his protégé took his breath away. Upon his return from the office to his home in Neuilly, he was greeted by a striking ensemble of black and white orchids illuminating his front hall, a gesture all the more delicate given Boussac's passion for orchids, which he grew in a hothouse in

Chantilly. Boussac hurried up to his wife's apartments. "Don't worry about tomorrow," he cried. "There isn't a florist in the world who could have created a bouquet as beautiful as the one I have just seen. I'm quite certain tomorrow will be a huge success!"

Back on Avenue Montaigne, meanwhile, those fine ladies were still hopping from one wedge-heeled shoe to the other, trying to keep warm. Their grumbling was becoming increasingly audible. Reinforcement for Ferdinand in his gray topcoat arrived in the form of Jacques Rouët's tall figure, and the crush began to ease. To keep their minds off the wait, people began to gossip. "It's all Boussac's money, you know." "Yes, they say he's put in sixty million." "I've heard it's more than that. Some say Dior got a billion! Boussac must be out of his mind. . . . Oh well, in for a penny, I suppose." There were murmurs of disapproval: three million people were out on strike, 250,000 of them in Paris. The garbage collectors were out too and the army had been forced to step in. "It's all because of the Communists, of course," came the familiar refrain. "Just look at what they've brought us to. What was the point of kicking out de Gaulle if it's come to this? And how much longer do you think they'll keep us standing here?" "I've just got back from London and I tell you, it's worse than Paris. It was freezing! Just like Siberia and not a thing in the shops. And they haven't got India to rely on any longer, either, don't forget."

Suddenly, however, the rush was on and politics abandoned. It was all eyes on feet as they surged toward the entrance, driven by an almighty crush. This was more like it, here we go . . . and at last they were in, the wait forgotten as they crossed the threshold into the inner sanctum, an entrance hall that quite took your breath away, and the flowers . . . heaven! not to mention the cloud of wafting fragrance as a string of lovely young women emerged from a little room all done out in cretonne to spray guests with the brand-new Miss Dior fragrance.

Seeing such excitement no doubt helped Dior maintain his composure. But suddenly he froze, his fingers tightening on a piece of wood in his pocket. The carpet had finally been tacked down and the workmen's din was gone. What was it Madame Delahaye, his clairvoyant, had said? "The last bang of the hammer will come as the first guest enters." The buzzing around him reached a crescendo and he felt strangely relaxed as he put himself in the hands of fate.

Suzanne Luling sets the scene. "It's hard to imagine what it's like if you've never been to a press showing of a new collection," she writes. "It's a final dress rehearsal, a tea party, a bullfight, and the Supreme Court rolled into one. In the midst of the chatter you're trying to find your seat, with one eye out for a little beribboned card with your name on it. You're saying hello and shaking hands left, right, and center, waving furiously at someone or other across the room, leaping up to get a program. Everybody's jumpy, there's a lot of gentle pushing, looking out for one's place. . . . And in this sea of delirium there's always someone complaining about where she's been seated, another one sitting on the staircase (because the salons are packed to the seams) who's pulled her stocking. It's all perfume, gossip, and frivolity . . . and yet, it's also a serious business. A damned serious business! With the exception of the odd friend squashed onto one of the steps, these people have been subjected to at least half a dozen showings like this in the past week. They are the ultimate arbiters, poised, pencil in hand, either to give the whole proceedings the thumbs-down or to hail the triumphant matador. Just like spectators at a bullring, they are flushed with heat, their legs have gone to sleep, and they use a special jargon to discuss the performance in front of them. They are allowed to take notes but not to sketch or take photographs. A camera here is as dangerous and forbidden as a cigarette in an oil refinery, because the showing of a collection is like the unveiling of a great revelation, one which, if it's a hit, is worth tens, even hundreds of millions. Anyone breaching the vow of secrecy can be severely punished by law."

All of a sudden, as if obeying some tacit code, a sudden hush fell. Framed in the doorway to the catwalk, where the first model was about to appear, stood the announcer, a sheet of paper in her hand. It was half past ten. Dior was out of sight, hiding behind the curtains.

"*Numéro un.* Number one!"

Marie-Thérèse came out to model the first gown but, dead with fright, she fluffed the turn and disappeared in tears, henceforth incapable of reappearing. But no matter. All the audience noticed was her show-stopping flounce and the way her pleated skirt sent cigarette ash flying as it swung open. Another gown appeared at the same tempo, then another and another. Skirts twirling, all twenty yards of fabric, tip-tilted hat and gloved hand, this flounce and flair was no apparition.

This was woman incarnate — unashamedly flirtatious in her nonchalant disregard of the stir she was causing, sensual, sensational, crazily chic and, above all, supremely sure of herself. This was the long-awaited image of Paris reborn, an explosive cocktail, a breathtaking fantasy. Conceived around the lines of a flower's folded petals and of a figure eight, the ninety outfits on parade gave a whole new grace to the female figure, accentuating and highlighting its natural proportions. Open-mouthed, the audience squirmed in their square-cut jackets and tugged unconsciously at the hems of their short, straight skirts as the applause mounted to an unstoppable ovation. As he stood behind his curtain, Christian Dior was forced to clap his hands over his ears. The chorus of "bravo"s was terrifying.

Both Carmel Snow and Bettina Ballard, the doyennes of the fashion press, were captivated. This had gone way beyond their wildest expectations. "We were given a polished theatrical performance such as we had never seen in a couture house before," wrote Bettina Ballard. "We were witness to a revolution in fashion and to a revolution in showing fashion as well." The *Harper's Bazaar* office in New York had been in a state of shock ever since Carmel Snow wired them the previous day, ordering them to "leave plenty of room . . . for Christian Dior." Snow was the first to throw herself on Dior: "It's quite a revolution, dear Christian. Your dresses have such a new look. They're quite wonderful, you know." Even before her famous phrase made it to the other side of the world, a messenger waiting on the street outside caught a note thrown down to him by the journalist from Reuters and the news reached the United States that same day. The French press had been on strike for a month, so it was the American and other foreign press who hailed the event. For once, even Bettina Ballard was effusive: "Magic . . . was what everyone now wanted from Paris. Never has there been a moment more climatically right for a Napoleon, an Alexander the Great, a Caesar of the couture. Paris fashion was waiting to be seized and shaken and given direction. There has never been an easier or more complete conquest than that of Christian Dior in 1947." Carmel Snow struck her most patriotic note (she had the well-earned nickname of "the French guard") with the words, "Dior saved Paris as Paris was saved in the Battle of the Marne." The American buyers who refused to believe her, and left for Le Havre before seeing the collection, barely sighted the Statue of Liberty in New York harbor before turning around and sailing back to France.

Thrust forward into the main salon to be greeted by a roar of applause, Christian Dior's face was soon red with a hundred lipstick marks. "Whatever happy event I might enjoy in my life," he wrote, "nothing will ever surpass my feelings at that moment."

That day unleashed an onslaught on the Avenue Montaigne that did not let up for months to come. A kind of madness seized the modest town house as a horde of women descended on Dior demanding to be fitted without delay. The poor saleswomen were at a loss to know where to start. Their traditionally exacting clients, difficult to please at the best of times, suddenly all wanted to try on the same number — the "Bar" suit, the signature of the collection, with its cream shantung jacket with peplum that hugged the figure like a marchioness's gown, worn over a black wool skirt with deep pleats that flared in a queenly fashion as you walked. The look was topped off with a saucy black pillbox hat. Olivia de Havilland bought the "Passe-Partout" suit in navy blue wool crepe, a collarless jacket with pockets on the bust and hips, worn over a slender skirt — the essence of the "figure eight" line. There were countless orders for the "Corolle" afternoon dress in black wool, with its bodice fastened down the front by five large buttons and its miraculously cunning pleated skirt. A blue taffeta version of those pleats appeared in "Chérie" and in several of the evening gowns. And the long gown "Africain" in panther-printed muslin had everyone sighing. Rita Hayworth ordered the "Soirée" evening gown, with its two tiers of navy blue taffeta pleats, and wore it to the premier of her latest film, *Gilda*. Vivien Leigh and Laurence Olivier came to see the collection with Christian Bérard. "Everyone there had a Chicago accent," remarked "Scarlett O'Hara" as she left.

Not only Chicago. They came running from London too, and from Rome, Buenos Aires, and Montevideo. For several weeks there was a marked predominance of women over men on the London-Paris air route. Nancy Mitford blazed the trail, closely followed by her sisters. When she found herself short of cash, the British embassy's elegant muse had no hesitation about selling her winter fur to buy a Dior coat, wrapping herself in it like a latter-day Anna Karenina, its meters of material a fair exchange for the warmth of her cast-off musquash. Dior's impact on high society was unprecedented. "I've been a member of the Jockey Club for forty years," exclaimed the Count of Lasteyrie, accustomed to remaining aloof from such frivolities, "and never once has anyone made mention of a designer: now all they talk about is Dior!"

Even more unexpected was the way Dior's designs captured the imagination of the mass market. His aim was anything but popular appeal. But within weeks the look had been embraced by a huge number of Frenchwomen. He was the first to be surprised at the voracious way in which the normally conservative sector of the public in both Paris and the provinces seized on his designs. There were no fashion boutiques; garment manufacturers tended to produce the most ordinary of apparel and barely followed fashion trends, leaving haute couture in its own rarefied little world. All of a sudden, women from all walks of life were wearing Dior's dramatic "corolla" skirts, narrow waists, and low-cut bodices, albeit with a few variations and alterations. It was as if all they had ever dreamed of, no matter what their social standing, was to play the femme fatale or the grand lady.

The instant transformation of the woman in the street was a result of the war. Women had become used to making everything themselves, and despite the newspaper strike and the absence of retail outlets responding to demand, most knew how to "make do" and create their own fashion. The real magic wand belonged to a fairy godmother by the name of Singer — that machine could remodel and restitch anything as long as there was material to be sewn. It wasn't always easy. Susan Train, soon to become assistant to Bettina Ballard at *Vogue* and now her successor, was a young student in Paris that year. "I found myself tearing my hair out trying to run myself up a long gray flannel skirt and not being able to sew!" Hebe Dorsey faced a similar problem: the future fashion editor of the *International Herald Tribune* was also just a student at the Sorbonne who was taken to the collection by a friend. She came out "transported." "It was like going to the opera for the first time. Dior really had won the war for France. There wasn't a single taxi driver, if you said to him 'Dior,' who didn't know right away where to take you. He was as much a household word as 'La Marseillaise'!"

There was something very French about *le New-Look,* despite the name! It was everywhere, even among the bohemians of the Latin Quarter, people like the singer Juliette Gréco, the star of her generation of antiheroes who spent her evenings giving husky renditions of *Si tu t'imagines* in the clubs of Saint-Germain-des-Prés. Gréco had no qualms about leaving the Left Bank to do a little shopping on Avenue Montaigne (a dress in those days cost around 120,000 francs, no small sum) and Dior was both flattered and appreciative of her patronage. "She had the rare gift of matching her own very unique style with mine. This new fashion really did belong to youth and the future."

But just why did young people take to Dior with such passion? What was it about the New Look, some kind of personal statement? Surely it wasn't the clothes — after all, it took a lot of nerve to flaunt such opulence in a country paralyzed by strikes, rocked by government crises, and seemingly doomed to perpetual gloom. The true power of this new fashion was as a catalyst for the universal longing for change, the need to forget empty bellies, run-down apartments, and a general feeling of tedium. It was the longing of forty million Frenchmen and women for a return to a normal, happy, healthy, and romantic existence.

There are times when all that is needed to turn things around is one simple crazy gesture. Take the triumphal procession from the Place de l'Etoile to the cathedral of Notre Dame ordered by General de Gaulle on the day after the liberation of Paris — an oh-so-daring enterprise that, in one fell swoop, reinstilled patriotic fervor in the people of France. It was as if Dior had unwittingly touched off a similar spark. The New Look was bolstered by a desire to hold one's head high, to shake off apathy and ennui and silence the grumblers. This was not the vulgar desire of the realm of the fast buck, of the profiteers and black marketeers, nor was it born of the cynicism of the new rich with their diamanté dresses and convertibles.

As the writer who was later to become France's minister of culture, Françoise Giroud, once wrote, "Every fashion dies from disenchantment and is born of desire, crystallizing all that is shimmering on the surface of a society." But never before had a fashion unleashed such a torrent, a fury in fact, of controversy. Cinema newsreels showed amazing scenes of women tearing off each others' clothes in the streets of

Paris. In a famous incident on Rue Lepic, a bunch of housewives in paupers' rags became enraged at the sight of a group of ladies in their new Dior dresses. They set upon them, pulling at their bodices until they were ripped to shreds and leaving the wearers half naked. It was long skirts and flower shapes against short skirts and mannish jackets, fine ankles and rakish pillboxes against wedge heels and cauliflower hats; Avenue Montaigne against the Flea Market.

Dior had chosen a floral motif but the collection he named Corolla was instantly dubbed the New Look, proof that not even he had anticipated its ramifications. He had simply followed his instincts, trying to revive a forgotten vision of beauty. If the role of fashion is to create a fantasy world, where else to turn, when the present is depressing and the future uncertain, but to the past? There was nothing calculated in his actions. But to unleash such a revolution he had to see his idea through to its ultimate expression. His real talent, the couturier in him, had taken him deep into the past as the only way to have real impact, to hit the right note and herald a return to another ideal. "Whereas fashion generally develops a step at a time with each collection, Dior's gift lay in jumping three steps ahead. He sensed that he needed to go for extremes," as Susan Train puts it. The result, to cite *Vogue* art director Alexander Liberman, was that "he hit the mark in creating a certain concept of womanhood." What was left to fuel a woman's dreams in the prevailing atmosphere of deprivation? Dior's magic touch anticipated her desires, gave her a means of expressing them, and told her it was all right to go ahead and dream again. It was that combination that was the key to his sweeping success; in a world starved of images the New Look was like some miraculous bounty. By reharnessing the power of the imagination, Christian Dior forged a special place for himself, one that no other designer since has been able to claim.

Every generation that has lived through dark times remembers the day they finally came to an end. To the wartime generation, the New Look was the rediscovery of happiness and they embraced it accordingly. This was enough for Dior: "I insist on using the word happiness," he wrote. "I believe Alphonse Daudet once wrote that he would like to feel that his works made him 'a merchant of happiness.' In my own modest field, I too pursue that dream. My first dresses were called

'Love,' 'Tenderness,' 'Corolla' and 'Happiness.' Women must have instinctively understood that I dreamed of making them not only more beautiful but also happier. And they rewarded me with their patronage." As for his own analysis of his success: "When I went to analyze this social trend I was responsible for, I realized that, above all, it stood for a return to the art of pleasing. . . . What was heralded as a new style was merely the genuine, natural expression of the kind of fashion I wanted to see. It just so happened that my personal inclinations coincided with the general mood of the times and thus became the fashion watchword. . . . It was as if Europe had tired of dropping bombs and now wanted to let off a few fireworks. . . . The birth of the House of Dior profited from that wave of optimism and the return to an ideal of civilized happiness."

And so it was that a man who had waited twenty years to find his true vocation came forward just as the time was ripe. Among the women who flocked to his door on Avenue Montaigne, women who felt themselves come alive again in their Dior designs, there was one group whose patronage was of special significance and immense clout. These were the professional buyers, the ones who Carmel Snow had summoned from New York with the announcement in *Harper's Bazaar* that "this new couturier Dior will produce some extraordinary things." Not everyone responded to her call. Only eighteen buyers turned up for the first collection while dozens more were to regret having ignored it. The news reached them en route to New York, bringing scowls to their faces and a certain dose of nausea at the sight of the ghostly silhouette of the Statue of Liberty emerging through the dawn. Six days on board ship and all for nothing, now that they had to turn around and go back again. "From that day onward," recalls Susan Train from *Harper's* rival *Vogue*, "it was no longer considered wise to 'disobey' our orders. The New Look took the buyers back in hand." As Norman Chosler, buyer for I. Magnin, declared: "I do not recall that we ever lived through such a cataclysmic event." Andrew Goodman from Bergdorf Goodman remembers, "It was a real sensation because the world had been closed to all possibilities of fashion creation." So it was that all the "greats" — Bendel, Marshall Fields, Bloomingdale's — found themselves lining up outside 30 Avenue Montaigne.

The writer Colette, ever alert to the talk of the town, described it thus: "It took one swish of the hips and America was won." The Americans and the British were closely followed by the Italians, who, to quote Dior, "were excellent clients from the outset, giving the lie to the myth of a fashion war between Italy and France. It never existed." A great lover of Italy and well acquainted with Venice, Dior knew all about the tradition of *la piavola di França* in the shopwindows of St. Mark's Square. Dating back to Marie Antoinette, the *piavola* was a doll whose costume changed every fortnight to show the Venetians the *dernier cri* from Paris. "Then came the Belgians, the Swiss, and the Scandinavians. . . . Shortly afterward, the South Americans, the Australians and, a few seasons later, the Germans and the Japanese."

To avoid overcrowding the salons, Avenue Montaigne was open day and night, receiving the buyers in the evening once individual clients had gone home. The saleswomen would remain to assist as the buyers studied the designs at leisure and pondered their orders. Dior was careful to stay away from what he termed "the carnage," where his dresses were passed from one to the next, pulled apart, turned inside out, and generally handed over to the "merchants of the temple." This necessary, and indeed normal, invasion by the world of commerce "sickened" him. At seven in the evening a buffet supper of sandwiches and champagne was set up, and buyers and sales staff worked into the night, often until two or three in the morning.

The premises had become too small to cope with demand. With Marcel Boussac's approval, two additional workrooms were opened and a seven story building erected where the old stables had stood, "probably the first time in this great horse-lover's career that he agreed to such sacrilege," wrote Dior.

Time came for Christian Dior to take a well-earned rest before embarking on his second collection. In keeping with his love of the rustic life, he drove down to the city of Tours on the Loire, stopping in tiny villages for copious meals in the tradition of another era. Suzanne Luling lent him her little Simca, which was driven for him by a young man he had met in 1946 on a trip to Cannes, by the name of Pierre Perrotino. The boy had just returned from a German labor camp and was looking for a start in life when Dior befriended him and suggested he return with him to Paris. One of Pierre's qualifications was knowing how to drive, something Dior steadfastly refused to learn. A few months later, needing a driver, he had Perrotino put on the payroll. But Perrotino was also a "friend" in the intimate sense. Dior liked his strong, solid physique, frank nature, and somewhat unpolished way of speaking, the legacy of his humble origins. There was an element of protectiveness in Dior's attraction to people with a touch of the "common," in the noblest sense of the word. Dior had always been discreet about his liaison with Jacques Homberg, who was to remain his real companion. But at the time Homberg was in England for two years. And in contrast to the elegance and aloofness of his official partner, the couturier preferred dalliances of a light-hearted nature. Perrotino was a case in point. He knew his place, and the country idyll proceeded without incident.

What went through Dior's mind once away from Avenue Montaigne? He confessed a reluctance to put the business out of his thoughts and would telephone Jacques Rouët daily for news. His previously carefree disposition was now a thing of the past.

He remembered the words of his friend Christian Bérard, only two months earlier. It seemed so long ago now. "Savor this moment of happiness," Bérard had told him. "There'll never be another like it in your career, nor will you be allowed to enjoy it as much as now. Tomorrow begins the anguish of having to live up to and, if possible, surpass yourself." Bérard had made the remarks over dinner on the evening of the first collection. His closest friends were there — Michel de Brunhoff, Boris Kochno, Marie-Louise Bousquet, and a few others. But it was Bébé, his "big brother," who made the toast after giving Dior a pastel drawing he had done of Avenue Montaigne. Dior had been so happy, surrounded by his loved ones and sharing his success with them. This celebration was for him, he was the one who had "made it." "I found such sweet pleasure in the murmurs of admiration and the applause that greeted certain dresses, that I swore I'd never tire of it." But the last few months, with all their stresses, had made Bébé's prediction ominously real, as if at the age of forty-two he were being stalked by the same fate as his friend. Dior knew only too well how Bérard had become a slave to his success, Bérard who never missed a ball, party, or play and never said no to a job here or a commission there, spreading his talents as a painter far too thin. Only a year later, having staggered from one attempt after another to kick his cocaine habit, Bérard was to die of his unrelenting fame, during rehearsals for a production of Molière's *Les Fourberies de Scapin*. Now, when Dior looked in the mirror, he saw the very image of the friend who had urged him never to fall into the same trap.

And yet those closest to him, those who knew him well, would testify that he did know how to say no, "refusing to be influenced in his professional life just as he protected himself in his personal life." Suzanne Luling is adamant. "I knew him inside out, he was my childhood friend and I knew he wouldn't stop being himself. No, Christian wouldn't change. Fame wasn't about to play tricks with him; he wasn't dazzled by it. What he liked, and what must have been the most precious crown of his success, was the fact that now he could pursue his own tastes with impunity. He had never compromised in that area. His very precise sense of judgment allowed him that very correct, but rare, notion that to have taste was to stick to your guns, that you needn't compromise by accommodating the likes and dislikes of others as if that would make your work better. . . . He had just been acclaimed as a man of good taste. Why should that influence his way of being and thinking? There was no way that success could turn his head."

Christian Dior was not one to speculate on what might or might not appeal. He followed his instincts. Once more turning his mind to the task, he thought of nothing but his creations, indulging his sense of extravagance just one degree further. The autumn-winter collection of 1947–48 did not rest on its laurels by limiting itself to reproducing the lines that had so revolutionized fashion just six months earlier, harking back as they did to the traditions of woman as an "object" of beauty. "This was a wild collection! It was long, it was wide! I took the famous New Look to the furthest extreme, . . . using an unimaginable amount of fabric and dropping hems right to the ankles." And once again, he hit the right note, further consolidating the New Look and establishing the Dior sense of taste even more firmly than before. It was a good strategy. But there was nothing calculated about it beyond Dior's stubborn determination to take his ideas, yet again, to their furthest point.

On August 6, 1947, the day of the showing, the town house on

Avenue Montaigne was bursting at the seams. No American buyer was going to miss it this time, an indication as much of professional instincts as of the significance of a collection bearing the Dior signature. The Californians in particular were only too aware of the market for Dior, with plenty of time to ponder it. It took a four to five day's trip just to cross America, on top of which there was the boat from New York to Le Havre and the final leg to Paris. One person who also had a hand in orchestrating this mass migration was the young American Harrisson Elliot, whom Dior had hired alongside Suzanne Luling to take care of public relations and the press.

It was another triumph, "breathtaking and supremely elegant," to use the words of Lucie Noel, correspondent for what was then the *New York Herald Tribune*. There was no room for doubt now. The first collection could have been a fluke, but this confirmed the supremacy of the New Look in the fashion world. The pièce de résistance, "Diorama," was a black wool dress with a skirt measuring 17 yards in circumference. So perfect was it that it has remained a fashion icon, one that is still periodically revived today when fashion has run out of things to say. It's the eternal return to the eternal feminine: the waist, the ankles, the breasts, the movement, the look . . . in short, desire at its most constant.

Dior made no bones about his intention of bringing fashion back to basics. "Abundance was still too much of a novelty for us to reinvent an inverted snobbery of poverty," he declared. This was a barely veiled dig at Gabrielle Chanel, with her mannish suits and elegant use of black (so admired by Dior). Mademoiselle Coco was not exactly enjoying the finest moments of her career. Following a fling with a German colonel during the Occupation she had closed down her headquarters and moved into the Ritz, which was flying the Nazi flag. When the purges began she was arrested, but escaped having her head shaved due to a few well-placed connections. She opted for exile in Switzerland but was getting restless in her bittersweet existence, making such scathingly Chanelesque comments as, "Dior? He doesn't dress women, he drapes them!"

But Chanel wasn't the only exponent of the kind of fashion Dior was so patently reacting against. Ever since Poiret in the era from 1910 through the 1920s, prewar fashion had followed a linear progression —

which Chanel had pursued with particular shrewdness — aimed at freeing women from sartorial regimentation and from the role of woman as object. After absorbing the modernism of the twenties, there was a general trend toward purified lines and functional, elegant fashion. To varying degrees, according to their talents, designers like Piguet, Lelong, Lanvin, Grès, Molyneux, and Charles James produced the type of minimalist fashion dear to the Bauhaus architects and their purist aesthetic, summed up in the motto Less Is More.

Dior's was a resolute departure from all that and an even more adamant rejection of what he termed "the extravagances of those surrealist trimmings," the giant crayfish transformed into an evening dress or the cutlet-shaped hat made all the rage by Schiaparelli. It was amusing to see the determination with which this male couturier politely annihilated the two grandes dames of prewar couture. Fashion may "always be right" but to Dior it was no longer a matter of "extending the frontiers of elegance till it bordered on the bizarre." This good shepherd had taken it upon himself to lead the lost flock back to more familiar pastures: "Couture wants to return to its true function — enhancing feminine beauty."

Such aesthetic values had long been Dior's inspiration, going back to his student days with his unsuccessful attempts at an artistic career and to tastes shared with fellow artists and friends like Cocteau, Bérard, Poulenc, Sauguet, Gaxotte, Geffroy, and Grandpierre. Throughout the revolutions of the twenties, they had held true to their classical aspirations, preferring for example the lyrical compositions of their friends Les Six to the new dodecaphonic music, and a nice easel painting expressing human sentiment to cubism and its deconstruction of the human face. Chanel's boyish styles might have been considered chic in their day and Schiaparelli's rendition of woman as window-dressing had not been without fascination. But when Cocteau announced his motto, Too Much Is Barely Enough, it was hardly surprising, after five years of total deprivation, that the uplifted breasts, jaunty little hats, and rustling skirts of Christian Dior's woman should have received such a chorus of accolades.

Strangely, though, it did not prevent people the world over from being disappointed in Dior himself, with his round face, pear-shaped body, and prematurely bald head. Not quite the man in the street but almost, he barely resembled the stereotype of the dashing French couturier. Cecil Beaton saw in him something of the "country doctor," a profession akin to the parish priest, the pardoner of sins in the anonymity of the confessional. The couturier too played his part in exorcising a few ghosts. As a Frenchman who had lived through the ignominy of defeat, Dior was as well placed as anyone to pick up on what was going on in his country at a subconscious level. France, traumatized by the Occupation, showed little desire to analyze its own behavior and, in the face of a less than illustrious present, looked squarely to the past, to the legendary brilliance of yesteryear. The floral women and the plunging necklines of Dior, the man and the artist, were his way of universally obliterating the monsters of Guernica.

What was then so stirring about that fragile, delicate figure, enshrined so miraculously in her clouds of silk, embroidery, and tulle, was the way in which she emanated a sense of heaven-sent security, the sweet comfort of "days gone by" in the face of an anxious future. For new dangers lurked on the horizon. The ink was barely dry on the Armistice when it looked as if World War III was on its way. The Soviet Union followed the United States' example and detonated its first atomic bomb, and before long the two blocs were at Cold War, in a frenzied arms race. The poet W. H. Auden, in his *Baroque Eclogue*, described it as "the age of anxiety." To the east, a malevolent regime exiled millions of its people to the salt mines of Siberia, depriving them of their freedom in the name of a new order. George Orwell's *1984* painted the bleak picture of a worker's trials in a society where love was banned as the unwanted legacy of a defunct bourgeois world.

From the west came the promise of purely material happiness: washing machines, nylon stockings, and mass-produced motorcars. It was the dawn of the age of television, already a reality in the United States and on the horizon in Europe. In 1950 France boasted a mere 3,794 television sets. But by the time of the first live broadcast — the coronation of Her Majesty Queen Elizabeth II — the number had soared to 60,000, and by the end of the decade television had reached some 1,500,000 households.

Christian Dior was well aware of what was going on: "In an era as gloomy as this one, when nations find luxury in cannons and four-engined aircraft, our kind of luxury must be defended to the last. I make no secret of the fact that this runs counter to the way in which our world seems to be going. But I think there is something quite essential there." And: "In the face of an uncultivated, hostile world, Europe is becoming aware of itself, its traditions and culture."

Europe might have lost its place at the center of the chessboard forever but its deliverers, the Americans, were only too present, helping in reconstruction and making their influence felt in the process. The conservative political climate favored a return to tradition. America was riding high, confident in its material values and its ability to bring happiness to the rest of the world. The GIs were home again, glad to see their sweethearts and relegate them to newlywed domesticity. The New Look timed it well, bringing a little color and glamour to the land of Uncle Sam, where everything had been khaki, even the packs of Lucky Strikes! There was a honeymoon feeling about Americans' relations with the Gay Paree they had encountered all too briefly before their return. And that air of longing and regret no doubt contributed to the speed with which the New Look caught on, duly Americanized with a touch of imitation Scarlett O'Hara. It was time to go back to the past.

9

The Reluctant Hero

Christian never dreamed of fame. However, when it came, no one ever knew
better or more instinctively how to
handle it.

— Bettina Ballard

As the applause that greeted his first collection gradually subsided,
Dior fled the capital to seek refuge in an old mill in the countryside,
which he had bought with his first earnings. Suzanne Luling, on the
other hand, threw open the doors of her Paris apartment on the Quai
Malaquais to hold parties that raged until dawn. The strains of gypsy
violins or Paraguayan balladeers filled its wood-paneled rooms overlooking the Seine. Suzanne, ever the life of the party (its very "atmosphere," to quote her regular guest, the actress Arletty), led the dancing.
Her "shindigs" always wound up with a nightclub-hopping session,
along the Left Bank to places like the Saint-Benoît and Tabou, or even
to Monseigneur on Montmartre, as the mood took her. She was a

veritable queen of the Parisian night and her patronage guaranteed instant success wherever she set foot.

It is hard to imagine Dior without this astonishing, explosive creature at his side. Everyone adored her: the American buyers whom she laughingly pestered for endless English lessons, the press with whom she was on a first-name basis and had been since her days in advertising, and all the other people for whom Luling was ready to bend over backward . . . virtually the whole world! Marlene Dietrich treated her like a sister and her diehard admirers included film stars Raf Vallone, Jean Marais, Arletty, Micheline Presle, and the writer-musician Boris Vian. Her fame had even spread as far as deepest Texas.

Paris after the war was a focal point for all those who had been uprooted by the years of conflict. The Ritz opened its doors to its former clientele — Argentine families connected by marriage to some French château, crazed Brazilian women with plenty of diamonds to flash around, and the international social set dropping in on their way to Biarritz, Monte Carlo, or the Lido in Venice. The fashionable seaside life picked up again, and the Riviera awoke from its languor. But it was the Americans who really stood out. There were buyers from the big department stores, GIs (five thousand of them) from the SHAPE forces, Marshall Plan officials, and New World heiresses, and their dollars flowed like water, dispensing good cheer throughout the capital. This was the Paris of legend, Paris of the hedonistic lifestyle, Paris there for the taking. A new golden age had dawned and the French capital was once again the cultural center of Europe. As the British historian James Laver once wrote, "Nothing is more remarkable in the French character than its capacity for revival after a catastrophe."

The American humorist Art Buchwald still remembers that "spectacular life." With his GI Bill of $75 a week, supplemented by a further $25 from the *New York Times,* he recalls living "almost like a prince." His earliest vignettes were based on observations gleaned in Montparnasse, where he lived at the Hôtel des Etats-Unis, and on the Champs-Elysées at the Alexander bar opposite Fouquet's or at Le Calvados, celebrated as the meeting place of the "Americans in Paris" like John Huston, George Plimpton, Sam Spiegel, John Steinbeck, and Lena Horne. "We fell in with people like [playwright] Marcel Achard, [producer] Anatole Litvak, [film industry agent] Georges Cravenne and the beautiful model Bettina, and would follow Edith Piaf to Carine whenever she sang there. She would turn up with a different boyfriend every night." The Little Sparrow was soon to make her debut in America, where she took audiences by storm. A pilgrimage to New York became mandatory for every French artist worthy of the name and, in reverse, Americans flocked to explore the streets of Montparnasse, Pigalle, and Saint-Germain-des-Prés. To some, it was a chance to enjoy a freedom unimaginable in the America of the conservative Truman years. For those whose indiscreet or scandalous behavior had seen them roundly condemned back home, Paris provided a safe haven.

America's romance with Gay Paree blossomed: a love affair with fine restaurants, sidewalk cafés, bridges, and squares, immortalized in Vincente Minnelli's *An American in Paris* (1951), in which GI and would-be artist Gene Kelly is swept up in marvelous escapades with the ingénue Leslie Caron.

Nostalgia was the order of the day. Society seemed so bent on reliving the brilliance of the prewar years, an era many feared had gone forever, that the beau monde reemerged with a vengeance, throwing huge balls and magnificent soirees with more than a hint of their old splendor. As in the prewar years, when people desperate to ward off impending tragedy partied as if there were no tomorrow, the survivors threw themselves into the festivities with gusto. First to make a splash was Christian Bérard, as much the magician now as he had ever been. At his "Bal du Panache" (Plumed Ball), "every feather that had ever graced a bird of paradise, ostrich, or osprey now adorned the prettiest heads in the world," to quote Christian Dior. Dior too was able to give free rein to his favorite pastime, dressing up. This time there was no need to improvise with a lamp shade and curtains as he had in the old days in Max Jacob's rooms or MacAvoy's studio in Cannes. Magnificent costumes were made to measure by the famous Madame Karinska or the young Pierre Cardin, who had gone into business producing theatrical costumes after a brief spell at Dior. He was responsible for the superb lion costume that transformed Dior into the King of Beasts for Etienne de Beaumont's "Kings and Queens Ball."

"They were ten to twelve years of great euphoria," remembers Pamela Harriman, recently divorced from Randolph Churchill at the time and spending those euphoric years living the high life, pursued by every man she met. "We had won the war. We had earned our playtime. We were indulging ourselves. We knew it but we felt we had a right to indulge ourselves. Dior came out of that indulgence. He established in France a certain recognition of the importance of tradition. . . . It was a glamorous time and Dior provoked it, understood it, provided it. He was a catalyst."

He was the couturier of his day, the sorcerer, the magician who dressed the Beautiful People of the 1950s in gowns inspired by Watteau, Veronese, and Winterhalter. It was their chance to enjoy "the past regained," to live out the fantasy of days gone by. At the legendary "Bal Beistegui" in Venice, for example, the Baroness Alix de Rothschild dressed as a shepherdess in yellow and caramel-colored shantung. Her gown, a Dior creation, consisted of a laced bodice worn over a wide crinoline skirt edged with black velvet ribbon. For a charity evening given by the Baroness de Cabrol at the Marigny Theater, Dior dressed his friend Henri Sauguet as Cardinal Richelieu. And the Viscountess de Noailles graced her own "Bal de la Lune sur Mer" (Moon-over-Water Ball) in 1951 in a barmaid's outfit by Dior — a black velvet open jacket with a frilly white collar over a straight skirt with a bustle inspired by Manet's painting *Bar des Folies-Bergères*. Dior made quite an entrance to that ball too. Accompanied by Marie-Louise Bousquet, Arturo Lopez-Willshaw, and the American ambassador David Bruce and his wife Evangeline, he went as a waiter with a cast of characters from a café!

Another memorable evening was Marie-Laure de Noailles's "Bal des Artistes" held for Mardi Gras on February 14, 1956. Dior dressed as the romantic nineteenth-century writer Jules Barbey d'Aurevilly, Nora Auric came as the Countess of Ségur, Francis Poulenc as the composer Emmanuel Chabrier, and Roger Peyrefitte as the Abbé Prévost, author of *Manon Lescaut*. André Roussin, a playwright and later a member of the Académie Française, was dressed as Alphonse Daudet, while the mistress of the house played Délie, the imaginary love of the sixteenth-century poet Maurice Scève.

Any resemblance between real people and the characters they portrayed may well have been purely coincidental, but a striking similarity did exist between the key players of pre- and postwar society. The parties were the same, the salons were the same, and the balls were still much-awaited events prepared for months in advance. The "Kings and Queens Ball" of 1949 was the last to be given by Count Etienne de Beaumont, a nobleman who had amused and entertained an entire generation at his town house on Rue Masseran. His passion for parties and fancy dress bordered on the absurd, including the time he dressed as a giant pink Cupid with wings, arrows, and a quiver (all six-foot-three of him!). The Count spent his leisure hours designing jewelry for Dior's collections and had been one of the very few French aristocrats in the prewar period to consider artists socially acceptable. The dusty opulence of his renowned gilt drawing rooms had seen the likes of Marcel Proust, who spent his last evening in society there, in 1922, and received a royal welcome. Such a gesture from a nobleman was an exception rather than the rule, as is clear from the Countess of Pange's *Mémoires d'une jeune fille de 1900,* in which she explains that Proust would never have been invited to the homes of the old aristocracy. If the likes of the "Guermantes" (Proust's exemplars of the aristocracy) invited writers at all, they would have been from the literary establishment, members of the Académie Française, not budding young geniuses.

But Proust's hour of revenge was nigh. Where once the old guard had risen up with one voice — mostly without ever having read a word he wrote — to protest at Proust's effrontery in describing a milieu he was not even familiar with, they now began to realize that Proust's version was actually far more interesting than the real thing. Prince Jean-Louis de Faucigny-Lucinge, who gave the first "Proust Ball" with his wife Baba in 1928, made the delightful observation that "thanks to him I was no longer so bored when I was in town." People stopped querying the virtues of the "past regained" and began feeding on it like some mood-enhancing drug. High society began to consume Proust too, fitting right into the mold he had created and enjoying the sight of its own kind at play to the point where no one wanted it any other way. The next generation would clamor for its own "Proust Ball," which was duly given, with incomparable brio, by Marie-Hélène and Guy de Rothschild at the Château de Ferrières on December 2, 1971. Such balls and the indelible memories they produced were like Hansel and Gretel's white pebbles, a trail sparkling in the moonlight left by one generation for the next as a visible sign of its passing, a lasting reminder of the way they were.

"Parties like these are genuine works of art," wrote Dior. There were those who saw the postwar period as a second Restoration, mirroring the brief splendor of the early 1800s when the French monarchy was restored to the throne. It certainly seemed that way in 1951, when Charles de Beistegui held the ball to end all balls at the Labia Palace in Venice. It was like a scene from the court of Louis XIV, with a guest list that read like the Who's Who of Europe. Dior and Salvador Dalí devised a show-stopping entrance called "the Ghosts of Venice," eight characters dressed as giants and dwarves in enormous pale masks. (Dior was the little ghost.) Jacques Fath and his wife arrived in a gondola, Fath standing regally in gold and white, dressed as no less a personage than the Sun King, as they were rowed down the Grand Canal. De Beistegui received his guests in the guise of the Commendatore of the Venetian Republic, towering over them at the top of the stairs in huge buskins like the towers of San Gimignano. The British ambassador's wife, Lady Diana Cooper, came as Cleopatra, in identical attire to the Cleopatra of the Tiepolo fresco on the wall behind her. The Baron of Cabrol was her Mark Antony. Huge buffet tables were set up in the city squares for the locals, but no members of the press were granted access to the ball.

Charles de Beistegui could not have cared less about journalists. Different times, different values. The public, meanwhile, had begun demanding its slice of the action, and the lives of royalty, those mythical beings, started featuring in color magazines. Events like the marriage of Princess Elizabeth and Philip Mountbatten in 1947 inspired an extraordinary level of public excitement. A similar moment, the royals' cruise on the *Agamemnon,* is used by the structuralist writer Roland Barthes in *Mythologies,* his perceptive account of these years, to demystify and deconstruct such icons of grand luxury and render them more democratic. Once it had ceased to be the exclusive prerogative of the upper echelons, the pursuit of luxury provided the perfect raison d'être for the department stores of the burgeoning consumer society.

*　　　*　　　*

Society is like the past. To remain vibrant it must keep reinventing itself. It is like a bouquet of flowers. You can keep the same vase forever as long as you continuously replace its contents. What gave zing to the old social arrangements in the years after the war was "café society," a new phenomenon which had couturiers rubbing shoulders with countesses, decorators with heiresses, models with racehorse owners. The old social order, meanwhile, was on its last legs. Only a few of its previous leading lights remained. Prince Jean-Louis de Faucigny-Lucinge was still in fine form (he had just remarried) but Count Etienne de Beaumont, recently widowed, was in gentle decline. Marie-Laure and Charles de Noailles, the idols of a golden era lasting some thirty years, were tired. He now preferred to spend most of his time in his gardens, while she played hostess to an adoring horde of young artists and musicians, bestowing the occasional favor to help them climb the social ladder.

Where once high society was out to dinner every night in full evening dress, more potent distractions came to the fore, at more vibrant venues, like the theater, art galleries, and fashion houses. The salons at 30 Avenue Montaigne buzzed with a constant stream of clients, none of whom thought twice about circling the globe each season simply to update their wardrobes. They wanted the Dior label, nothing less — plus their favorite saleswoman, of course. The only question was which of those two suits to choose. . . . Oh hang it, I'll take both. The fitting rooms were the last stop on the social merry-go-round, a perfect place to catch up on the week's events: who was seeing whom, who had broken with whom. No one ever lost sight of the real purpose of the exercise, of course, which was to choose an evening dress other women would kill for, a plunging neckline *he* would be unable to resist, or a hat that would leave all the others gasping. Dior's genius offered the perfect tools for seduction.

Everyone who was anyone was there — Ali Khan between actresses, Porfirio Rubirosa between cars, Gianni Agnelli between yachts, Barbara Hutton between "suicides," Pamela Churchill between lovers, or Elie de Rothschild between a spot of polo and a round of golf, if not also between affairs. Then there were those Dior called "our great foreign visitors, more Parisian than the Parisians." These were the brewery barons, tin or copper kings, lively types who adored Paris, loved drinking in its bistros and listening to its chansonniers. Particular favorites of Dior's were the South American Arturo Lopez-Willshaw and his wife Patricia, an elegant woman with the fineness of a Tanagra figurine. The Lopez-Willshaw residence in Neuilly was the scene of countless extravagant parties held in their amazing ballroom, which was decorated from floor to ceiling in seashells. There were others who remained forever tourists, shielded from any contact with the outside world by their refusal to speak anything but English. The Duke and Duchess of Windsor belonged to this category, holding court at the palace in the Bois de Boulogne graciously placed at their disposal by the Republic of France. The Duchess had her redeeming features, however, like the habit of spending every afternoon at fittings or the hairdresser's. She was also much loved by the jewelers of Paris. The inimitable Charles de Beistegui was another, a prince even among the many who pursued a princely lifestyle. No one could eclipse him when it came to holding a party. His "Venice Ball" would live in everyone's memory, not least for all the gowns that had to be designed especially for it. He instituted a whole calendar of festivities, alternating among his remarkable seventeenth-century château at Groussay, his town house on Rue Constantine, and the Labia Palace in Venice. He was the last to entertain on a scale worthy of Louis XIV, before modern technology gave rise to the jet set and altered the billionaire lifestyle forever.

On the surface, the mix seemed familiar — nobility, artists, great minds, rich foreigners, women for the taking. But the comforting feeling that everything was "just as it used to be" added a gentle note of abandon. Jean Cocteau's love affair with Jean Marais both on- and offstage was public knowledge, the ménage à trois among composer Georges Auric, his wife Nora, and the young aristocrat Guy de Lesseps was quite open, and while it was a well-known fact that Louise de Vilmorin was part of a threesome at the British embassy with Ambassador Duff Cooper and his wife Lady Diana, it did not seem to stop her engaging freely in more than a few dalliances on the side. No one batted an eye when Henri Sauguet was invited to dinner along with Jacques Dupont as though they were a married couple, nor when it was discovered that Arturo Lopez had set up the young Baron Alexis de Rédé at the Hotel Lambert. Everyone knew he preferred young gentlemen to his beautiful wife Patricia. There was, however, a very strict code of etiquette in these matters. "If you slept with the Duke of Westminster, you would always greet him as 'Your Grace' if you bumped into him the following day," Marie-Hélène de Ganay, who ran the boutique at Dior, pointed out with all the style necessary to carry off that sort of remark. In this era, such games seemed as innocent as the masqueraders frolicking in the shrubbery at Versailles in the era of Madame de Pompadour. Everyone applauded the Marquis de Cuevas when he created his ballet company, with the financial assistance of his wife, a Rockefeller. The writer Louis Aragon and his wife Elsa Triolet, famous Communists of the era, were all the rage when they decided to come in from the cold of the postwar period and "warm up" a little at a few society dinners, most notably those given by Philippe de Rothschild, the poet and proprietor of Mouton-Rothschild. As the satirist Philippe Jullian put it in his *Dictionnaire du Snobisme*, café society attempted "to combine the facilities of a brothel with the appearances of an embassy."

The perfect observation post was Maxim's. Suzanne Luling had a permanent table there. "I can always find a way to bring together lovers of fine entertainment and lovers of fine clothes," she said. The satirical society columnist Henri Calet concluded on a visit to Maxim's that the bejeweled vamps of yesteryear had made way there for a new breed, ladies of social repute, "not to be confused with women of ill repute, of course," he notes. "Society types get up early, the other sort sleep late. But the whole lot of them, baronesses, countesses, and duchesses alike, real or fake, take their chosen career very seriously."

The upper middle class, in fact, had developed a taste for employment, especially in couture houses. It was no coincidence that Dior's name was on everyone's lips at dinner parties — countesses and ambassadors' wives alike, they all had their eye on a sales position at Dior. It was a swarming place for beautiful names: Andrée de Vilmorin, Marie-Hélène de Ganay, Carmen de Boisgelin, Baroness Turkheim, Countess Edouard de Segonzac, and Madame Bonnet, wife of the French Ambassador to Washington, all did a stint as saleswomen at Dior.

Christian Dior had a weakness for titles. When the time came to replace his charming American publicity genius Harrisson Elliot, he engaged the Marquis de Maussabré. The influx of all these aristocratic names was not viewed kindly. The other saleswomen often looked on askance as these well-connected young ladies who had never done a day's work in their lives sauntered in with their signet rings, upper-class accents, and Hermès little black books crammed with addresses. With its luxury, fine perfumes, and overwhelming beauty, they saw the couture house as a perfectly natural extension of their lives. Dior, who called all of his women his *chéries,* describes their chief characteristic thus: "Accustomed to adjusting their level of warmth to the social standing of the person they were dealing with, they were in turn courteous, haughty, impertinent, or gushing in their welcome, in the way the staff of a couture house have of assuming an air of great self-importance. It is very important to know how to say 'no' in every language!"

How times had changed since Maurice de Rothschild was asked to extend an invitation to one of his balls to Madame Louis Cartier, wife of the acclaimed jeweler. She may well have been a well-born Hungarian but Baron Rothschild's famous reply was biting. "I never invite my tradesmen!"

Now all that was reversed. Well-born ladies courted the couturiers while models set their sights on inherited wealth and royal titles. Once designers had been far from socially acceptable, with the exception of Lucien Lelong, who was born into high society and married a princess, Natalie Paley, whom he had employed as an occasional model. Chanel had broken the barrier too, but by virtue of her generosity as a patron of the arts.

With the arrival of Dior, such questions were no longer an issue. Couturiers had become veritable pillars of the best society and it was not long before the satirists had a field day with this new social scale.

Dior himself got his name in lights on November 12, 1947, when the ballet *Treize Danses* by Roland Petit and Boris Kochno opened at the Théâtre des Champs-Elysées. Not only was a very young Leslie Caron costumed by Dior, he was also responsible for the music. The amusing idea of bringing Dior back to his first vocation came from Christian Bérard. Bébé suggested it to the manager of the theater, Gabriel Dussurget, who immediately agreed. The score was an arrangement by Dior of an eighteenth-century work by a composer named Grétry. The sets were also Dior's creation, again at Bérard's suggestion — a white background lit with colored lights.

For Suzanne Luling, this was "the first major Parisian soirée since the war," a sign that artistic and social life had resumed. In the best traditions of Paris society, the front of the house rivaled the show on stage. Count Etienne de Beaumont was in charge of the invitations, along with Carmen Colle, whose connections nicely complemented Suzanne Luling's, making for quite a guest list. The ladies pulled out all the stops in choosing their evening wear, to the point where even Etienne de Beaumont was amazed.

As the final curtain came down and the applause rang out, Dior heaved an enormous sign of relief. He had spent a nightmare evening in the wings watching as his costumes, which had been sewn by Madame Karinska under his direct supervision, tore with the dancers' every movement. He had to stitch them up hastily every time the girls came offstage. The public was blissfully unaware of the drama but Dior never got over it. He had worked so hard for this moment! He was, however, delighted to see his designs on stage. The young lead Dominique Blanchar, who had made her debut in Giraudoux's *L'Apollon de Bellac* the previous April, insisted on "wearing the most deliberately New Look costume," Dior remembered. "I loved that dress so much I named it 'Chérie.' It had a nymph neckline, a sylph waist, and eighty meters of white faille in its huge, almost ankle-length skirt, a twirling fanlike affair with a thousand tiny pleats."

"To me the New Look and the rebirth of Paris were one and the same," said Hebe Dorsey of the *International Herald Tribune*.

While France's fashion, painting, and cinema were doing big business in the United States, its literary achievements were also getting their share of acclaim. Americans had already had their brush with Sartre, de Beauvoir, Boris Vian, Antoine Blondin, and Jean Genet at the Café de Flore and Tabou. They were all part of a generation whose "universal" themes traveled well, and soon the two continents were embroiled in a debate over "responsibility," "freedom," and "engagement," the catchwords of the day. Albert Camus even made it onto the *New York Times* best-seller list, and its *Book Review* section ran a regular column headed "Imported from France." Antoine de Saint-Exupéry's

Little Prince sold one million copies. Paris was home to American writers like James Baldwin, Hemingway's friend Peter Viertel, and Irwin Shaw. André Gide was awarded the 1947 Nobel Prize for Literature and the trade unionist Léon Jouhaux received the Peace Prize in 1951.

French popular music had also found an export market. Yves Montand performed his "Les Feuilles mortes" and "C'est si bon" live in New York, Charles Trenet's "La Mer" had them humming on both sides of the Atlantic, and Edith Piaf became an international household name.

Dior had always been enthralled by the vibrant atmosphere of the art world and show business. He was reticent, however, about designing for theater and film. Creating the costumes for films like Roland Tual's *Le Lit à colonnes* and Claude Autant-Lara's *Lettres d'amour* in 1942, and René Clair's *Le Silence est d'or* and *Pour une nuit d'amour* by E. T. Gréville in 1946, allowed him to indulge his passion for period costumes. But his meticulous concern for quality and perfection proved too great a burden. He was not like the professional costume designers who opted primarily for effect at the expense of fine detail. Gradually he stopped accepting any work in the performing arts arena, though he made an exception in 1947 for Marcel Achard's play *La Valse de Paris*, based on the life of Offenbach. It was a marvelous chance for a little nostalgia and Dior created some magnificent crinolined gowns for the star Yvonne Printemps. He made a final concession in 1953 for Giraudoux's *Pour Lucrèce*, which opened in April of that year at the Marigny Theater with Madeleine Renaud, Edwige Feuillère, and Simone Valère in full Second Empire regalia created according to the rules of haute couture in the workrooms at 30 Avenue Montaigne.

There was plenty of Dior in the movies too, of course. His most faithful client was Marlene Dietrich, who wore his creations in films like Alfred Hitchcock's *Stage Fright* (1950) and Henry Koster's *No Highway in the Sky* (1951). Dior was well ahead of his time with the muslin body stocking he had made to shape Dietrich's figure, legs and arms included, under her slinky gowns, and no one at Dior will ever forget the painstaking fitting sessions involved in measuring the star for the tuxedos she wore for her concerts. Well before the invention of latex, incredible care and toil went into cutting a trouser leg that would allow for as much exotic movement as possible without sagging afterward. But there was nothing they would not do at Avenue Montaigne for Marlene Dietrich, great friend that she was of Jean Cocteau and Jean Marais, Dior's neighbors in the country. On Sundays they would get together like a little family. Dior also became a close friend of Olivia de Havilland, another excellent client. Looking back now, she calculates that she bought two hundred dresses from Dior over the years! Dior created her clothes as well as those of Myrna Loy in Norman Krasna's *The Ambassador's Daughter* in 1956. In the same year he also made fourteen outfits for Ava Gardner in Mark Robson's *The Little Hut.*

Christian Dior rarely left Avenue Montaigne for his famous clients, however. Idol though he was, he preferred to stay in the wings, not out of coquetry or a desire to cultivate an air of mystery, but as a way of avoiding jealousy among his clients and, primarily, in order to dedicate himself to his creative task, his raison d'être. Try as they might to meet him, thank him, congratulate him, he refused to make an appearance. The best present anyone could give him was to wear his designs.

It was precisely for these reasons that when the producer Christine Gouze-Renal came to ask for a meeting, she was met by Jacques Rouët, Dior's financial manager and right-hand man, rather than the great fashion genius in person. She had come to tell him about an up-and-coming star. Gouze-Renal described her long, sensual blond tresses, her child-woman's body (which would seduce an entire generation), her husky but naive voice, her rebellious gaze, and her soft, come-hither eyes. She had already made sixteen films, but the one about to be released would be the turning point in her career, putting her name on everyone's lips and her photograph on every magazine cover. Her name was Brigitte Bardot.

The producer then came to the point. In Bardot's next film, Pierre-Gaspard Huit's *La Mariée est trop belle,* she would play a young fashion editor who makes a name for herself. She also gets married in the film and, of course, needs a truly fabulous dress for the occasion. Part of her triumph consists in her choice of designer, the greatest ever. . . . Dior, of course. Would the House of Christian Dior be prepared to give them a dress in exchange for the obvious publicity value of having such an acclaimed actress wearing one of its creations?

Jacques Rouët listened carefully. While he could not promise anything without first talking to Monsieur Dior, the only person who could decide in such matters, he did not hold out much hope of a favorable response. The producer asked him to give it his best shot.

As Rouët had expected, Dior refused. He loved the cinema and considered it a great art. But couture too was an art and also needed to grow and prosper. He needed to sell his dresses, and there was no reason why his clients should spend huge sums of money on his clothes if they could then turn around and see the same dresses on the screen, on loan or given as a gift.

Although annoyed and surprised by this refusal, the producer was undeterred. She offered to bring Bardot to Avenue Montaigne in person, convinced that meeting the star, BB in the flesh, would melt Dior's resolve. But no amount of cajoling would dissuade Jacques Rouët. He knew there was nothing to be gained by disturbing Dior a second time. As he showed his visitor to the door, he assured her gallantly that the world's most beautiful women were always welcome at Dior but that unfortunately Monsieur Dior's mind was made up.

It is hard to understand the logic of such a decision today. Indeed, Pierre Balmain did not think twice when asked to supply the bridal gown in question. But the world of couture had its own rules and codes. There was no way Dior would risk incurring the displeasure of some of his most elegant clients by allowing his dresses to be put on vulgar display on the screen. The ladies who purchased them from his couture house felt privileged in acquiring something quite special and unique. Besides, it has to be said, Dior was a snob. He adored countesses and duchesses and loved to dress them with full regal pomp and ceremony in gowns inspired by the Empress Eugénie and Madame de Pompadour. He ranked living, breathing aristocrats far higher aesthetically than their pale imitations on stage and screen and considered it far more prestigious to design a ball dress for Princess Margaret's twenty-first birthday than for a celluloid queen. (And in those days, of course, princesses were blue bloods who would never have dreamed of an acting career.)

The beautiful young Margaret appeared on the cover of *Paris Match* in that coming-of-age ball gown, photographed by Cecil Beaton. More than three hundred hours had gone into making its wide silk organza skirts with a bustier bodice and floral motifs embroidered in a prettily asymmetrical fashion (the Oblique line) over one shoulder, spreading across the front of the dress in a sheaf of straws, gold stars, and mother-of-pearl. Before commissioning the design Dior consulted the princess herself. "Does Your Highness feel like a gold person or a silver one?" "A gold person," she replied.

There is no greater memory in the history of the House of Dior than the fashion show at Blenheim Castle in 1952 at the invitation of the Duchess of Marlborough. Imagine fourteen drawing rooms, one after the other, including a room hung from ceiling to floor with tapestries celebrating the defeat of the French at the hands of the English. Such majesty was in perfect keeping with the lady of the house, who came in person in her Red Cross uniform (she was its president) to ask Dior whether he would agree to do a show for her charity. Suzanne Luling, with her excellent English, was put in charge of organizing the event, and recalls how the venue simply took her breath away. The size of it, however, meant that "we had to devise a show that would not make the models look like thoroughbreds who had just run a steeplechase!"

As the day drew near, a dense fog shrouded the palace gardens and driveway. The news came through that Balmain had been forced to cancel a London show because poor visibility had delayed his gowns and models at Orly Airport. The Duchess of Marlborough was quick to sound the warning. "There will no doubt be those who will say, 'That would never have happened with Dior.' You mustn't let them down. The fog may last. Tell your models to take the train."

Suzanne Luling remembers the day itself. "It was quite fantastic. Seeing our girls striding down that amazing catwalk, with their usual distant, nonchalant, haughty look, made me quite giddy.

"Finally the doors of the music room opened. There was Princess Margaret, sitting in a room decorated with French and British flags entwined in a gesture of fraternity. They were playing 'La Marseillaise.' It was a beautiful, uplifting, unexpected moment. The Duke of Marlborough, who was sitting next to me, leaned forward and whispered, 'Many things have happened in this palace but I have never seen anything like this: a French flag, "La Marseillaise," and . . . dresses!' "

*   *   *

How many other couturiers could have declared, as Dior did, that "I hardly went out of my way, but the ones who came to me were exactly the kind of clients I dreamed of"?

Here they all were clamoring for fittings, all the women whose names had been on Dior's secret list of ideal clients, drawn up with fingers crossed prior to the launch of the first collection. The Duchess of Windsor waited one season before joining the throng, just so as not to be like everyone else. But once she did become a Dior client, she won universal admiration for her firm adherence to styles she knew suited her understated elegance, simple evening suits worn to best set off her jewelry and her amazing sense of Less Is More. The dusky Mexican beauty Gloria Guinness, a Balenciaga client, was another woman with her own particular style who occasionally wore Dior, and always in black or white. To Christian Dior she was the very soul of elegance, as much at home stepping out of her Rolls Royce in a little black wool coat as she was pottering among her apple trees at her farm in Piencourt, watering can in hand, or walking her dog. She was the only client, or at least one of the very very few, for whom Dior would actually come down to the fitting rooms, an honor he did not extend even to Elizabeth Taylor. What a wonderful existence it was for a couturier to see women with the pure-bred elegance of Babe Paley, the flowerlike grace of Margot Fonteyn, or the classic curves of Ederica Gazzoni and Laurella Arrivabene (who was related to the film director Luchino Visconti), who had figures like antique vases. Nothing, in Dior's eyes, could surpass a truly elegant Italian woman. And "it will not be long," he predicted, "before you'll see the prettiest society women putting themselves forward as potential models."

There were already a few well-born girls who could match Dior's models when it came to glamour — that indefinable art that relies not on beauty alone but more on an ability to highlight the lines of a dress and on a face that photographs well. One such candidate was the daughter of the English painter Lady Rhoda Birley and Count Alain de la Falaise. Maxime de la Falaise, long and slender like a schoolboy, posed in a series of Dior gowns for some of America's top fashion magazines. Martine Dewavrin was another society model, beautiful and blonde with a pink and white complexion. But she found the whole thing exhausting and did not last long.

Jacques Fath was the first designer to turn his models into stars in their own right. There was the diaphanous, poetic Louise, whom he dressed as Sarah Bernhardt; a girlfriend of Aly Khan's, the beautiful Bettina, who moved very quickly, unsmiling and a little sad; the tall, graceful Sophie, who would marry the Russian-American producer Anatole Litvak; Paule of the huge blue eyes, who later married the photographer Willy Rizzo. Fath and his dazzling wife Geneviève often entertained at their château at Corbeville, just outside Paris. Their parties were Brazilian galas or glittering Hollywood-style affairs, and in ambiance and guest lists were more like a nightclub than the masked balls of high society.

Dior launched a model called Tania whom he described as "one of the most gifted and natural models I ever found: . . . a model turned woman rather than a woman turned model." He saw himself as something of a Pygmalion when it came to his models and had to fight unanimous opposition when he decided to employ one tiny, dark girl called Victoire. She was completely different from the others and had no idea how to walk. In two seasons he made her into a star.

It was no surprise to hear them complain that he "undressed them with his eyes" with his "fearful professional gaze." No, he retorted, he did not undress them but rather "dressed them in something else." In an era when elegant women changed their outfits four times a day, couturiers had a field day. Some creatures, rather a gift from heaven, ordered three of everything — like the wealthy widow Mrs. Thomas Biddle, who was well connected politically and held salons at her residence on Rue Las-Cases. She liked to have one dress for Paris, another for New York, and a third to travel in! The milliner Claude Saint-Cyr, who had once helped the impoverished Christian Dior out of a spot by purchasing some of his sketches, now made hats to go with Dior's dresses. She recalls being asked by Mrs. Biddle to make the same hat nineteen times, "in nineteen different colors and materials; she wanted it in antelope, in velvet, in satin and in felt, even in black, to go with every one of her outfits. And very often she would phone me at seven in the morning to say, 'Madame Saint-Cyr, I am going to the opera this evening and I don't know what to wear on my head.' When I arrived, her chambermaid had laid out every one of her magnificent evening dresses, and we watched her go through them asking, 'What would you suggest I wear with this? or that?' "

Like Mrs. Biddle, women soon discovered that following fashion and Dior in particular was not simply a pastime for the wealthy but a full-time job. The Duchess of Windsor's hairdresser, Alexandre, recalls his client's hectic daily schedule. "She would have her hair done on her way home from lunch. She would then go to her fitting sessions, which included selecting shoes, hats, and gloves to match every one of her outfits. It was not uncommon for me to be summoned to her house in Neuilly early in the evening to redo her hair if she were going out that night."

An elegant woman would never go to the theater or a concert in the same suit she had worn to an opening at the Charpentier gallery, let alone in the hat donned for lunch at Maxim's. That little afternoon dress was fine for window-shopping for antiques, a stroll by the Seine, or a walk in the Bois de Boulogne, but once five o'clock came around it was time to bring out the mandatory pearl necklace for tea at the Ritz or the Pavillon Trianon at Versailles. That was followed by a quick session at the hairdresser's before going out for the evening. Then there was the matter of choosing an evening bag, gloves, and an osprey feather, with the vital assistance of one's chambermaid, whose job it was to lay everything out. She would then help her mistress into a cocktail gown after having duly corseted her and chosen her furs, her perfume, even her pocket handkerchief. The difference, of course, as Alexandre put it, was that "in those days they had what no one has now — time!"

The trials of the elegant woman were many. There was all the business of reshaping one's figure, which entailed encasing one's waist in *guêpière* girdles or "waspies" and pushing one's breasts up for Madame Pompadour necklines. (Dior, in fact, spawned a whole new industry, far more successfully than his predecessor Marcel Rochas.) The name on everyone's lips was Madame Marie-Louise Lebigot, who reshaped busts to order. She could push them up or flatten them or fill them out, according to the requirements of the dress. Her secret weapon was a series of foam inserts molded and personally fitted by her husband. Mr. Lebigot was also responsible for the strategic placement of these "endowments," assisting the young ladies at the same time in the forgotten art of lacing themselves up, teaching them to breathe right in, just like their great-grandmothers. "We loved being pulled in like that!" laughs Patricia Lopez-Willshaw. Rosine Delamare, the theatrical costumer who was Harrisson Elliot's wife at the time, is a little more blunt. "We were all thin to start with. None of us had eaten for four years." But wasp waists were the thing. "Pulled in?" exclaims the dancer Zizi Jeanmaire, "We didn't bat an eye. We felt good because we felt beautiful!"

Zizi won Dior's heart during her performance of the ballet *Carmen* at the Marigny. As he was later to tell an American television station in a rare interview, his type of woman was "the small, brunette type." He completely fell for Zizi Jeanmaire's ragamuffin style to the point where, having befriended her and her partner Roland Petit, he quite sincerely declared that "if ever there was a woman I ought to have married, she was the one." It was a strange confession from someone who usually looked at women from quite a different perspective, with the famous gaze which "dressed them in something else" (usually something very feminine and reminiscent, of course, of his mother). Zizi Jeanmaire was quite a different proposition. She was a woman in flesh and blood who exposed and used her body for her art. Ever since his youth Dior had been haunted and fired by the ecstasies of dance. But Dior's confession was odd in many ways. He felt no need to re-work Jeanmaire's image. This was one woman who was just as he would have liked her if . . . if ever he had contemplated a relationship of that kind.

When he heard that she was to go on tour to the United States he invited her to come and choose a wardrobe. "It was the first time I had ever been to a fashion house," she recalls. "Dior gave me a huge black cape and a little matching cap. The Americans thought I looked wonderful. I will always remember it."

"All the girls dreamed of wearing Dior," related *Vogue*'s Edmonde Charles-Roux, "far more so than Molyneux or Balenciaga who looked down on you so much that all you wanted to do was run away! Dior, on the other hand, just loved dressing young girls." Only twenty at the time, and fresh on the fashion scene at *Elle* (she went on to a long career with *Vogue* and a long devotion to Chanel), Charles-Roux was persuaded by Dior to purchase a floor-length crinolined gown, on sale, which weighed something like sixty pounds. "Take it," he urged, "I know it needs courage to wear it." The dress consisted of a butterfly bodice atop a mountain of canvas-backed taffeta double pleats. "It was superb for being photographed by *Vogue* on Nicolas de Gunzburg's arm," Madame Charles-Roux remembers, "but I couldn't dance one step in that dress!" Even in retrospect, however, she finds nothing ridiculous about any of it, including the fact that an invitation to a country ball meant carting a huge trunk just to carry your finery plus a chambermaid to help you into your gown (with the knowledge that when you finally did decide to go to sleep that there mightn't be a soul around to help you *out* of the damn thing!). The most illustrious fashion victim of all, Queen Marie-Antoinette, once went to the extraordinary lengths of *kneeling* in her carriage all the way from Versailles to Paris to preserve an enormous tower of a hairpiece constructed by her whimsical coiffeur for an evening out.

The writer Nancy Mitford, one of the first to wear the New Look in London, described the women of the time as being under the influence of a "magic potion." They certainly were quite delirious. The photographer Willy Maywald relates an incident at the House of Dior involving a former model, a Swedish girl who had married an extremely wealthy South American. Maywald was there to photograph her.

"Carmel Snow was there and congratulated her on her dress. 'Yes,' replied the client, 'it is the most amazing dress I have ever seen. I can't walk, eat, or even sit down.' Without batting an eye Carmel Snow asked her what else she had picked from the collections. 'Three evening gowns,' she replied, 'five cocktail dresses, six coats, and twelve suits, all from Dior, but I have also bought a few other things from other couturiers.' 'That's all?' exclaimed Carmel Snow as the girl completed her list. She blushed as if she had committed a sin, saying by way of excuse that she lived in Rio where it was very hot and so she couldn't wear all those dresses there. She had simply bought them to wear when she was in Europe."

It must have been grist for the mill of the feminists, who were later to take to the streets in protest at the treatment of women as objects. There is certainly no excuse for the extravagance of women like Mrs. Biddle or Mrs. Hilsen, who used to order up to three hundred outfits a year. At Jacques Fath's "Black and White Ball," held at his château at

Corbeville, one guest danced all night in a Dior dress that cost one million francs. Christian Dior himself, in fact, was momentarily stopped short. "How can they buy all these dresses?" he wondered.

Jean Cocteau, meanwhile, began to see red. "When one thinks that the fields of art and architecture have lost all sense of proportion and that in 1953 a few inches off women's hemlines could revolutionize the world . . . No one saw the ridiculousness of it all. People talked of Dior's bombshell as seriously as if it were the atom bomb." At several points in Cocteau's memoirs, his irritation is evident: "All talk is of Dior," he writes, when the eyes of the world should have been on the Geneva Conference. "In the midst of such a tragedy, the wife of the French prime minister, Madame Bidault, ordered a few Dior dresses . . . to wear to Geneva!"

Balenciaga remembers being solicited to fasten Bettina Ballard's Dior dress when he went to her home for dinner. It had thirty tiny buttons all the way down the back. Her husband had refused to assist. The couturier decided Dior had gone too far. "Christian is mad, mad!" he exclaimed, according to Bettina Ballard's account.

None of this deterred most women from undying devotion to Christian Dior. Pamela Harriman professes her eternal gratitude to him for persuading her to wear red, her favorite color. For years she had refrained from wearing it because her mother believed it was wrong for her type of skin. "Dior had them fetch a whole lot of red samples down from the workrooms to show me how well it suited my complexion. He changed my life!"

There were some less favorable reactions, however, including some very unpleasant letters from the depths of the United States. "Stay out of Topeka, you bum!" read one such missive from an irate gentleman in Kansas, while another, in Idaho, informed him that he had "disfigured my wife with your genius. I want to make you a proposition. Why don't I send you the remains? She is about a size 46." The American husbands were decidedly the most outspoken.

Mrs. Randolph Hearst, a young bride in 1948, had gone from her previous couturier Charlie James to Dior, on James's recommendation. "Dresses are much better than a psychiatrist. Clothes give an image which can help a woman enhance her opinion about herself." She was completely won over the minute she stepped in at Dior. "You were sure to make a stunning effect. I loved the construction of the figure, the finishing work on the cloth underneath, the four layers at least that held the jacket: it was great art!" Hélène Rochas was also amazed by the workmanship. "We used to study the inside of the clothes; they were quite wonderful."

Some women completely lost their heads. The most serious clinical case was that of Lady Mariott, daughter of the financier and patron of New York's Metropolitan Opera, Otto Kahn. Married to a British general, "she was petite, slim, smartly-dressed, and intelligent, but she sacrificed her life for her figure and her clothes," recalls Baroness Liliane de Rothschild. "She lived on a rusk and a chicken leg." Was this Dior's ideal client? She would book in at the Plaza, spend every afternoon at Dior from two to seven P.M., and order around a hundred outfits a year with no prospect of even wearing them all. "The rest of the time," according to Frédéric Castet, made a workroom head by Dior at the age of twenty, "Lady Mariott was on her own. She would dine alone at the Ritz, she'd be seen all alone at the Lido in Venice, you'd even see her looking alone in photographs of some ball or another, sad beneath her fancy dress."

No doubt Dior was thinking of Lady Mariott when he described a client who was "dress mad, . . . addicted to clothes the way other people become addicted to gambling. She can tell you how many rows of straw braid there are on a hat or how many checks on a plaid coat. She goes to sleep at night thinking of the dress she will order the following day and her dreams are interspersed with hats that might go with this wondrous creation. The minute she wakes up she calls to make an appointment with her saleslady, even though she has probably already made five or six. 'Her' dressmaker (for it is her dream to get him all to herself) becomes her mentor and guide."

Ironically, even Dior found himself reacting against such feminine excess. When one salesgirl boasted that she had sold three lace dresses to an American client, he demanded immediately that she phone her to cancel two of the three. "It's ridiculous," he fumed. "You can't do that. Not three of the same type."

Although he had made it a rule not to go down to the fitting rooms, he still knew everything that was going on. "Make sure Princess Troubetskoï pays her account before we make her any new outfits," he wrote in a note to Jacques Rouët. They were such a wicked lot, his *chéries*! And they also needed educating. After each collection he would shoulder his moral responsibilities as the headmaster of this "girls' school" and attempt to restore a little order to the general atmosphere of frivolity by dedicating a dozen pages or so in his first book, *Je suis couturier*, to a lesson on fashion etiquette. "What are the duties of a client toward her couturier? To choose dresses that show her to her best advantage. If they should fail to do so, she is doing a disservice both to herself and the good name of the firm."

With his taste for portraits and masquerade, he appeared to enjoy painting thumbnail sketches of the different types of women he observed: "the client who is never satisfied," the ones who don't "know their own minds," or "the perfect little client who knows what she can afford and what it is she wants, and doesn't bother anyone."

The world of a couture house is a great source of entertainment and Suzanne Luling's diary relates some of its funniest episodes with much panache. "There was the client who said, 'Jacques is the one I live for, you know.' . . . but it was Pierre who paid the bills! One day, alas, she got her appointments mixed up." As Dior, who has also immortalized this story, writes, "One of her lovers bought her dresses at Fath, the other from me. One day she arrived at Avenue Montaigne in a suit by Fath, on the arm of a different man from the one who usually accompanied her. It wasn't until she was halfway through her fitting session, just as she was putting on her skirt, that she stopped to ponder for a moment and, whipping out her diary, exclaimed, 'How silly of me! I thought it was Friday.' "

"Buying dresses really brings out the woman in them," Suzanne Luling continues. Even she and her agile mind were sometimes at a loss, like the time a devastated client had to face the prospect of taking only twenty dinner dresses that year due to financial problems, it was hoped of a temporary nature. How on earth could she avoid being seen twice in the same outfit while away on holidays? Confronted with such a ghastly dilemma, Suzanne attempted a suggestion, "You will just have to cut short your holidays. Dreadful, of course, considering how much you need a break . . ." "No, we could not possibly cut short our holidays. We'll just have to change our hotel three times," the woman replied, demonstrating how resourceful one can be in a crisis.

The famous "Bar" suit, the essence of the New Look, February 12, 1947.
(Sketch: René Gruau, Christian Dior archives)

"Fortunio," for autumn-winter 1948, featured a shimmering yellow satin bodice over a black velvet skirt. The success of the New Look was pushed to the limits.

Sketch of the ensemble by René Gruau.

(Photographs: Laurent Sully-Jaulmes/Willy Maywald, ADAGP)

Ball gowns—"Schumann," above, and "Offenbach," opposite—for spring-summer 1950. Dior's collections were inspired by artistic themes: here, "harmony restored."
(Photographs: Dahl Wolfe, Hearst/Willy Maywald, ADAGP)

The "Rubempré" suit, spring-summer 1950.
(Photograph: Willy Maywald, ADAGP)

"Plein Ciel," an outfit from spring-summer 1957. Every season Dior would present a new line—from Oval to Oblique to the Scissors look . . .

(Photograph: Henry Clarke, ADAGP)

"Favori," a gray flannel suit from autumn-winter 1950, above, and "Bleu de Perse," opposite, an outfit from autumn-winter 1955, illustrating the Oblique line and the Y line respectively. Dior used geometry as inspiration for his designs.

(Photographs: Irving Penn, Condé Nast/Regi Relang, Christian Dior archives)

Above: sketch for "Miss Dior" perfume, done by René Gruau in 1949; opposite, advertisement for "Diorissimo" in 1956.

(Photographs: Christian Dior archives)

"Dauphine," spring-summer 1949, modeled in the Dior boutique. The decor, using cretonne material for the curtains and walls, was designed by Christian Bérard.

(Photograph: Willy Maywald, ADAGP)

"Haiti," from the autumn-winter collection of 1954; this little black tulle dress was a great favorite at American debutante balls.

(Photograph: Willy Maywald, ADAGP)

"Zémire," an evening suit in pink satin from autumn-winter of 1954: the color is reminiscent of Dior's childhood home. *(Photograph: Regi Relang, Christian Dior archives)*

Illustration by René Gruau for *Fémina* Magazine, April 1948.
(Loden-Frey collection; photograph: DR)

"Diorama," autumn-winter 1947, a dress that epitomizes Dior's definition: "A dress is a piece of ephemeral architecture, designed to enhance the proportions of the female body."

(Photograph: Blumenfeld, Condé Nast)

Suzanne Luling's diary offers quite a cross section of experiences, from the strangest stories to the most mundane, including "the story of the poor dear standing in the fitting room in foundation garments and suspenders saying, 'Angina is dreadful. My husband has it,' in just the same way she would say, Jaguars? Oh yes, my husband has one. 'It's extraordinary, though,' she added, 'He comes home every night just dead on his feet, literally. But when he has to go away for work — Pfff! Gone! It's as if he had never had a single attack.' If only she knew," Suzanne adds. "Poor thing. Her husband never goes away on his own and, gentleman that he is, he always dresses his girlfriend at Dior . . . almost as extravagantly as his wife."

Dior would have loved to dedicate himself exclusively to the women he called his "queens of the day." "They are our glory, our muses, the ones we fight over, envy, love, and admire. These are our true 'Parisians,' regardless of whether they were born in Boston, Buenos Aires, London, Rome, or even . . . Passy!" As for the others, he could take them or leave them; the nice ones who think all you need to be elegant is to buy your wardrobe from a top couturier, and the unfortunate ones who buy outfits best suited to someone else — the women they think they are, the women they would like to be or, worse still, the women they used to be. Then of course there are the seriously disturbed types, the ones who would go bankrupt just to fill their wardrobes with Dior.

But Dior was certainly not one to complain. He might have been a snob but he never forgot the fundamentals. "Who could begrudge them?" he writes. "Not I, for one." If the House of Dior had become a tourist attraction to be visited like the Eiffel Tower or the Folies-Bergère, was that such a bad thing? In any case, it was too late to do anything about it. According to Dior's own calculations, twenty-five thousand clients came through each year. That was not counting the waiting list, those who dreamed of making the pilgrimage to the Dior shrine or penned countless letters to Dior that he never had time to read. Not all of these missives were of an inflammatory nature like those of incensed American husbands rebelling against the "dictatorship" of a couturier ten thousand miles away. Dior also received the occasional billet-doux. One English housewife wooed him by mail, vowing she would one day appear at 30 Avenue Montaigne in person.

"If only I were Balenciaga!" sighed Dior privately, longing for the modest, exclusive establishment of his dreams. His more austere colleague had long since chased the merchants from the temple and now presided over a stable of elegant women who hung on his every word and venerated him as if he were the pope. Shrouded in silence, he looked somewhat askance at the hotbed of frivolity over on Avenue Montaigne, assailed as it was by the demons of publicity and the press.

One wonders whether Dior realized just what effect the electrifying appearance of the New Look had on his fellow couturiers. He could hardly have failed to notice the number of established couture clients who spun around like weathervanes in the direction of Avenue Montaigne, dropping their old allegiances without a backward glance. Stung by such treachery, Balenciaga refused henceforth to appear after his collections to greet his audience and accept their acclaim. He was disgusted by such feminine fickleness and by the fact that the "faithful clients" who once professed to swear by him and him alone were no longer present in the same numbers as before. His workroom head Madame Renée was even more devastated by their ingratitude than her employer and certainly, proud Spaniard that he was, Balenciaga gave no open sign of his feelings. Dior remained unaware of them but the Spaniard did confide in fellow designer Hubert de Givenchy. While most of his clients eventually returned to the fold, Balenciaga never forgot the affront and decided from then on that it would be beneath him to debase his talents by accepting their deceitful applause.

Dior secretly envied Balenciaga but openly admired him, calling him "our master." In July 1949 when workrooms around Paris were brought to a standstill by strikes just a week before the collections, Dior went to see his revered colleague, accompanied by Jacques Rouët, to offer him the assistance of his seamstresses. (Dior was not a member of the Chamber of Couture and hence was not affected by wage-bargaining disputes.) Balenciaga was touched but declined the offer.

Balenciaga was too much of a noble heart to bear a grudge. His real bone of contention with Dior was artistic. Purist that he was, Balenciaga was appalled by the way fabric was treated at Avenue Montaigne, backed with canvas, lined several times, or stiffened with tulle. As his pupil Hubert de Givenchy put it, Balenciaga could "make a piece of fabric speak." Failing to respect or highlight the individual qualities of a piece of cloth was a crime in his eyes. Such patrician intransigence set the Spaniard apart from the rest in the realm of fashion, "like some Elizabethan malcontent meditating on the foibles and follies of fashion," to quote Cecil Beaton. For Beaton, Dior was the "Watteau of dressmaking, full of nuances, chic, delicate and timely" while Balenciaga was "fashion's Picasso."

Dior versus Balenciaga . . . many were delighted at the contest. Nancy Mitford remembers the excitement of a taxi driver who once drove her to a fitting at Avenue Montaigne. "At last we have another dressmaker to rival Monsieur Balenciaga," he enthused.

The debate they sparked did them great honor, but also went beyond them as individuals. Fashion could no longer exist without either. Each found his own response to the eternal dilemma of haute couture — art for the elite or art for the masses? — by carrying his philosophy of fashion to its logical extremes. As fashion historian Didier Grumbach wrote, "They were like two venerable cats, sitting on the two most comfortable cushions in the drawing room, close and yet remote, separated by an insurmountable barrier of mutual respect and affection."

The ultimate expression of this unspoken respect was Dior's reaction when Balenciaga announced he was closing his business. Dior was so disturbed at the thought of "such a huge loss for the prestige of Paris couture" that he persuaded Balmain to go with him to see Balenciaga at 10 Avenue George-V and entreat him to change his mind. The pair arrived with a Braque drawing as a present for Balenciaga.

When they were not being couturiers, fashion's Watteau and fashion's Picasso were uncannily alike. Both lost no time in seeking out their origins the minute they had a chance to rest. Bettina Ballard remembers with emotion the simplicity of Balenciaga's childhood home, which he had kept intact in the little fishing village where he was born, Guetaria near San Sebastián. Only his closest friends were invited there. They would gather in the kitchen with its clean smell of floor polish and sparkling silverware. He had imported the latest refrigerator and washing machine from America but never plugged them in! He and his guests dined at a huge wooden table on *angulas* (eels) sautéed in garlic, drinking good Asturian wine and talking late into the night.

Dior too would disappear after the collections. Exhausted, he sought refuge in his garden, surrounded by flowers and shrubs. Having played his part and put on the usual spectacular show, he considered it time to beat a well-earned retreat. His first material reward came when he spent his first share of the profits on the purchase of an old mill, the Moulin du Coudret at Milly-la-Forêt. As houses went, it was nothing but "a hole in a swamp," to quote his companion Jacques Homberg, who was with him the first time Dior saw the place. But this was his big chance to take up his missed vocation as an architect. By the following year he had patched up the tiny group of cottages that stood around the millpond like a little village, and planted flowers and a vegetable garden. This was his sanctuary, a place where he could rest in peace on weekends and potter around his garden in his shirt sleeves and gardening boots, blissfully happy, surveying his irises and dahlias.

Cecil Beaton, a gentleman to whom life had been more than kind (and who showed his gratitude by photographing it magnificently in all its aspects), confessed his surprise at discovering a sense of understatement in Dior which he had previously considered uniquely British. "Dior enjoys the trimmings of life. A bourgeois with his feet well planted in the soil of reality, he has remained as modest as a sugar violet in spite of eulogies that have been heaped upon him. His egglike head may sway from side to side, but it will never be turned by success. Dior does not make the mistake of believing in his own publicity, though when he arrived in New York he received as much newspaper space as Winston Churchill. He is grateful that when fashion tires of him (and even the greatest can hold the throne for no more than several decades) he has been lucky and wise enough to save a nest egg on which to retire to his farm and cultivate his gardens."

10

The American Love Affair

> Our culture is a luxury, and we fight for
> its survival.
>
> — Christian Dior

*C*rossing the Atlantic was not something Dior had in mind. He usually dreaded moving away from home. But the managing director of Neiman Marcus had invited him to Dallas, Texas, to receive its "Oscar for Couture." The homebody in Dior made him reluctant, to say the least, at the prospect of traveling but his natural business sense made him only too aware of the significance of Stanley Marcus's gesture. His biggest buyers were all Americans and meeting them on their home turf was definitely a worthwhile exercise. His couturier side was also curious to get to know American women a little better and was flattered to learn that this was the first time the "Oscar" (which had been inaugurated during the war years) had been awarded to a Frenchman, and for his first collection, what's more. Spurred by a strong sense of patriotism and his memories of the way in which French couture had almost gone under forever because of the war, he felt like a man on a mission. Not

175

only had he roused French fashion from its postwar stupor, now he had the chance to restore Paris to its rightful preeminence. All these most worthy reasons aside, Christian Dior's ever fertile imagination had already been kindled by the thought of setting out to discover the much talked-about New World.

And so in September 1947 he set sail on the *Queen Elizabeth,* delighted to be traveling under a British flag. Despite the "ghastly kind of luxury common to all big ships . . . an English liner just reeks of all things English. There is no other country, besides my own, with a lifestyle I like as much. I love English customs, the sense of tradition, the politeness, the architecture and, amazing as it may seem, English cooking. I dote on Yorkshire pudding, mince pies, and chicken with sage stuffing, and an English breakfast of tea, porridge, eggs and bacon is an absolute delight." Besides the joy of indulging in such Anglophile pleasures, Dior discovered a small group of traveling companions with whom he was to strike up a firm friendship over the days at sea. These were Iva Sergei "Pat" Patcévitch, *Vogue* president since the death of Condé Nast, art director Alexander Liberman and his wife Tatiana, and Bettina Ballard — the entire *Vogue* team, in other words — and in the course of sunbaking sessions, games of bridge, and gossip about New York, a warmth was established that allayed some of Dior's fears about what might await him once he stepped ashore. He was traveling alone, without anyone from the couture house, and the pleasant five-day interlude was a chance to unwind before the Statue of Liberty loomed before him, glowing in an Indian-summer dawn.

His first glimpses of the city's skyscrapers filled him with childlike wonder. To Dior, "the zest for life and self-confidence of those thousand obelisks thrusting against the sky" somehow embodied the power of this giant continent where everything was forty to one hundred times bigger and better. He drank it all in, afraid to miss a single thing and eager to retain the freshness and impact of his first impressions. Dior had no hesitation about talking up his whole adventure and indulged in a string of superlatives to describe its every minute. "Quite carried away by my enthusiasm, I completely forgot the ancient continent of my birth. My Eiffel Tower and the lacelike beauty of its structure seemed so very far away. I was quite intoxicated by it all." It was to be an expedition full of discovery and surprises.

The first of these occurred even before he stepped ashore. While checking his papers, the immigration officer gave him a broad wink. "Well, you are the designer? What about the skirt length?"

Dior was dumbfounded. He had thought his arrival would pass quite unnoticed. Realizing that his reputation preceded him, he decided to use his couturier image to get him through the rest of his stay. After all, playacting was his forte. Once he understood that America was waiting to see Dior the famous couturier, he hammed it up for all it was worth, embellishing his account of his American adventures with the escapades of Dior the buffoon, the country cousin lost in the big city, chasing after lost suitcases, patting his pockets for lost papers, and wandering down labyrinthine corridors only to be rescued by the sound of his name being called over the loudspeakers. His description of what awaited him is a wonderful indication of Dior's sense of comedy. Little Mr. Everyman finally emerged from his corridors, to be greeted by the popping of flashlights and the glare of spotlights. A posse of journalists and photographers had been lying in wait for him. He was thrust into the restaurant for his first press conference — his initiation into the role of media personality, American-style.

To his great relief on this occasion, however, a familiar soul emerged from the crowd and hastened to his rescue. It was his friend Nicolas Bongard (whom he had last seen in the days when they shared an attic room without running water just above Le Boeuf sur le Toit). Bongard was now doing extremely well in New York as a partner of Jean Schlumberger, the jeweler. His presence made Dior feel a little more comfortable as the microphones came out and the questions began and he launched into his first performance in the role of "the French designer abroad." The press lost no time in putting him on the spot, and continued to do so throughout his stay. The question was always the same: Why the devil did he insist on hiding women's legs? It was not a trend Americans were keen on.

These first experiences were just a foretaste of what was awaiting him in Dallas. Flying on after two days' rest in New York, he arrived in Texas to face a crowd of 3,000 people. There was nothing lighthearted about the American anti–New Look movement. The famous scenes in Paris's Rue Lepic, where housewives had set upon a group of women in Dior dresses, seemed like hysterical bickering in comparison to the air of genuine revolt fueled by the very well organized network of protesters who dogged his every step in the land of suffragettes. It was a force to be reckoned with, and had branches right across the country. First to sharpen the battle-ax was a Mrs. Louise Horn of Louisville, Georgia, who had the unfortunate experience of catching her new, longer skirt in the automatic doors of a bus. She found herself being dragged for a whole block before the vehicle came to a stop. As the first serious victim of the infamous New Look, she vowed not to let the matter rest and immediately enlisted a further 1,265 women to sign an anti-Dior petition. They called themselves the Just Below the Knee Club and their fame soon spread. A former Dallas model, a Mrs. Woodward, also took up the fight, saying, "Whoever dreamed up this fall's gruesome styles has been reading too many historical novels." Washington, too, was home to a league aimed at abolishing long day-dresses. In Albany, Dallas, Oildale in California, even Toronto, the message was the same. Advocates of practical dressing felt, as one protester said in a *Newsweek* interview (September 1, 1947), "long skirts are dangerous. With to-day's speed, you can't even catch a streetcar in a long skirt. And how can you drive an auto?" It was no time before the most militant among them had decided Dior's brand of fashion amounted to a conspiracy against sexual equality. "American women have attractive figures," said one. "Why disfigure them with padded hips? And even if people like the slender waist put forward by the New Look, how many women are prepared to put up with the torture? I put on one of those new corsets and after fifteen minutes I had to take it off again. I have never felt worse in my life."

Even husbands became embroiled in the battle. Their arguments were more pragmatic. They declared their outrage at the exorbitant bills they would be forced to run up if their wives followed the new fashion, with its decadent use of copious fabric. They formed a group known as the League of Broke Husbands and claimed a membership 30,000 strong.

Now that they had been let loose on their prey, Dior's public had no intention of letting him escape without being taken to task. The Christian Dior for which America was waiting was a "mythical, revolutionary, diabolical creature," according to writer Françoise Giroud. The real thing proved something of a disappointment. "This dumpy little fellow with the balding head and dressed like an office clerk would not do at all!" As Giroud notes with irony, "There was nothing prestigious about this little Frenchman, who was so discreet in appearance as to be nondescript. . . . He was hardly a symbol of Gay Paree, nor was he the gallant, mustachioed type with a monocle or a dynamic young man in the pseudo-American mold. He was something of an enigma on this side of the Atlantic. No one quite knew what kind of Frenchman he was supposed to be. . . . He must be some kind of historical monument, they decided!"

On arriving in Dallas, Dior found out he was to receive his Oscar in front of an audience of 3,000 people. The fact that he would also have to stand up and make a speech from a gilt rostrum kept him awake all night. He was hardly reassured by the knowledge that a similar fate awaited Italian shoe designer Salvatore Ferragamo and the MGM costume designer Irene, who were each also to receive an award. But when the moment finally came, his past came to the fore with appropriate inspiration. Those wild evenings with friends like Henri Sauguet, Christian Bérard, and Max Jacob spent impersonating the hedonistic nineteenth-century romantic writer Alfred de Musset, the French mass murderer Landru, even Queen Victoria, all counted for something. "What did they expect of me, after all? To behave like a French designer abroad. . . . And so when they called my name it was not I who got to my feet but a character from a game of charades." The audience clapped and roared with laughter. He was a resounding success. It was a great routine and he trotted out his new act at every gala and reception to come.

Stanley Marcus, for his part, was quick to seize upon the whole anti–New Look controversy. Among the designs on parade after the awards, a few of the dresses were wittily fitted with a system of pulleys that could bring a hem up from the ankles to the knees in a jiffy.

Any fears Dior might have had about the crowds and the aggressive questioning of American journalists soon abated and he began to realize just how valuable such controversy could be. Newspaper headlines, public debate, and groups of women hurling insults and telling him to go home were in fact the best kind of publicity he could have gotten. "The battle of the New Look is all the rage," he wrote to

Jacques Rouët on his return to New York. "There are two American designers by the names of Adrian and Sophie Gimbel who have gone on the offensive against *Vogue* and *Harper's Bazaar* and, indirectly, against me. It's wonderful publicity. I don't think our name has ever been as widely known as now."

Along with all the demonstrations, the New Look was a topic of social debate and frequently made the front pages. Even the *Wall Street Journal* broke with its more sober image to run a survey indicating that a majority of people were in favor of the new line, a result that must have been a great relief to self-conscious citizens. Nevertheless, the success of such an aberrant fashion remained a puzzle. Here were American women who had fought for the right to vote, to drive automobiles, and to go to work, suddenly opting to go back fifty years in time to dresses with twenty yards of fabric in the skirts, whalebone in the corsets, hats so wide they barely fit through doorways, long gloves, and strings of pearls — all far more suitable for an outing in a carriage than for sitting at the wheel of a motorcar. Here was a couturier with the gall to turn his back on nylon, washing machines, and weekends of leisure in favor of a resolute return to the past. Only those who were old enough to remember 1914 and the scandal unleashed with the first bob cut had ever seen anything like the political emotion generated by what seemed to be mere fashion.

Life magazine joined the action, running a series of articles over several weeks tackling the issue in depth and from every angle — financial: "Fashion turmoil: drastic new styles will make most existing clothes obsolete"; sociological: "Skirts: up or down? Argument rages over year's major style change, which returns feminine knee to prim seclusion"; and political: "Major fashion turning point is marked by public furor." In the best tradition of American journalism, no stone was left unturned when it came to finding another way to stir up debate. The views of both sides were canvassed, famous people were asked to comment, graphs were published showing the changes in hemlines over the last two hundred years . . . and on it went.

Ultimately the real value of the exercise became clear, at least for those in the know and certainly for Stanley Marcus, a merchandising genius who had been running the biggest deluxe department store in the

States since 1906. Neiman Marcus is a legend in itself, a life-size projection of the American dream. (No one will ever forget the time the store's Christmas windows featured the ultimate gift — twin private jets, "his and hers.")

Stanley Marcus was the first to realize how the fashion industry could benefit from the introduction of a radically different style. He realized it the minute he saw Dior's first collection. "I had never seen anything so sensational," he recalls. His judgment was all the more astute for having sat on the War Production Board, a wartime committee entrusted with the task of limiting the new fashions to appear each season, in an attempt to discourage people from updating their wardrobes too frequently. The board laid down very strict guidelines for the garment industry under L-85, a ruling that banned evening dresses, three-piece suits, pleated skirts, and puffed sleeves. The New Look appeared just as L-85 was being repealed.

Stanley Marcus and Christian Dior struck up an immediate rapport. Marcus was fiercely intelligent and groundbreaking in his own right. His fashion "Oscar," for example, was an excellent way of attracting celebrities from all over the world to Dallas. "You don't get artists just by paying for their trip," he explains. (Dior paid his own way to America, with Neiman Marcus covering only the cost of freighting and insuring the gowns.)

Marcus's first meeting with Dior was a pleasant surprise. "I offered to show him around the city and its best neighborhoods. 'With pleasure,' Dior replied, 'but I want to see the slums, too. I'm interested in seeing how people live.' " This down-to-earth approach revealed much about Dior's character that appealed to Marcus. Honoring Dior was also a smart move on his part. He realized the New Look would bring a much needed breath of fresh air to the American fashion industry, a view shared by the all-powerful Carmel Snow at *Harper's*. As she later wrote, "My friends on Seventh Avenue confirm me in my belief that American designers didn't really come into their own until after the war, when their release from the restrictions of L-85 gave them impetus, and renewed contact with Paris stimulated their imaginations." As the unchallenged oracle of the fashion world, when Snow told *Harper's* readers to wear the New Look, all of America ended up obeying.

Meanwhile, though, there was a lot at stake. The stores were holding millions of dollars' worth of dresses and coats in stock and no one was buying. In some sectors, sales were down 40 percent on previous years. Something had to be done. If this damned Frenchman made the whole lot unfashionable, there would be mass bankruptcies. On the other hand, if women came running like bees to honey to buy his designs, it would spark off a powerful new interest in clothes that would really get things moving again. Old rivals buried their differences. Saks Fifth Avenue called Henri Bendel, meetings were held at Marshall Field in Chicago and at Bergdorf Goodman. Even the powerful, exuberant septuagenarian Hattie Carnegie, who shrugged her shoulders at first, got on the plane to join them after hearing an effusive Carmel Snow on the radio. "Dior has done for Paris fashion what the Paris taxis did for France at the Battle of the Marne!" said Snow. What were a few hours in a plane in comparison?

Christian Dior's trip to the United States proved to be a formidable propaganda tool. Wherever he went, the press went too, never failing to work up a little more debate on the New Look question. He could not have dreamed up a better publicity campaign. The "little Frenchman" was a hit. Although he hardly made a striking first impression and his accent made people smile, his one-liners were terrific. What people did not know was that he rehearsed his facial expressions on the train or airplane en route from Dallas to Los Angeles, Los Angeles to Chicago, Chicago to Washington, and back to New York, and honed his skills at the game of question and answer. "The rule is to give an answer without offending anyone and always along the lines the interviewers expect. Whenever you encounter an obstacle, do a swift about-turn. The skill is in being amusing, either in what you say or how you say it."

Wherever he went, the questions were always the same: What do you think of our women? Are they the most beautiful? "I always say yes," Dior noted, "but inevitably add that French women are not all that bad either."

In the land of the mass media, Dior turned out to be a "pro" and soon won over the American heartland. Free of preconceived ideas, he never came across as arrogant, but listened, observed . . . and said "thank you" a lot. He really hit his stride by the end and, much to his audience's delight, once made an off-the-cuff remark to the effect that he was "a self-made man." It won them over completely. He also had a soft spot for Americans, particularly for their ability to "switch quite naturally from business to warm-hearted camaraderie." This first trip proved to be the start of a lasting friendship with Stanley Marcus, a relationship built on shared sensibilities. Marcus, who knew quite a few designers, was surprised to discover in Dior a man with "a statesman's stature" very much in the mold of Lucien Lelong, and someone "who is far more cultivated than his peers, in literature, art history, and typography." Marcus and his wife Betty were also impressed with Dior's courtesy and finesse, qualities they themselves considered fundamental, always stressing elegance in taste and attitude.

Wherever Dior went, the routine was the same — "press conferences, hasty tours of endless stores, frenzied cocktail parties, fork lunches (Dior was on a diet of sandwiches and orangeade, there being, sadly, never any wine!), and hundreds of anonymous letters from people calling themselves the 'opponents' of uplifted bustlines, rounded hips, or long skirts . . . in short, of the New Look. Unperturbed, I faced a battery of flash bulbs, smiled, waved, sipped orangeade, and became increasingly assured in the role I had created for myself in Dallas."

In San Francisco "a thousand people greeted me at the airport. A thousand invitations awaited me, leaving me with the dreadful task of trying not to offend anyone. At one club I was presented with the keys to the city, in gold cardboard, while a crowd awaited me at another club for the same ceremony."

Chicago was quite a different experience and he was actually forced to go incognito. His train drew in to a sea of placards saying "Christian Dior, go home" and his minders' expressions were enough to conjure up all sorts of scenarios. "It was as if we had narrowly escaped an assassination attempt," writes Dior, most amused. Photographs of his Chicago visit offer the strange sight of Dior pushing his way unmolested through a mass of threatening placards and screaming suffragettes, none of whom even recognized him.

"My serious, unruffled appearance soon dispelled any risk. I'm not sure what sort of mental image the crowd had of me — a Petronius, a pinup boy, or some other stereotype straight out of a movie or play, no doubt. Meanwhile this solid middle-class Norman went through the lobby without causing the slightest ripple, or even the faintest breath of curiosity. I was almost disappointed!"

By the end of his stay, the New Look had definitely won the day. The department stores gave him a star's welcome and the huge American fashion machine was overwhelmingly behind him. "The most exciting collection in my entire life. It arrived at the right time. Just like being hungry and having a lot of food to eat. I wanted to try every dress I saw," remembers Stella Hanania from I. Magnin. Norman Chosler, another I. Magnin buyer, adds, "Dior was the most important source of inspiration both in fashion and merchandising." Andrew Goodman, chairman of Bergdorf Goodman, had this to say: "Dior? Unique! Not only brilliant in his creative ability, but we also met a charming, down-to-earth person. He was a kind of anchor in a stormy sea."

What an effect it must have had on Dior when he saw his own designs on the streets. The New Look was all over the department stores, and at what prices!

"It only took three months for the clothes to become available," recalls Stanley Marcus. Sophie Gimbel, the designer who had attacked both *Vogue* and *Harper's Bazaar,* adapted the look to American mass production and came up with the "Margrave" cocktail dress, from the 1947 autumn-winter collection. Priced at $400, it was a black dress in wool crepe and faille with a wide décolletage. The fitted bodice was highlighted with three wide bows, in decreasing sizes, which allowed glimpses of skin between the bands of fabric. The wide skirt was a classic "Corolla" style, and used at least fifteen yards of fabric. The dress was first seen in the windows of Bergdorf Goodman and Henri Bendel in New York but was soon copied, recopied, and adapted to sell for as little as $110 . . . still with the same look but entirely in rayon, with a zipper instead of the original twelve buttons and a skirt reduced to eleven instead of fifteen yards of fabric. By December the New Look had really gone down-market and was available at Orbach's for a mere $8.95. By then, the openwork bodice had disappeared, replaced by three bows stitched onto a conventional top. But at that unbeatable price, millions of dresses were sold in the space of a few weeks. This amazing process was the forerunner of the more regulated practice haute couture designers later adopted, selling patterns under license to foreign markets.

Dior's reaction to all this was interesting. He could have been outraged at the thought of his New Look dress being thus adapted for the American mass market. Then again, he might have been flattered by the sight of it on every street corner. He could have not recognized it, of course. And the variations dreamed up by the rag trade might well have offended his artistic sensitivities. For not only did Americans adopt the new style, they also reworked it to fit in with their own sartorial heritage. It was quite reminiscent of the femininity immortalized at the turn of the century by Charles Dana Gibson in his captivating portraits of the "Gibson Girl" encased in her long skirt and tucked or frilled blouse, suggestively submissive beneath her air of Victorian composure. The August 15 issue of *Life* that year described the Americanization of the New Look in exactly those terms. Thanks to his new friendship with *Vogue* art director Alex Liberman and his wife Tania, Dior began to understand these subtleties. "Americans are fascinated by the waist," said Liberman, "so Dior's concept of womanhood really hit the mark. Prudish Americans were wary of the more seductive, but enveloping a woman in satin, lace, frills, and flounces was just the right way to appeal to Anglo-Saxon timidity, unveiling her beauty in a subtle, delicate fashion, a little like a perfume coming out of its box." Liberman's metaphor was a pretty one, with its image of a woman as a precious gift to be handled carefully in her silken wrapping. "Balenciaga hated women's bodies," Liberman continues, "and hid them. He dressed them all like old ladies." It is certainly true that the austere Spaniard almost boasted that "a distinguished lady almost always has a disagreeable air."

This American fascination with tiny waists touches on the whole symbolic relationship between fashion and sexuality. If fashion à la Dior brought the erotica clothes of the Belle Epoque back into vogue, with its laced corsets, fitted waists and bodices, plunging necklines, fine lingerie, petticoats, and frills, then clearly this method of packaging sexual desirability touched on something quite universal. England too, as we shall see, was soon to be consumed by Dior fever.

*   *   *

Dior was not in the least upset to see America seize on his designs and reproduce them to suit its taste and its markets. But he had no intention of leaving it at that. The trip had proved quite a revelation and this continent with its jumbo-size values excited his keen sense of curiosity. His head was buzzing with a million new ideas. Everything he saw was food for thought. The latent architect in him had been stimulated but so too had his interest in town planning, sociology, and indeed commerce. He recorded a detailed description of every town he visited: Los Angeles, which he disliked, San Francisco, which delighted him, Chicago with its gangster air, Washington with its slight stiffness, and New York and its café society. While he was fascinated by the architecture and urban design, what he found most intriguing was the way people lived. Housewives arriving at work in air-conditioned Buicks immediately made him think of putting in air-conditioning on Avenue Montaigne. He waxed lyrical to Jacques Rouët about the "wonderful workrooms and office canteens" enjoyed by American workers. Nothing escaped him. He devoured America with its many faces, varied climates, and diverse characters and, aware of just how much he could learn, decided to stay as long as possible.

His first observation was that Americans were far more mobile than the French and that American women did not necessarily confine themselves to one wardrobe, as styles and seasons differ so greatly from the East to the West Coast. He also realized what an important role department stores played in the wider picture, determining fashion trends, offering fast, trouble-free service to the majority of Americans, no matter how isolated or different their horizons and backgrounds might have been. The chief problem, as he saw it, was that "the women are badly dressed and never in the right attire. They buy everything ready made and have no concept of what it is to be properly fitted for an outfit." Even the positive had its negative sides: "The garment industry was rich and varied, making for huge choice, but sadly undiscriminating. It was only too evident that a hat bought here, a coat there, and a dress from somewhere else again . . . might be a means of clothing oneself but did not constitute an outfit." As he finally concluded, "America may not be the land of grand-scale luxury but Americans certainly spend on a grand scale." And "American women . . . would rather have three new dresses than one very beautiful dress. They do not linger over their purchases because they know they will soon tire of them. . . . The Americans may seem a little hasty to us in their buying habits. They certainly are at odds with our more frugal and methodical ways. . . . Why is such a wealthy country so cheap when it comes to fashion?"

Gradually he began piecing together the various things he had observed during his stay. It had almost been like a course at business school! Now it was time to sum up what he had learned. American women's reaction to his designs and the battles waged over the New Look made him realize one thing: not only had he put to the test his dresses, his savoir-faire, his perfectionism, even his own personal sense of style and poise, but he had also discovered fashion's power to communicate. The success of the New Look was in fact the first time that a cultural concept had truly transcended its own borders and taken the lead at a global level. A simple fashion had triggered a massive public reaction and attracted media attention to an extent usually reserved for the theater, cinema, major concerts, or sporting events like the Olympic Games. Dior had initially been motivated in his study of the United States by his belief in the uniqueness of French traditions of style and taste. Subsequently, though, it made him determined to set up a system of commercial fashion distribution in America. The consumer society was not yet even in its infancy but Dior had already seen the potential of the luxury goods market.

It was while he was in the States that he made his famous pronouncement about the role of couturiers and designers. "We are merchants of ideas," he declared. And with the benefit of distance and because America was so very unlike his beloved France, he saw a way to translate the germ of an idea into reality and create a commercial empire that would be a first both for Europe and for couture.

Pragmatist that he was, and ever anxious to see his ideas through to their logical conclusion, he began envisaging his New York house, "a clothing establishment of great class" where his designs could be reproduced for a mass market and, more important, adapted for places as diverse as California and Boston. While still in the States he phoned Henri Fayol, Boussac's right-hand man, to discuss the project, and he referred to it in one of his letters to Jacques Rouët. He was already thinking in very real terms about how to license his designs. In New

York he had noticed Schiaparelli stockings sold in her trademark shocking pink boxes and immediately revised his views on his own arrangement, whereby he used Prestige hosiery in his collections in return for a fee of $5,000 and joint publicity paid by the American company. "I am not really keen on promoting American stockings," he told Jacques Rouët on his return. "Couldn't we make our own?"

When he finally disembarked at the French port of Cherbourg to be met by Jacques Rouët and Jacques Homberg (chauffeured there by Pierre Perrotino), he no longer had anything in common with the "nondescript little Frenchman" who first landed in America. He had been infected with its entrepreneurial fever and dynamism. The "little establishment" he had once dreamed of now seemed so very far away. "Overcome by the fuss of my sudden popularity, I did miss it just a little," he confessed, but there was no turning back. "With its marvelous ability to generate energy, America had inspired me to take action." He was driven as much by the will to succeed as by the desire not to miss a moment of an adventure in which he, Dior, for the first time, found himself in the starring role. Seeing his name on the front page, his New Look all over the streets of New York, San Francisco, and Paris, and having discovered that in a matter of seconds anything is possible, he may not even have been aware of how much he had changed.

"Where is my new car?" he demanded, barely off the gangplank. Before leaving he had ordered a new Citroën Quinze 6, a convertible model with a black leather interior. Pierre Perrotino's face assumed a strange look. The new automobile was at a garage for repairs to its brand-new chassis after a rather too close encounter with a chestnut horse, and a Citroen 11 had been hired in its place. Dior was furious, "ready to kill me," relates Perrotino. The storm soon subsided but a new, rather more temperamental Dior had been born.

Jacques Rouët soon found himself reeling from the onslaught that invaded his office. Dior was full of plans, ideas, questions: he wanted air-conditioning for the salons and a New York branch ... and the business was barely a year old. "Not so fast," his partner was obliged to tell him; most business ventures are at their most vulnerable in their first few years. As Jacques Rouët confirms, "The Boussac group had decided to wait to see how the second collection went before making any further investments." True, between 1947 and 1949 Boussac would increase his investment ten times over. Then again, the amazing success of this fledgling operation was enough to make even the most cautious investor, let alone a racing man, want to double his stake.

In its very first year the House of Dior returned a profit. Its turnover for 1947 was 1.2 million francs (the equivalent of 4 million francs, or some $800,000, today). In 1948 it increased to 3.6 million and in 1949 to 12.7 million. Sixty percent of that figure consisted of foreign earnings, though overseas licensing contracts were still in an embryonic stage, and the pretax profit was around 15 percent. Boussac had already put in almost half his total outlay of 60 million francs (the 1990 equivalent of 13.7 million francs) by 1947, most of the money going to set up the American outlet. For, in fact, the plan was approved and two people were dispatched to do the preliminary work while a manager, Mrs. Helen Engel, was hired on the ground in New York.

It was another example of Boussac's legendary business flair, which had never once let him down. The House of Dior was a new, very different prize for the stable of the man whose jockeys wore the orange and gray silks and who had made such a name for himself at racecourses on both sides of the Channel. Boussac was most adept at irritating the English; not only had he topped the list of winning thoroughbred owners in France for seventeen consecutive years, but he was now beating the British on their own turf. In 1949, the year of his greatest triumphs, Marcel Boussac raked in 94 million francs, 41 million of them won in just forty-eight hours. (In one fell swoop he had recouped most of his total investment in Dior!)

"Dior was never more than one bright little flower amid my many business activities," he told *France Soir.* It was a subtle way of defining the distance between Boussac's various commercial interests and between the two men themselves. It is interesting to note that they only ever met the one time, at that initial interview. Ostentatious as he might have been, Boussac never thought to invite Christian Dior to his sumptuous apartment in the smart Paris suburb of Neuilly, although Dior would have been most taken with the very eighteenth-century decor and in ecstasy over the marvelous orchids, Boussac's one indulgence, which he grew in a greenhouse in nearby Chantilly. Nor was Dior ever a guest at King Cotton's hunting parties, which he used to entertain his political contacts, as if to the manner born. It was each to his own world, although, as Jacques Rouët stresses, Boussac was "perfectly aware of the prestige he gained from Dior."

Backed by his newspaper, *L'Aurore,* Boussac was a man of influence who moved in the highest circles. When he embarked for the United States — in November 1947, just as Dior was on his way home — it was not, despite his position as a textile manufacturer, to tour department stores as his partner had done, but to meet privately with President Truman. On the agenda with "Harry" was not business or trade, although the president had begun his working life in men's shirts, in Kansas City. Boussac had come to discuss with Truman his anxieties about the future of Western Europe and to plead for aid to Germany, threatened as it was by galloping inflation, and France, where unemployment was rampant. After three-quarters of an hour at the White House, Boussac stopped off in New York to open a branch of his Cotton Industry Trading Post (CIC in the French acronym). There were those who immediately jumped to the conclusion that Boussac's real plan was to provide backup for Dior and launch a range of raincoats or bath towels with the Boussac name on them. No such scheme ever existed.

It may, however, seem surprising that haute couture's foremost figure never once worked in tandem with Boussac's multifaceted textile empire. To understand such autonomy, one needs to go back to Henri Fayol and the mentor role he played in founding the House of Dior. It was he who was the guardian, as it were, of what started off as a small-scale enterprise. Every week he would meet with Jacques Rouët at CIC headquarters on Rue du Faubourg-Poissonnière and go through everything to do with the House of Dior and its future directions. All decisions affecting those directions were made by Henri Fayol, subject to Marcel Boussac's endorsement. The fact that Marcel Boussac and Christian Dior did not meet face to face was all part of Fayol's skill as an administrator. His experience in business management taught him not only that it would be disastrous to put two such powerful personalities together but that their management styles were too vastly different for them to see eye to eye. Boussac's industrial empire was run on classic hierarchical lines, with a centralized management structure headed by a supremo whose word was law. The wisest option was to keep Avenue

Montaigne well away from the cogs and wheels of the Boussac machine. "It wouldn't have worked any other way," Jacques Rouët points out, "given Monsieur Dior's personality. He was a manager cum artist and he dominated everyone else through his stature, his intelligence, and his talent." With Henri Fayol in an overseer's role, adept, as Boussac's deputy financial controller Pierre Jarry explains, "at delegating responsibility to his colleagues on the basis of clearly defined goals," Dior always felt perfectly in charge. "The only concern," Jarry adds, "would have been if the business failed to earn enough money and Boussac decided to cut off his contribution." It was for this reason that Fayol paid so much attention to his "baby." His dynamic approach, coupled with the fact that he and Jacques Rouët were very much on the same wavelength, really formed the cornerstone of the business at Avenue Montaigne and its development. In the meantime he used all his powers to encourage Marcel Boussac to continue his investment. As Jacques Rouët confirms, Boussac "realized that Dior brought an element of prestige and a certain reputation that reflected indirectly onto his entire textile empire." So everyone was happy. Dior, a small star really, became the jewel in the Boussac crown, and while the former put it down to good fortune, the latter continued to believe that it was attributable to his amazing foresight.

The finest irony is that the greatest success of the billionaire's career was the area in which he was least involved. He only visited his "jewel" once (Boussac never went to the collections). It was when extensions were being built to 30 Avenue Montaigne. For forty years he had conducted similar inspections in his factories in the Vosges and Nord *départements*. The machines had to be gleaming, the floors shining like mirrors, the workers standing to attention, and the foremen poised, checking every detail. The boss's eagle eye would inevitably spot some irregularity . . . and his visit to Dior proved no exception. He had been through the workrooms and was on his way down through the salons when he suddenly bent to pick up a thread from the carpet. "The upkeep on this place is very poor," he commented.

Nonetheless, Boussac had the greatest respect for Dior's talent. He was able to admire it in private thanks to his wife, who did, of course, attend the collections. Madame Boussac liked to order evening dresses to match her eyes, which were blue, and in keeping with the glittering world she had once been part of, as a singer. Her regular day wear consisted of unremarkable suits and berets, always with a raincoat over them, none of which gave the slightest indication that her husband owned a couture house. She was quite indifferent to all the theatricality associated with couture and was always quite startled when she inquired, out of curiosity, as to the price of this gown or that. She is, however, remembered at Dior as a charming woman who had a collection of wonderful gowns for evening wear.

Things were well under way in New York. The new Dior was to be managed by Mrs. Helen Engel, half Russian, half Swedish, and a longtime resident of the United States. But when Dior arrived in New York to design his first American collection, there was nowhere for him to work at the new Dior premises at 730 Fifth Avenue, on the corner of Fifty-seventh Street. He had no choice but to do a makeshift conversion on a little brownstone he rented on Sixty-second Street and set up shop there with his whole team. The drawing rooms became workrooms, the bedroom the models' dressing room, and the conservatory Dior's studio. Dior, of course, reveled in the impromptu nature of it all. The Harlequin in him was always ready to improvise a few steps on the bare boards of the *Commedia dell'arte.*

Sumptuous flower arrangements greeted guests at the showing of the first Dior collection in America on November 8, 1948. "Every elegant person in New York was there. Marlene Dietrich came with her entourage, dripping with diamonds." Frances Weisz, the locally hired chief assistant, remembers it all with great emotion. "We loved Dior. He was a true gentleman. We worked like dogs for him." The interiors of the House were designed by Dior's friend Nicolas de Gunzburg, the wealthy son of a banker, one of those swallows of the *beau monde* accustomed to flitting from one side of the Atlantic to the other as the season took him.

One particular suit with a peplum jacket, called "Bobby" after Christian Dior's dog, was an instant hit and became a huge best-seller. It stayed at the top of the charts for eight seasons! These were interesting lessons for Dior, who had been trained to think that fashion demanded constant change.

In Paris he was a designer of haute couture. In New York, his name became synonymous with deluxe ready-to-wear and garment manufacture. It was the start of Dior's semi-annual trips to New York, complete with the Zehnacker-Carré-Bricard triumvirate, to design a collection in situ that was then sold to department stores like Bergdorf, Saks, Lord and Taylor, and a few select "specialty stores." The dresses were a little larger than their French counterparts (size 12 instead of 8) and adapted for different climates. Most of the garments were made by Dior's own workrooms, the rest by carefully chosen American manufacturers. The Fifth Avenue couture house functioned rather as a showroom for a series of sales outlets. When, for example, Cary Grant came to 730 Fifth Avenue with his wife Betsy Drake, they were shown the collection and she was able to try on the dresses she liked, but she could not purchase them directly from Dior.

The reasoning behind this courageous step was as follows: "I wanted to remain autonomous, the only situation I could see that was compatible with the dignity, distinction, and supremacy of Paris couture. I also considered it was only fair for me to run the same risks and put myself on an equal footing with other, fully American companies." To his credit, he managed to induce his backers to invest in the project. It is not easy to get a foothold in an industry that is effectively a spin-off of haute couture, and many French couturiers have gone under in the process. Dior, however, having observed the way in which American fashion operated, was able to benefit from its advantages and avoid its disadvantages. He did so by using its distribution system — adapting as needed to American cost structures, work practices, trade unions, and the like — without giving up control, in that the House of Dior continued to run the company.

The advantage for Dior was that he could exploit the pulling power of the Dior label while using the powerful American fashion system. Its tight infrastructure was designed to reach some two hundred million consumers and was backed up, for example, by the magazines, which gave lavish and useful advice on how to wear each new fashion, including the New Look. Parisian couturiers found this "collusion" quite outrageous and were known to protest vigorously, especially when the collections came out. In 1956 Givenchy and Balenciaga actually banned journalists from their fashion shows on the grounds that they exercised undue influence over the buyers.

Above all, however, Dior's direct creative link with his market, which gave him the ability to adapt to the tastes and needs of American women, also allowed him to defend couture's integrity and prestige in the face of the greatest scourge, Seventh Avenue's uncanny ability to lift and rework designs. A Balenciaga coat bought in Paris, for example, could reappear in New York — in two different versions, one for day wear and another in shantung for the evening. The collar might be altered, lifted from a Fath design perhaps, while the sleeves might be pure Dessès. . . . The result was not necessarily an abomination! *Women's Wear Daily* commented on the way in which Dior was able to maintain the integrity of the "Parisian touch" by keeping a close eye on any attempts to copy his designs, down to choosing the fabrics that could be used or, at least, demanding the right to approve any alternatives chosen. His supremely chic fashion shows, where the models used the brisk pace and haughty stare of the Parisian catwalk, added the pedigree touch, the refinement of the Dior label. Once the system had been road tested to the satisfaction of Paris headquarters, it was ready to be used as a model all over the globe. Jacques Rouët, the Dior globetrotter, was then able to sign licensing agreements in other countries, like England, where Dior London opened in 1952.

It seemed highly unlikely that British women would be even remotely interested in the New Look. They had never been particularly bothered by the vagaries of fashion in peacetime. Not that they were not elegant, original, or indeed highly individual in their attire — and certainly a lack of interest in fashion should not be confused with a lack of style. A perfect excuse for their attitude was the "utility wear" of the war years, which had imposed a virtual uniform on Englishwomen and also served, at least temporarily, to mask any of the class distinctions attached to the way women dressed. Above all, though, England was so drained by its war effort, the fiercely cold weather, and ongoing power cuts and coal shortages that the last thing on anyone's mind was a New Look. The only mentions of it came in the women's magazines, and then only in the harshest, most critical terms. "Paris forgets this is 1947," wrote Marjorie Becket in *Picture Post,* going on to describe the latest fashion as a pure scandal. Imagine an evening gown costing two hundred fifty pounds in a country with two million people out of work and clothing purchases limited by a newly introduced coupon system. In addition to the restrictions, there was the very male attitude of ministers and senior civil servants like Sir Stafford Cripps, head of the Board of Trade, who roared, "What New Look?" when urged by fashion journalist Alison Settle to consider lifting fabric quotas. "Out of the question!" was the emphatic response from the future Chancellor of the Exchequer. Prospects for the New Look seemed grim. But a hearty combination of courage, humor, and ingenuity assured something of a Cinderella ending to the tale.

No one is quite sure how, but that year the Dereta fashion house managed to find some fabric on top of the existing quotas and turned out seven hundred New Look suits. They sold out in just two weeks. While mothers balked at using twenty yards of material for a New Look dress instead of the usual three needed for a conventional outfit, their daughters were determined to see this new fashion take off, come what may. King George VI remained adamant that his daughters Elizabeth and Margaret abide by the restrictions, but the court couturier, Captain Edward Molyneux, managed to take a coat of Princess Margaret's and create a New Look garment by inserting a series of black velvet bands. It was a clever way of overcoming the lack of resources and following the fashion of the day.

Here too Dior was lucky. The future queen and her sister were captivated by the New Look dresses, which they saw as something straight out of an old master like Gainsborough or Velásquez. In the autumn of 1947, while Dior was in London showing his collection at the Savoy, he was most astonished to receive a message from the French embassy passing on a very special request: the Queen Mother would like a private showing. Dresses and models were bundled out of the hotel as unobtrusively as possible, through the service door, and taken to the home of Madame Massagli, the French ambassador's wife, where the Queen Mother, Princess Margaret, the Duchess of Kent, and her sister Princess Olga of Yugoslavia were all seated in anticipation of the clandestine fashion show. It would be quite another story in 1951, four years later, when Dior openly designed Princess Margaret's ball gown for her twenty-first birthday party — elevating the New Look to the status of "By Appointment to the Queen."

The rest of England had to wait until 1948 before Dior-inspired garments appeared in the shops. It was all too clear that this was more than just a matter of hemlines. It entailed the complete transformation of the female figure. A collective initiation into the new lines came courtesy of a fashion show organized by the John Lewis department store. The author Diana de Marly quotes the John Lewis *House Gazette*'s report on the event and its presenter: "Miss Rowland, smiling more than ever, held up an enchanting little corset, pink satin and lace, which she assured us must be faced by all as the necessary foundation for the smart figure. This little garment was then girded on to a slim model with such vigor that the blood rushed to her face, while Miss Rowland exhorted her to greater efforts. 'Pull yourself *in* a little, dear' and we all held our breaths in sympathy."

It was not until 1952 that Dior finally opened his London house in a delightful town house in Mayfair. In keeping with the system already in place in New York, two collections were designed there each year and Christian Dior–London soon had fifty-five sales outlets across Britain.

Jacques Rouët, meanwhile, was tying up licensing deals with department stores or specialty boutiques in Mexico, Cuba, Chile, and Canada. The Cuban outlet, El Encanto, was the most luxurious in Latin America, boasting its own Dior salon, a perfect replica of Avenue Montaigne. In Canada a partnership was set up with the Holt Renfrew company and its seven stores. Holt Renfrew president Alvin J. Walker was a diehard Dior convert. Such was the pace of expansion, however, that it soon became impossible for Dior to attend the launching of his label in each new country — there were not enough days in the year!

On the other hand, it was decided in 1952 that the New York atelier would have to be closed. Dior could not keep up with the schedule of two visits a year, and the whole exercise was proving far too costly, both in travel and accommodation (Dior was in the habit of staying at the Pierre with his whole team). In just a few years, the New York house had increased its agencies from 160 to 250, with Mrs. Engel acting in the same capacity on the local market as Jacques Rouët worldwide. Still it failed to make a profit and Henri Fayol was forced to step in and ask Rouët to find a solution. In the end it was decided that the design and preparation of the collections would be brought back to

Paris. The finished dresses would then be sent to New York. An entire studio at Avenue Montaigne was thus devoted to the American market, under the supervision of Marguerite Carré, who was also responsible for monitoring the standard of garments made under license in the States. Dior's four New York models, Mary, Marjorie, Maple, and Marcia (Dior had given them all names beginning with his lucky letter, M) were brought to Paris to be fitted for the gowns. "The Dior girl is generally sleek, suave, sophisticated and often beautiful," wrote *Women's Wear Daily,* "though not necessarily so. . . . The very fact that some of the best suffer the limitations of 'ordinary women' . . . shoulders a bit too broad, legs a bit thick, [reminds] the retail buyer [that] Dior clothes are *not* designed exclusively for the perfect figure. And naturally, there are many more customers with imperfect [than] with ideal figures. Particularly in the income brackets able to afford Dior clothes."

At this point Jacques Rouët came up with an idea that was to prove highly successful. He suggested selling Dior patterns, to give buyers exclusive reproduction rights. The practice already existed to a certain extent but Rouët argued it should be extended across the board. Given the fact that Dior's ideas were being copied anyway, no matter how hard the House tried to stop it, why not make a little money by selling what could loosely be called "rights of interpretation"? All buyers attending the collections at Avenue Montaigne paid a deposit of 60,000 francs, to be applied to their first purchase. Patterns were made available in two ways. A *toile* included details of the original fabric, buttons, and other trims, plus the address of an agent to guide the buyer. The finished product was then entitled to display the Dior label, so that an American client ordering a dress from, say, Bendel would find "Christian Dior" in large letters on the label and "Bendel" smaller. For the less "top of the line" designs, a simple paper pattern was provided and the manufacturer was then free to choose his own fabric and colors. All designs were protected by French copyright, while every model garment to leave Dior in Paris was numbered and registered against a corresponding description, and the name of the client. The list was then supplied to Customs to coincide with the departure of the haute couture jet that flew off once a season to New York, full of dresses and patterns!

*   *   *

Despite such precautions, the House of Dior was still unable to thwart the pirates. Try as it might to regulate its agents and step up measures to protect its label and clients from forgeries, it never could keep pace with cunning tricks like stolen labels and "model renter" scams. For Dior, there was nothing more repellent than fraud and he became quite enraged at such behavior. Many was the occasion when a gatecrasher or woman with a sketch pad was bodily removed from the collections. Unlike Chanel, who considered it a form of flattery, saying, "Fashion is made to be copied," Dior likened copying to theft. "During one press showing," he writes, "one of our workroom heads, who was watching . . . through the curtain to gauge reactions, came to alert me to the presence of a couture dressmaker in the room. As each dress appeared, she would quickly sketch it in a little notebook. I was so incensed that I left the dressing room and marched over to her, took her by the wrist, and led her to the stairs. I then came back into the salon where, in front of everybody in the room, I tore up both her invitation (no doubt fraudulently obtained) and her sketches. I felt quite pale. Perhaps I was a little hasty but copying deserves rough treatment."

While Dior had hoped to conduct business on the same footing as the Americans, and abide by their rules, he felt nothing but frustration with this aspect of their fashion industry. "Like all respectable American houses, I was convinced that the system not only authorized but actually encouraged stealing the artistic creations of others. There seemed to be no effective way of stopping it." It was a major blow to his enthusiastic vision of the land of free enterprise! His memoirs also relate his encounter with the Antitrust Commission, which summoned him one morning to explain his buyers' exclusivity contracts. While he accepted the episode with good humor, making fun of such excesses of bureaucratic zeal, he did not mince his words when it came to criticizing America's lack of fair play and what he saw as commercial hypocrisy. While it gave with one hand, via the Marshall Plan, America imposed what Dior termed "almost prohibitive customs duties from a supposed champion of commercial freedom but which ultimately benefited only America, with all the selfishness of a child who will only play if he is allowed to win."

Notwithstanding such gripes, his label was everywhere. In its first five years, half of Dior's turnover came from the New World, clearly a springboard for what followed. On October 28, 1948, he launched Christian Dior Perfumes in New York, also based at 730 Fifth Avenue. In 1949 he signed his first licensing deal for hosiery manufacture with Julius Kayser and Co. under the name Christian Dior Stockings and launched the "Diorama" fragrance. In 1950 a deal with Stern, Merritt and Co. underwrote Christian Dior Ties and Cravats. There followed Christian Dior Fur Inc. and a special Christian Dior Diffusion department, the coordinating body for all wholesale, export, and licensing deals. Christian Dior Export was also set up in New York to look after hats, gloves, handbags, jewelry, and ties. There were contracts with Mexico's Palacio de Hiero for the exclusive reproduction of made-to-measure and ready-to-wear designs. There were even licensing deals with Australia. In 1951 the Christian Dior Export Corp., Christian Dior Fur, and Christian Dior Stockings Paris were established in Canada and Cuba. Then in 1952 came Christian Dior Models Ltd. in London, followed by a hosiery licensing deal. Italy followed in 1953 . . . and so it went, every year seeing another Dior flag planted at some new point on the globe.

The Americans could not get over it. Here they were, the epitome of economic progress, the business management experts par excellence who sponsored study missions under the Marshall Plan to teach the less fortunate their methods, and this little French company was showing them all. Elsewhere in the States, too, French garment manufacture was taking off. One Albert Lempereur came up with the concept of prêt-à-porter — ready-to-wear — essentially as a means for the haute couture industry, which clothed only 25 percent of Frenchwomen, to find new outlets in the American manufacturing sector. While on the one hand the French clothing industry was taking inspiration from American work practices, Christian Dior beat Seventh Avenue hands down when it came to quality and expertise. He was the subject of long articles in the trade papers, in particular a series of stories analyzing his success in *Women's Wear Daily* (July 13 to 20, 1953, under the headline "The Dior Story"). In 1957, he was consecrated on the cover of *Time*. The consensus was that the House of Dior was in a class of its own. Some industry professionals, like Ginette Hallot Steinman, a buyer for I. Magnin in Canada, talk in particular of their amazement at the quality of workmanship in each garment. "Looking inside a dress was a revelation. I used to tell the girls in my workroom to press them with love, that these were dresses that had to be looked after and that every last detail in them had been carefully planned." Eleonor Graham, a designer with Canada's Holt Renfrew chain, remembers how generous Avenue Montaigne proved to be in imparting information about the profession. Norman Chosler, another I. Magnin buyer, in this case for San Francisco, also valued the closeness of Dior's collaborative efforts and the way in which Dior assisted the department stores to fulfill their chosen goal of "inculcating in our clientele dedication to quality." This was not a battle to be won in a day. Jacques Rouët worked like a Trojan in the course of his long and repetitive trips around the world to establish and then control Dior's enormous distribution empire. Dior too was constantly on the lookout whenever he traveled, as evidenced in his letters to his right-hand man. In November 1948, for example, he told Rouët, "When you ask the price of something, it takes a while to get a response. I cannot help stressing to you that our business does not solely consist in making dresses. When things are quiet and we find ourselves working hard to keep our clients, we must never feel that at any stage we treated any of them too casually."

It was no mean feat for a Frenchman to succeed in the United States by demonstrating the sort of qualities not typically associated with the French national character — things like modesty, strict professional standards, and an emphasis on quality above all else. What most intrigued the Americans about the whole business, however, was Christian Dior himself. He taught them that fashion can also be a game.

The archetypal fashion designer in America's eyes was Jacques Fath. He arrived triumphant, handsome, suntanned, and so sure of himself that no one was allowed to applaud at the end of his fashion shows until he himself stood up to receive his due. The average American, who felt gauche at the best of times in matters of taste and style, found this most intimidating, and for this very reason imported fashion was often considered quite daunting. Dior was quite the opposite — and won them over completely. To cite Andrew Goodman of Bergdorf Goodman, Dior was "detached, down to earth, and committed" but also "ultra retiring, quiet, restrained, and introverted." At the same time, he had the admirable ability of rising to any occasion and milking it for all it was worth. For those in the industry, it was important to capitalize on the concept of the "latest fashion" with the seasonal appearance of new collections. Dior gave them an additional hook with which to catch public attention — the "suspense" of waiting to see just where hemlines would be. It had worked with the New Look, getting the feminists' backs up in the process, and in a land where commercialism comes naturally, this sort of "tease" would go on working. The strategy fooled no one but it kept them coming! As each new season approached, the suspense would mount as America awaited the dictator's latest edict. Hems up or down? As Andrew Goodman put it, it was "a publicity gimmick so that the press around the world would have something to talk about." To an English fashion journalist who appeared to be taking the whole question very seriously, he retorted, "This is ridiculous. I am sure a creative genius like Dior does not have to depend on moving a hemline down or up one inch." After all, he added, all a woman would have to do is tip a couple of glasses of champagne down her dress after a good lunch and her hemline would go up a couple of inches all by itself!

When you are on to a good thing, you should stick to it. When Dior took skirts way up again, in 1953, he unleashed a furor reminiscent of 1947 and its skirmishes in the streets. This time he had a few followers, however, including a whole troupe of Hollywood stars vowing never to hide their legs again. (Dior's fashion constantly made waves in the film industry, causing producers to agonize over their actresses' outfits, "fearing half-finished mid-calf pictures might have an outmoded look," as *Newsweek* put it.) Once again, the battle lines were drawn, with the opponents of this latest change united in their call for a boycott. It was front-page news again, too, with headlines like "The Great Hemline Hullabaloo" and "The Battle of the Bare Calf." "Will the ladies obey Mr. Dior?" asked the *Saturday Evening Post* of October 17, 1953, indignantly. "Christian Dior, tyrant of the hemlines, decrees short skirts for American women. Can he bend the female will to his will again?"

There is no rest for the wicked in the fashion world. By fall of the very next year, all bets were off once again when Dior brought out his H line. Baptized the Flat Look by Carmel Snow, it did just that — flattened the bust. America was all up in arms again. The cover of *Life* announced, "Flat Versus Buxom Look in Paris" (September 6, 1954), going on to say, "Even disinterested observers joined in the storm of protest against what sounded like a supremely un-American attempt to eliminate the female bosom and bring back the shapeless flapper mold of the Twenties." Others adopted more threatening tones: "Dior's Flat Proposals Likely to Estrange Bosom Friends" and "Dior Will Never Crush US Womanhood" and "Film Beauties Fit to Bust at Dior Deflation Policy."

Dior pleaded not guilty. "I wanted to get rid of corsets. How many times have I heard men complain that, while dancing, they were not able to feel the living body of women under the yoke which imprisoned them." (*Time,* August 10, 1953.) But this time he had gone too far! The American public rose up with one none-too-diplomatic voice. In *Time* (August 9, 1954) a particularly buxom TV starlet named Dagmar stated, "Frankly, honey, the instrument hasn't been made that can flatten me out." Marlon Brando, who had already made known his opposition to the New Look with the words "Emphasizing women's hips is like putting falsies on a cow!" said this time, "Any girl who goes for this flat look should have her chest examined."

Dior, on the other hand, did his best to avoid the publicity spotlight. Not only because, as Suzanne Luling put it, "Christian put all his Norman care into fencing off a little corner of his private life. It was quite a coup to get him to attend a lunch or a dinner." He was like a blushing snail backing madly into his shell when forced to face an interview, let alone the CBS cameras in a special report on him in 1955 in which he comes across as awkward and highly nervous. To circumvent this intolerable grilling, he put on an act just as he had that very first time in Dallas, replying to such questions as "What will women be wearing this year?" with entertaining answers like "This year women will be wearing their thighs on their shoulders." (His "chicken thigh" cut for sleeves left them wide at the top and narrow at the elbow.) He would rather amuse them than bore them. "A joke always works best," he maintained.

His public relations department had a hard time of it. Suzanne Luling never quite knew how to soften him up. Arranging an interview was either a marathon, a steeplechase, or a game of chance with often unexpected results.

Luling recalls trying to accommodate a group of Brazilian journalists who had turned up at Avenue Montaigne. Summoning her courage, she proceeded up the stairs to Dior's studio, turning over in her mind all the possible arguments she could use to persuade the master of the house to talk to them — Latin politeness, the French influence, etc. etc. The reply was direct. "All right, but as long as we do it in Portuguese." Once again, this was Dior drawing attention to something other than himself.

A correspondent from *Fortune* had the even more disconcerting experience of not only being granted an interview but being summoned to Dior's own home to conduct it. Imagine his consternation when he was received in the bathroom, with Dior in the tub, stark naked. He was even allowed a photo — a coy one, naturally. Dior loved practical jokes of that nature and used the bath tactic more than once. During a very long and dull reception in Cincinnati, when assailed by a posse of admiring fans, he was asked where he got the inspiration for his designs. "In my bath, madam," he replied. "In my bath."

The public response to Dior was overwhelming, record-breaking in fact. Never had a couturier been so popular. Ever since Walter Winchell's 1948 radio proclamation "Flash! The romance of the year is between Carmel Snow of *Harper's Bazaar* and Christian Dior" (which earned Snow a dozen American Beauty roses with a card inscribed "To my 'fiancée.' Tian."), the U.S. press had its own love affair with Dior. His New York office counted his name between twelve hundred and fourteen hundred times a month, in the American press alone.

It was a name that sparked similar reactions the world over. José Llopis Lamela, who was in charge of launching Dior in Caracas before going on to head Dior Perfumes, remembers the extraordinary success of the House of Dior when it opened in Venezuela in 1953. "Dior arrived amid the popping of flashbulbs and a fifteen-minute standing ovation. It was clearly a great moment for him."

Each time the Dior collection visited a new country the couturier named one of his dresses for it, in a gesture designed to acknowledge the hospitality accorded such a powerful guest. One day, however, schedules were so tight that no one remembered to change the name of the dress christened "Havana" in the Cuban collection to "Santo Domingo" for the next port of call. Relations between Cuba and the

Dominican Republic happened to be at an all-time low, and when the gown appeared, all eyes turned embarrassedly to Dominican President Rafael Trujillo y Molina and his wife, who were in the audience at the Hotel Jurugua. For a second, everyone thought he would get up and leave. Fortunately, however, a diplomatic incident was averted and an apologetic telegram was hastily sent to repair any lasting damage.

"Dior is a great publicist, a kind of King Barnum of fashion," wrote *Time* in a cover article on the couturier. He certainly stirred them up. In far-off Paris, colleagues like Balenciaga guarded their establishments like a holy shrine and frowned upon all this fuss. Perhaps it was time, though, to bring fashion down from its ivory tower and adapt its aesthetics to the needs of the modern world. Silent till now, the rest of the profession began reacting to this bold and intrepid knight.

11

A Wealth of Treasures

> Christian Dior . . . was a son of the land
> of King François I, the country that built
> Versailles, a place where genius goes
> hand in hand with harmony and
> rigor. . . . He is the product of twenty
> centuries of cheerful culture, clever
> craftsmanship, and restraint.
>
> — Françoise Giroud

*I*t was an electric blue New York morning and Christian Dior was
walking down Fifth Avenue with Jacques Rouët. They drew level with
54th Street and turned in toward B. Altman. Christian Dior ties were
selling well here, under a contractual arrangement of which Jacques
Rouët was justifiably proud, whereby Dior was allocated its own
exclusive area in the store, with four counters. Negotiating the deal
had been no mean feat. Rouët had been forced to relinquish some
aspects of creative control in exchange for a couple of particularly
favorable clauses and, in fact, Altman's actually designed their Dior

ties themselves. There had been a point at which Jacques Rouët had expressed his doubts about some of the patterns, including a gray spotted tie he considered ordinary, to say the least. The licensee had begged him not to veto it, using the powerful argument that it happened to be very popular with President Eisenhower, who ordered that particular tie regularly!

Jacques Rouët had not been down that way for a while and decided to drop in. "Come and I'll show you some of our ties," he told Dior.

"If I see our ties," replied Dior, "I am afraid I might hate them. Then I would have to make you break the contract!"

Rouët was certainly used to unpredictable reactions from the couturier but was a little taken aback all the same. At times Dior behaved like an artist, at others like a businessman. And although he was indeed both, the two aspects of his character did not always jibe. Rouët knew it was best not to insist. He would drop in at B. Altman some other day, alone. In the meantime, he had just the way to lift Dior's spirits. There was one thing the pair had in common over which there was never any argument, and which gave them great enjoyment, and that was good food. (Jacques Rouët's dream was to become a member of the prestigious gastronomic fraternity Le Club des Cent, and he had already put down some promising wines in his cellar.) "Why don't we go and have lunch at La Côte Basque?" he suggested. "My dear Jacques," came the reply, "let's go this instant!"

Jacques Rouët was full of admiration for Dior and considered he had learned a great deal from him. There was a little piece of paper he was never without — he carried it about with him in his wallet — on which he had copied a few sentences from a letter Dior had written him on September 17, 1946: "I don't think I would have had the fortitude to run this couture house on my own. And the future of the house will be the result of our work together. Let's hope we succeed. . . . You, Raymonde, and Suzanne form a trio upon whom I rely more than anyone else." Dior might have been *le patron* but he knew how to give credit where it was due. He showed the same sense of respect and gratitude toward those who worked for him as he had for the artists and other talented people who surrounded him in his youth, and was particularly indebted to Rouët, to whom he dedicated the following lines in his memoirs. "His native Norman finesse helped him to avoid the charming yet cunning traps inevitably laid for him by our delightful '*chéries.*' . . ."

Who are these "chéries"? Almost everyone, from the seamstresses to the models, from the sales ladies to the journalists, and even the clients at times. The word was short for the entire realm of couture with its charming perversities: all smiles and sweetness on the outside, covering up for the petty jealousies, intrigues, and nervous fits that are its daily fare. These sweet and sour feminine epithets have always been part of the language of haute couture. And if the word betrayed Christian Dior's homosexuality, it would never have been heard in the mouth of Jacques Rouët. The lieutenant's job was to keep order in the house and be tough when necessary with the female population. It was certainly not unusual to see women leave his office in tears. And just because you were with Dior did not mean your wages were higher than elsewhere. With all the arrogance of those who know they are on the winning side, Dior and Rouët made it perfectly clear that if you were not happy, there were ten people waiting to take your place. "They needed Rouët to be tough," said Llopis Lamela, who set up Christian Dior in Caracas.

Although deeply and genuinely attached to his employees, Dior knew how to deal with human nature. With a timid and anxious temperament, he had spent a lifetime watching others, and now that he was in a position of power, he demonstrated his natural talents as a "manager of human resources." Imperious at times, firm in his commands, he took pleasure in using his keen psychological sense to maneuver people, and he could even be disarmingly direct about it. Rouët has no shortage of stories about his employer's idiosyncrasies — not least his fixation on astrology and clairvoyants — but of all the memorable moments, one stands out above the rest.

It was their first meeting. Christian Dior was considering hiring him and had asked him to come by Avenue Montaigne. It was June 1946 and the lease had only just been signed. The town house was strangely silent, a little like Sleeping Beauty's enchanted wood, plunged in semidarkness, its rooms empty with an air of subtle neglect. Dior took him by the arm and led him toward a suitable sofa corner on which to perch. "He then began telling me what he expected of me," Rouët relates. " 'Let me be frank with you,' he said, 'first and foremost, I want a manager who has never worked in couture. Secondly, since I am experienced in the field, I must always be made to look good. You will be my right-hand man, but whenever there are difficult decisions to be made, you will be seen as the one who has made them. Of course I will support you, as we will decide things together. But no one is to know that and you will find there are moments when you will have to take the blame.' " Rouët did not mind playing the cop, and that may have been the quality that Dior spotted immediately.

Suzanne Luling was already on board at the time and remembers the day he came for his first meeting with Dior. His looks and appearance were such that she would not have given him the slightest chance to get the job. "He had such an awkward way about him. And the poor fellow was wearing a suit he had dyed black especially, a hand-knitted jumper his mother had made for him, and dyed yellow shoes!" But Christian Dior was never one to judge a book by its cover. He realized instinctively that there was potential in this dark-haired beanpole of a fellow, barely thirty years old at the time, all got up in a hat that made him look like a police sergeant (over the years he gradually became a little snappier in his dress). Rouët was the son of a court officer, and the strange reason that led him to seek a career in the fashion industry was in fact the war. As a civil servant, he had spent the war years as an employee of the collaborationist Vichy administration. After the Liberation, like many other people who needed to protect themselves against an "anti-collaborationist purge," he undertook to find a position in the private sector and was introduced to Dior by Boussac. As it happened, the Boussac group was looking for a competent fellow to assist Dior in managing his new enterprise. Given Rouët's lack of relevant experience, it was decided to put him to the test by asking him to price the renovation work to be carried out at Avenue Montaigne. When he managed to come up with tenders that were 30 percent cheaper than the original calculations, the job was his.

Dior's intuition did the rest. Jacques Rouët did, of course, possess one essential attribute: he too was from Normandy! The relationship between them was a harmonious one: "In all our ten years together," Jacques Rouët says, "Dior never undermined me in my managerial role." Dior saw to the big picture, the development of the French concept of taste and elegance into a commercial business. Rouët was the one who not only ran the organization daily but traveled tirelessly to take the Dior label to the four corners of the globe. Their collaboration developed into mutual affection. "Your letters give me great pleasure," Dior once wrote to him, "but please do not adopt too respectful a tone. It irks me to think that I might not enjoy your affection. Let me however reassure you of mine."

It almost seemed Christian Dior's natural flair for comedy had a hand in the often bizarre role reversals that came about over those years. The prime example was the relationship between Dior and Boussac. King Cotton was the one who clung to the traditional notion of a high-class fashion house with an exclusive clientele while the designer seemed bent on exploiting his name to the maximum. Similar contradictions emerged between Boussac and Henri Fayol. Fayol, who had been hired to restructure the management of the textile group, ended up diversifying operations (unbeknownst to his employer) to such an extent that, when the Boussac empire collapsed twenty years later, the fashion house was the only business left standing. The fairy tale ending, however, belongs to Jacques Rouët, the hero who finally got his reward. He might have been a bailiff's son in an ill-fitting suit, but after his employer's death he took over the reins and continued Dior's work for a further thirty years.

Waxing lyrical at the memory of those early days together, Rouët sums it up. "They were extraordinary years. Just think. We were the first everywhere we went and everything we turned a hand to was a success!"

Such glowing words had his competitors frowning. They were used to managing businesses handed down from father to son without the slightest change. They could accept Dior opening a house in New York, given all the obstacles such a move would present. But the licensing deals they found most disturbing. Dior and Rouët were stirring things up in a profession that clung to tradition with the same fervor as a believer clings to religious dogma.

As mentioned earlier, even before the House of Dior opened its doors Christian Dior accepted an offer worth around ten thousand dollars from the New York hosiery manufacturers Prestige for the right to use the Christian Dior name. When the contract came up for renewal, Dior decided a flat fee was no longer desirable, and that instead the licensee should pay a percentage of its turnover to Dior as owner of the name and label. Jacques Rouët then entered into discussions with Julius Kayser & Co., and in 1949 the first Christian Dior hose appeared on the American market. Dior demanded a direct say in quality control, even designing a special reinforced foot so that it did not twist. The stockings were elegantly presented in layers of tissue paper inside pretty gray boxes, with a Louis XVI seal and the name Christian Dior printed on the tops. After all, they were competing with Schiaparelli's shocking pink boxes, which really set the tone when they were released in New York in 1940.

An American textile manufacturer by the name of Benjamin Theise had been equally fast on his feet, turning up at Avenue Montaigne even before the renovations were completed to secure the Dior name for his silk ties. Unprecedented though such a concept was, Dior agreed to allow Rouët to negotiate with Theise, who then introduced him to his biggest client, Mr. Lou Mansfield of Stern, Merritt. A deal was done and two historic contracts were signed, the first of many hundreds to come. Jacques Rouët had found his niche . . . and he was off. The flood of prospective deals that followed did cause Dior a little soul-searching, but Rouët soon found a way to overcome his scruples. As the sole statutory director of Christian Dior Ltd., Dior's chief concern was turnover (he would get a third of the profits, prior to tax and depreciation). When the first licensing deal was proposed, Rouët pointed out that revenue earned in this way would not accrue to Christian Dior Ltd. A new contract would have to be drawn up between Dior and Boussac which enabled Rouët to ensure all monies earned through licensing deals came directly to Dior, who took royalties of 30 to 40 percent.

Once the ball was rolling other licenses followed, for lingerie, scarves, gloves. Distribution manager Hervé du Périer de Larsan recalls how Dior monitored the whole process. He was "keen to see it turn into a major enterprise. He weighed up each new product carefully before deciding whether to go ahead." A proposed agreement with the French firm Scandale to manufacture brassieres caused Dior some embarrassment at the thought of combining his name with the word "brassiere." After considerable deliberation he came up with a suitable alternative for the new product line: Gaines et Gorges Dior — Dior Foundations. Next to come was hosiery. Manufactured by Grimonprez, a subsidiary of the Masurel group, Dior stockings took a couturier's name for the very first time into a French department store — the well-known Galeries Lafayette.

Clearly all this was to be the subject of great professional jealousy. As Didier Grumbach relates, "His colleagues followed the 'deployment' of his label with caution, uncertain just how they should react. In 1952, however, when Jacques Rouët signed a licensing deal with a German firm in Pforzheim for the production of costume jewelry, it was considered the last straw and open hostilities broke out. In the middle of a meeting of the Chamber of Couture, its president Jean Gaumont-Lanvin accused Rouët of being 'nothing but a bumblebee upsetting a very hardworking hive.' "

A united front was formed to counter Dior. While the press seized on the controversy, public authorities swung into action to have the German contract revoked. "How can these great couturiers fail to realize that by exploiting the prestige of their name in such a way they are flying in the face of tradition and sounding the death knell of a craft that is centuries old?" asked columnist Lucien François. "It won't take long," he predicted, "before haute couture clients will turn their backs on houses whose name has thus been devalued and which no longer hold any international clout." The minister for industry even summoned Jacques Rouët to tell him that the House of Dior would have to cancel the contract rather than allow the Dior name to fall into German hands.

To the House of Dior, however, even the guaranteed minimum sales promised under the Pforzheim contract were worth twice the existing earnings for export sales of French jewelry to Germany. It was a case worth fighting! Well schooled in the bureaucracy from which he himself had come, Jacques Rouët refused to be intimidated by the dictates of the industry minister and immediately set about playing one minister off against another. He requested an interview at the ministry of finance, where he was received by two departmental staff members by the names of Valéry Giscard d'Estaing (future president of France) and Michel Poniatowski [later a senior government minister]. Being slightly more "free market" in their views, they promised Rouët the minister's support.

There was no shortage of other couturiers keen to jump on the bandwagon. Jacques Fath, for one, had no hesitation in openly acknowledging that "his real success began with Christian Dior." Moreover, as fashion historian Didier Grumbach relates, Fath's manager Henri Winter "once confessed to Jacques Rouët that for every licensing deal Dior signed, Fath would immediately be offered an equivalent contract from a rival licensee." Once a year Fath would go to New York armed with a few sketches, which were then adapted to his licensee's needs, and the sixty gowns subsequently produced would carry the label "Jacques Fath for Joseph Halpert." With the money he earned through couture he went on to launch his own line of fragrances in 1948, and a year before his death, in 1953, he established the Jacques Fath "Université" label — an early model, in its revolutionary new approach to production, for André Courrèges, who created a series of inexpensive ready-to-wear lines in the 1960s and 1970s.

Dior was the spark that set the whole profession ablaze. The New Look had already launched a new golden age for Parisian couture; and designers like Fath and Lanvin were employing between 1,000 and 2,500 people. Five hundred copies were sold of one single design, Jean Patou's "Joy," and shoe designers, bootmakers, milliners, feather workers, embroiderers, and other vendors of fancy goods also felt the impact. It was the start of a brand new era and Dior was the driving force behind the up-and-coming generation. The old guard, meanwhile, had disappeared with the war: Lelong had closed down, followed by Molyneux, the English designer who worked out of Paris; the spectacular Elsa Schiaparelli had departed to conquer America; Robert Piguet's pink Napoleon III salons had fallen silent, and Marcel Rochas passed away, leaving an ailing business to his wife, the beautiful Hélène. She went on to make her husband's name famous by successfully attaching her poetically evocative image to fragrances like "Madame Rochas."

Pierre Cardin, who worked for Dior for a time before a rather abrupt departure, credits his former employer with the knack of opening up new horizons and inspiring others to ambitious plans of their own. Although long since forgotten, there was one particular incident that prompted Cardin's resignation from Dior in 1948. The House had become aware that someone was leaking information to copyists and had gone to the police. In the course of his inquiries, the investigating magistrate called Cardin, along with many others, in for questioning. His manner was clumsy and Cardin, furious at being considered a suspect, took umbrage and left. Dior was in the United States at the time and was unable to intervene. On his return he was most distressed to learn of Cardin's departure and, determined to make it up to him, was the first to walk through the doors of Cardin's next enterprise, a theatrical costumer's establishment. When Dior rang the doorbell at the workroom on Rue Richepanse with the intention of commissioning a costume, Cardin greeted his former employer with tears in his eyes. His first client ordered a King of Beasts outfit for Count Etienne de Beaumont's "Kings and Queens Ball."

One lesson Cardin certainly learned from Dior was not to hold back — and everyone knows what that led to. Cardin's creative genius has succeeded in transforming his name into a potent symbol. He early realized that his signature was more important than the painting. By merchandising it on everything, from socks to sinks, he has certainly become the richest designer in the world and perhaps the worst.

The powers of the licensing deal have since become an entrenched addiction for all the big fashion names. With his taste for taking risks, Christian Dior would certainly have been the first to get hooked, if it had not been for Jacques Rouët's restraint. One day Dior's managing director was called in to be asked whether he had registered the Dior trademark for food products as well. Rouët was at a loss to know how to respond. "I've been thinking about this a lot," Dior continued. "After all, fashion . . . well, one day you're a hit, the next they shoot you down in flames. And you know I am really interested in anything to do with food. I know lots of recipes and, who knows, one day I might need something to fall back on. We could do a Dior ham . . . or a Dior roast beef, perhaps?"

Rouët was reluctant to pursue this rather risky idea but the House of Dior did register a wines and spirits trademark on March 12, 1956. It was allowed to lapse in 1962. A book of Dior's recipes called *La Cuisine cousu main* (*Hand-stitched Cuisine*) was published by Jacques

Rouët in 1972, with illustrations by René Gruau — evidence of Dior's interest in the pleasures of the table.

Although the House of Christian Dior made healthy increases in turnover, it was never as good a money-maker as Dior Perfumes. The latter produced a profit margin of around 30 percent while the House of Dior only made about 15 percent. That figure then had to be reduced by 30 percent for Dior's personal share. Nor were the various licenses the universal cure-all. Of the average 4 percent paid to Dior in royalties, 1 percent was lost in administration, leaving a profit margin of a mere 3 percent. Serge Heftler-Louiche's fragrances, on the other hand — "Miss Dior" followed by "Diorama" — were distributed in eighty-six countries.

Dior was anxious for success. As his distribution manager Hervé du Périer de Larsan testifies, "Dior loved paradox and was no doubt amused by the situation vis-à-vis Boussac. He was well aware that Boussac was not interested in developing the Dior name, which made him all the more determined to launch something innovative. He also had a very clear vision of what he hoped to achieve. 'We set a lot of store by this licensing business,' he told me, 'because we know we are dealing with very short-term markets and we want to build up the label. We will start small but we intend reaching a stage where a considerable proportion of our overall revenue comes from licenses.' "

Like all pioneers, Dior had to suffer his share of setbacks, and quite a few mistakes were made before the House of Dior hit pay dirt. The aim, of course, was to make good taste accessible to the widest market possible. But Dior found the slow and sometimes uncertain progress of his empire frustrating. Hervé du Périer continues his account. "Dior Hosiery was launched in a very sudden and highly complex way. It was actually flying in the face of conventional wisdom to start with the wide distribution of a product without backing it up with a strong design element. And Dior only wanted to use top sales outlets like regional couture houses, which meant we had to make up deliveries of three, maybe a dozen cases at a time. It was a real headache! We made two fundamental errors at once: we had our market wrong and our product wrong.

"I remember a meeting in 1949," du Périer goes on, "at which Dior expressed his disappointment at the poor sales figures. 'But

Monsieur Dior,' I reminded him, 'remember your instructions. You only wanted Dior hosiery in couture houses!' "

The policy for the French market was then revised and the House of Dior became a wholesaler. A hosier in Lille was contracted to manufacture the stockings and they were sold through a series of agents. This meant wider distribution while still remaining selective.

As Jacques Rouët continued his unstoppable ascent, he transformed the House of Dior into a complex creative structure. It was the first time that the French concept of a *griffe,* a label or literally "signature," had formed the basis of a gigantic network — in this case, eight companies and sixteen affiliated firms employing seventeen hundred people over five continents — while retaining tight control over its activities. The development of this giant organization was ad hoc in the extreme. This was at a time when trademarks, standard contracts, product image, and house style were still unheard of in the fashion industry. At issue here was the need to set a standard of quality control that also allowed for a few variables, given the number of sales outlets in each country and the variety of products involved. "Our overriding philosophy," explains Jacques Rouët, "was to spread the French idea of elegance and good taste while being pragmatic about the degree to which standards of living had developed in different parts of the world. Dior was also most determined and he was quite prepared to run the risks this strategy entailed. While he proceeded with utmost caution in France, for example, he understood that a licensee in another, far-off place could not necessarily conform to the same criteria when it came to quality." The whole licensing policy was sustained by these dual concepts of pragmatism and control. "The idea was that the name Dior should signify 'the very best' in the country concerned," says Hervé du Périer. "We were like policemen. We'd even stop production when the quality didn't come up to scratch rather than let something go through."

The task of setting up appropriate structures to manage all this naturally fell to Jacques Rouët, who had to make it up as he went along. In 1950 a licensing department was created alongside the distribution department. To head the new section Rouët appointed Christian Legrez (who went over to Chanel in 1963) with Geoffroy de Seynes as his assistant (later his successor; de Seynes is now with Nina Ricci).

Under the guidance of Jacques Chastel, the head of Christian Dior Paris, Legrez's first task was to draw up a standard contract for all negotiations with outside companies. He also devised a trademark registration procedure aimed at thwarting pirates and plagiarists, and put in place a very tightly constructed system of checks and balances — guaranteed minimum sales, security measures to guard against fraud, promotional conditions, and cost-sharing mechanisms for publicity and advertising. All this was done with the assistance of law firms in both Paris and New York, and everywhere else as well.

There was also a policy on uniformity of image. The House of Dior put out a "house manual" for its retailers covering every aspect of presentation of the Dior name, and codifying house style. Everything emanated from Avenue Montaigne, from the way in which windows were dressed to shop fittings, René Gruau illustrations, Trianon gray, Louis XVI medallions, and the like. Every two years representatives from all over the world were brought together for a series of seminars. Comprehensive financial analyses were also instituted, and from 1958 onward, quarterly figures were presented for every country and every product.

By virtue of such stringency, the Dior name began to take the lead. In 1954, seven years after it was launched, the House of Dior published a brochure — set in the "Nicolas Cochin" font that Dior himself had chosen from the outset as his signature typeface. It was the start of a groundbreaking communications policy that confirmed Dior's place, after its somewhat tentative beginnings, as an established name in the luxury goods industry. The brochure itself was a kind of annual report. It described all the activities of the House of Dior, from the way in which the collections were created down to details of its buildings and employee services. It plotted the expansion of Dior around the world, listing all its sales outlets outside France and featuring graphs showing turnover in each part of the world. There were descriptions of the various commercial sectors, from fragrances to lingerie, and a rundown of the activities of the Dior *griffe* abroad. On the first page was a pencil portrait of Dior by his friend Nora Auric.

The keystone of this great edifice makes no attempt to conceal his pride: "Christian Dior had reached the age of reason," he wrote in *Christian Dior and I.* "It was his seventh birthday. He now occupied five buildings, comprising twenty-eight workrooms and employing more than a thousand people." Dior then takes us on a guided tour of the labyrinth extending across the corner of Avenue Montaigne and Rue François-Ier. He paints a picture of a model employer who loves his employees like a family and for whom his business has finally become his life. With almost childlike pride he guides us through the show-rooms and workrooms, through the ultramodern infirmary (which he himself designed with the architect Chaysson), the models' recreation room, the retirement home at Vaire-le-Grand (the necessity of which he stresses as he passes) and, still leading the reader by the hand, goes back over the glassed-in bridge straddling the administration area and proceeds down to the basement where the staff canteen is housed. There is one canteen only for all one thousand employees, a model of social democracy. Each person pays according to his or her salary level, apprentices paying one twentieth of the amount expected from the upper echelons of management.

"But the best day to visit 30 Avenue Montaigne," Dior concludes, "is Saint Catherine's Day.* I visit every department and give a little speech to each workroom in which I express my sincere and tender affection for all those who have joined their efforts to mine — whatever their part, big or small — to see our endeavors succeed. Something in the welcome I receive on that day, the way the rooms are decorated, the imagination that goes into the costumes and the organization of the event, seems to capture the pulse of the place. There is nothing more moving and yet more joyous than Saint Catherine's Day. There are musicians playing in every workroom and it is one continuous party throughout the building."

In a profession still in the process of inventing itself, there was no simple, no predetermined profile. It was certainly no surprise to find at its head a man with the gift of reading people's minds and a taste for seemingly strange appointments. (One wonders how he was able to see

---

* Saint Catherine is the patron saint of students, philosophers, seamstresses, and all unmarried girls twenty-five and over! Saint Catherine's day is November 25, when it is customary to wear fancy dress.

in Jacques Rouët's square appearance a potential as a roving ambassador for the Dior name.) Dior was a bit of a magician. His own life had been transformed from a tragedy to a fairy tale and yet there was nothing mythical or illusory about it. Life was a carnival. Ever since he was a child he had been convinced of that. Put on a mask and it is easy to let your hair down. Set your sights on a goal and your team will fall in behind you. Dior at the helm was all the motivation needed at Avenue Montaigne.

When Hervé du Périer de Larsan came to see Dior about a commercial position and presented his resumé, Dior exclaimed with delight. "You were a lieutenant with the paratroopers in Indochina? Oh, the women will love that!"

Aged twenty-two, tall, slim, and with a film-star look, du Périer had been forced by the war to abandon his studies in political science and now found himself in an uninspiring position with the Kléber-Colombes concern. Family connections with Jacques Rouët brought him to Dior, where he was put in charge of licensing. His first foray came with ladies' hosiery. It was clearly no coincidence, however, that Dior selected upper crust candidates to promote his label — young men like Hervé du Périer and Geoffroy de Seynes. Even on the commercial side of the business, Dior was partial to aristocratic names. In matters both of etiquette and of affinity, it was only logical that a couture house should be staffed with people possessing the kind of education and refinement extolled by the establishment itself.

Although he now presided over a large concern, he still felt sincere affection for his employees and a sense of responsibility toward them: "Every collection has the wages of nine hundred people riding on it!" he once said. Along with the justifiable pride he felt in his endeavors came the desire to see his workers continue to prosper, and he made a concerted effort to promote the talents he observed around him. The fact that he had spent so long finding his own calling and had experienced such difficulty establishing an outlet for his creative talents no doubt heightened his awareness of others' ability and inspired him to act as a mentor — even a patron. As a result, the House of Dior became a breeding ground for young talent, nurturing and encouraging many a vocation.

It was a long list. There was Victor Grandpierre, who got his big break in interior design from Dior; André Levasseur and Gaston Berthelot, who were appointed as milliners for the boutique collection at the tender age of twenty; Frédéric Castet, who found himself being offered his own workroom at twenty-four and who later took charge of Dior Furs; Jean-Pierre Frère, who was given carte blanche to design "lifestyle" accessories for the boutique; and Jean-François Daigre, who was mad about the theater. Dior gave him his break by allowing him to work a little magic on the window dressing.

"We were totally in awe of Christian Dior," says André Levasseur. "He was the all-powerful one. He made every one of us tremble and we never dared show him anything that was less than perfect. He played on that and found nothing more amusing than to play the grandpa spoiling and teasing his grandchildren, waiting to see how you would react and enjoying having you at his mercy."

This tendency to demand total submission from his subjects, in the tradition of Louis XIV, was particularly prevalent during the weeks leading up to the launch of a collection. Work took on a frenetic pace and the staff never had a minute to themselves, going home only to snatch a few hours' sleep and never thinking to ask for payment for all those extra hours' work. This ascetic existence simply became part of the ritual of haute couture, as did what became known as the "Dior look," a grayish tinge to the complexion that seemed to afflict most Dior women in the run-up to launch day.

Dior might have been an ogre who destroyed his workers' health, but he knew how to reward them. Whenever a dress came out particularly well, he would summon the workroom head: "Was it you, little one, who made this dress?" "Yes, sir," she would reply, blushing from head to toe. "Let me congratulate you," he would continue. "It is very beautiful indeed." And everyone around him would chorus their approval.

The many branches of design in which the House of Dior was now involved provided ample scope for creative talents. Besides the 250 outfits in each collection, there were clothes to be designed for the boutique, another 50 outfits for Paris, 90 for London, and 110 for New York. Then there were all the designs and objects that never even got past the prototype stage. The way the licensing system had been set up meant that the lion's share of ideas had to be channeled through the couture house, and there was certainly little room for any direct input from the licensees. As Dior milliner Gaston Berthelot put it, since Dior was "generous in his admiration for his coworkers, he was keen to see their work recognized." It was no wonder Avenue Montaigne acted like a magnet for the likes of a shy young man from Algeria (a French colony at the time) by the name of Yves Matthieu Saint Laurent, and it was quite natural that he should find himself standing at the door one fine June morning in 1955, the culmination of his childhood dream.

The shoe designer Roger Vivier had been under the Dior roof since 1953 and already had his own display window on the corner of Rue François-Ier. For his first collections, Dior had gone to the two "big names" in the pantheon of ready-to-wear footwear, Salvatore Ferragamo and Andrea Perugia, although he had balked at some of their more daring styles. Their stiletto heels went perfectly with the New Look, and the classic lower-heeled pumps lengthened women's figures in a gentle way, making shoes a functional accessory to the total look rather than a simple ornament. Roger Vivier had made two attempts to join Dior. He had originally offered his services as a milliner, after having worked in that capacity for Bergdorf Goodman in New York where he had fled during the war to join the bright young colony of French exiles there and play the multifaceted artist, making shoes in the morning for Delman, acting as a photographer's assistant for Hoyningen-Huene in the afternoon, and working as a milliner in the evening to make ends meet. Once back in Paris, he was drawn by Dior's success. He had dinner with Dior in 1949 and hats were discussed, but nothing ever came of it. Mitzah Bricard had closed off that avenue by opening her own millinery workroom. In the meantime, however, Vivier's supporters in the Dior entourage continued to pull strings for him and eventually Madame Raymonde Zehnacker, the central pillar of the Dior trio, organized the decisive luncheon at her home at Mougins in the South of France. An exclusive contract was then signed with Delman in New York under which Vivier would design for Dior, on Dior's premises, but under the Delman name.

Vivier's custom-made shoes were used in the collections and also sold in the Delman-Dior boutique at Avenue Montaigne. Here as elsewhere Victor Grandpierre was responsible for the interior design, and the classic lines of the shoe showroom mirrored those in the rest of the House. A large molded scroll with a bow on it, bearing the names of the new partners, Delman and Dior, was attached to the wall between two display windows. The same logo appeared inside the shoes along with the figures of two characters in period costume, a man pursuing a woman in a rococo pastoral setting. There was nothing of Roger Vivier in any of this — the prime concern of the House of Dior was to promote a single image for all its merchandise, all bearing the name Dior. In his book on Roger Vivier, Pierre Provoyeur describes the look: as if on a stage, "a single shoe lay in the kind of solitude generally reserved for a religious idol, surrounded by layers of fabric, beneath awnings decorated with pompons, behind plaster moldings worthy of the Louvre." Each shoe was a little masterpiece in itself — a pump in black on white nylon tulle embroidered in silver thread, sequins, and pearls by Rébé with a hollow Louis XV heel, or an extremely plain evening sandal whose simple beauty lay in the arrangement of a few elegant straps. Vivier's shoes took the architectural concept of the foot to its highest plane, while retaining the purest, most austere and yet distinctive lines. He was a master of invention too. For the coronation of Elizabeth II in 1953, he created a sandal in gold kid studded with rubies and sculptured like a pre-Renaissance jewel. It was (Pierre Provoyeur again) "the only liturgical shoe Roger Vivier was ever to create."

Then there was the other space on the ground floor, the Dior Boutique, presided over originally by Carmen Colle, the Mexican-born widow of Dior's great friend. Dior was already "Tio Christian" to Carmen's three little girls (immortalized, like their mother, in a portrait by Christian Bérard). Dior adored them, giving them dolls in New Look outfits, even dressing up as Father Christmas for them and dreaming up amazing costumes for their fancy dress parties. Following Pierre's death, Dior became something of an adoptive father to the three girls, taking a role in family matters like school reports, holiday plans, and Marie-Pierre's first communion — including the design of her communion dress. Carmen Colle remembers her time at Dior as "the best years of my life." "Come on, Carmen," he urged as he announced his decision to let her run the boutique, "work a little Popocatepetl magic on it."

She knew just how to rise to that sort of challenge, with all the lighthearted seriousness and spontaneity so typical of the early days at Dior. She gathered a little gang of helpers — a decorator, a couple of friends with taste, a few ideas, and some style — and it was, Let's do it! "Our friends lent a hand with advice, criticism, and encouragement," she says, ". . . people like Francine Weisweiller, Liliane de Rothschild, Dora Maar, Elsa Triolet, and Nora Auric." Liliane de Rothschild, for example, came up with the idea of a little cushion for the backseat of a car, shaped like a license plate with a registration number on it in petit point. "I was very proud of the fact that Dior used my idea," she said. The boutique was done out in chintz, which gave it all the charm of a little drawing room.

In June 1955, however, Dior decided to pull out all the stops, closing down the "small" boutique on the Avenue Montaigne side one evening . . . and reopening the next day at 15 Rue François-Ier with all the speed of an impromptu ball at the court of the Sun King. In charge this time was Marie-Hélène de Ganay (Carmen Colle, now Madam Baron, having retired to look after her family), and the decor was once again by Victor Grandpierre. For sale in the Grande Boutique was a range of accessories produced by "a whole bunch of young enthusiasts," as the former window dresser Jean-François Daigre puts it. "There was the most marvelous atmosphere, the natural result of Dior's exceptional gift for dealing with people. Christian Dior completely shaped my life. He was what you would call a real gentleman in the seventeenth-century sense of the word."

"At half past nine the next morning, clearly unaware of the transformation that had just taken place, our first client walked in to buy a coat," Christian Dior relates. In front of her was a full range of jerseys, pullovers, belts, shawls, scarves, all sorts of knickknacks, trinkets, and gifts — sweet-smelling sachets for storing gloves, heart-shaped ashtrays, little cushions, velvet frames stitched with braid, fireplace accessories, tortoiseshell handkerchief boxes, cloth bags for slipping into your suitcase, and, just across the way, simple, reasonably priced summer dresses. The dresses were designed by André Levasseur under Dior's supervision and produced in the workrooms in the off-season for an unusually low 30,000 francs (3,000 francs at today's rate). "I had always hoped that a woman could leave my boutique clothed from head to toe and carrying a gift as well," wrote Christian Dior. "The range before me was the proof that I was not far from achieving my wish." And the shoe shop next door, "where my friend Roger Vivier was busy making shoes for the most elegant feet in the world, helped make my dream come true — to dress a woman in 'Christian Dior' from head to toe."

This wonderful adventure was moving along too fast. It was time to take a break and write it all down. Dior had already put pen to paper once, for the book *Je suis couturier* (translated as *Talking about Fashion*), a series of interviews put together by *Le Figaro*'s Alice Chavane and published in 1951. In 1956 he wrote *Christian Dior et moi*, which came out the following year in translation as *Christian Dior and I,* with a preface by his friend Pierre Gaxotte. In it Dior described the process of designing a collection, life inside a couture house, and how he saw the significance of his work. While Dior might have seemed detached from the glory surrounding him, it is quite apparent that he saw himself as a man with a most exalting mission. He knew that he had brought his profession out of the "ghetto," the narrow realm of the craftsman. His prime aim was to see "the supremacy of French quality and the talents of our designers" launch a new wave of economic activity — the commercialization of the products that symbolize its culture and way of life. Convinced of the value of his own experience, Dior became something of a public speaker. At once professor and popularizer of fashion, he drew on the Dior example to hold forth on how best to exploit France's artistic and cultural legacy.

He took the line that haute couture had a dual function. While it was the exalted domain of the craftsman, providing a workshop for the best creative energies, it also had to act as a means for promoting and exploiting TALENT (he always wrote the word in capital letters in his notes). It is not often one sees a businessman openly outlining his strategic thinking — innovative thinking at that, and still perfectly valid today — and his efforts did not go unnoticed in the United States, where Dior continued to receive the highest accolades.

The American press had devoted many column inches to Dior from the outset, well aware of just how original he was in every sense. "The Dior worldwide empire is no easy-money production designed to take advantage of one designer's success and capitalize on it for fast profits," wrote *Women's Wear Daily* at the time. "It is a long-range undertaking aimed at creating a continuity of design creativeness and, logically, long-range profits to the concern itself." In 1957 the Dior success story made the cover of *Time* magazine, the ultimate honor.

In France, however, Dior did not enjoy the same level of recognition — or at least, not in his own lifetime. The French Republic became aware of the case for rewarding the couturier when the Ministry of Trade came out with figures for 1949 showing that 75 percent of Parisian fashion exports bore the Christian Dior label . . . as indeed did a full 5 percent of the total volume of French export sales. A Légion d'Honneur was in order. But it was to be years before Dior was acknowledged on his home turf as the visionary, pioneer and, indeed, inventor of a whole new profession, based on his own discovery of couture as a cultural gold mine.

There is no arguing that Christian Dior could not have gotten where he did without Marcel Boussac's backing. But what no one realized was that the couturier and his partner belonged to two different generations in terms of economic perceptions. Dior's idea of the marketplace was as something where the consumer reigned supreme. Marcel Boussac firmly believed that a manufacturer imposes his methods on the consumer. He refused to acknowledge any other economic model. Such a system might have remained viable during the postwar reconstruction period when widespread shortages guaranteed a market for manufactured goods, but by the end of the fifties, with the opening up of the Common Market and the end of the colonial era, it was passé. With his newspaper *L'Aurore* and government ministers and politicians at his beck and call, the all-powerful Boussac was convinced he could alter the course of events, and put all his energy into undercover opposition to the Treaty of Rome, the foundation agreement for today's European Union. He had the sultan of Morocco deposed, he played off Edgar Faure, who maneuvered to defend the status quo and France's colonial empire, against free-trade advocate Mendès-France . . . but his political blindness was ultimately his downfall. He might have done well to take notice of what was going on right under his nose, at 30 Avenue Montaigne, where all eyes were on the future.

In the 1970s, Dior revenue was to prove a godsend when the

textile side of the Boussac group suffered massive losses. Jacques Rouët was powerless to save it. A series of French governments flew blindly to Boussac's rescue with public subsidies but were unable to turn back the tide of bankruptcy that engulfed both his empire and Boussac himself, the man who in 1947 was the wealthiest in France. But that's another story. . . .

Dior was just as misunderstood by the governments of the Fourth Republic. At the 1957 Paris Trade Fair he made a speech declaring his support for organized free trade and advocating the same sort of legal protection for the applied arts as already existed in industry and other fields of artistic endeavor. He called on the authorities to take action to protect "the sacred ground between the Place Vendôme and the Place de l'Etoile, which sets the tone and provides the artistic atmosphere for the entire world. Requiring very little infrastructure at all," he concluded, "the prestige of France will bear fruit, and our country will be like the laborer in the fable who discovers a treasure buried in his own field." If only they had listened, back then! There is no escaping the fact that, forty years later, nothing has effectively been done to guard against piracy — the scourge of Dior's existence — which costs French design billions of francs each year.

For his words to have had an effect, Dior himself would have had to be recognized as an industrialist. But no academy was prepared to grant him that honor. On the contrary, for years French governments have echoed former president Pompidou's condescending attitude toward "the France of champagne and perfumes," while concentrating their energies on the Concorde and Bull information systems. There is no exception here to the old proverb . . . yet another prophet crying in the wilderness!

There was one quite simple reason for such shortsightedness — the French are far too Cartesian in their thinking. The idea that Dior could combine artistic talent and managerial knowledge was most unsettling to his peers. It gave the lie to the cliché that says creative types have their heads in the clouds and hold wealth and money matters in contempt.

Perhaps it is time to take another look at this unusual character.

12

Smiling Gowns

Dior was like a magnificent painting you hang on the wall.

— Yves Saint Laurent

Dior fell into the trap of permanently having to alter his line.

— Marc Bohan

*M*itzah Bricard was never to be seen at Avenue Montaigne before midday. She possessed that *je ne sais quoi* that made men ashamed of the irresistible attraction they felt for her lioness-like allure. There was "a certain something" about her that annoyed other women, who tended to look down on her rather than confess to being jealous — jealous of her ability, and effrontery, in getting everything she wanted and being forgiven no matter what.

She was never seen without her turban, her pearls, and her stiletto heels. She never wore briefs and was only ever found in one of three places — at home, at the Ritz, or at Dior. Wreathed in a cloud of mystery peopled with Russian princes and admiring billionaires, a childhood in Romania . . . or perhaps England . . . she was thought to be of Austrian descent. It was said that she had once performed in a nude revue and had worked for a while at Balenciaga and Molyneux, but could anyone be sure? She materialized as if from nowhere. No one could imagine her any other way, let alone having to put up with the tedium and minutiae of everyday life. It was impossible to think of her being hungry or overtired, or with a face crumpled from sleep first thing in the morning. She was one of those people who manage to slip between the raindrops in a downpour, whose hair is never out of place even in a gale.

She was unfailingly, spontaneously creative, conjuring up a hat — "get me a few straws" — or finding exactly the right accessory for an outfit, a dog collar perhaps or a little bit of chiffon tied casually around the neck just to soften the look. She could take something quite run-of-the-mill, like the leopard-print scarf she wore at her wrist, and give it great style. (The leopard print was actually to hide a scar, but she was the sort of person who turned everything into a fashion statement.)

Christian Dior could not be without her. To those who complained about her grand airs, his response was simple. "Would you prefer to see her in another couture house? I'd rather have her here." While his fellow designers needed their special pair of scissors to make a dress, he needed Mitzah. She was a living image, an immutable yet changeable portrait. "She was his dancer and courtesan," remembers Alexander Liberman. "With her rustling silks, her poses, her pearls, and her points of view on everything and nothing, she was feminine seduction incarnate."

Mitzah Bricard was Dior's lifeline, a direct connection with his ideal image of womanhood — the women of his childhood, those who had left him with "the memory of their perfumes, perfumes that lingered in the elevator, more clinging that those of today. Figures muffled in furs, gestures à la Boldini,* bird-of-paradise plumes, and amber necklaces . . ." One of the Diors' neighbors in La Muette was a

---

* Italian-born Boldini was the "painter of fashion" in the early decades of the century.

marquise who left trails of powerful scent in the elevator and filled Christian "with an extraordinary emotion."

Mitzah was Proust's Odette, the *grande cocotte* Lantelme, and the daring soubrette Gabi Deslys* all rolled into one, *rara exotica* every one of them, "symbols of a moment of elegance that earned them a certain place in eternity," as Dior puts it in his preface to the French version of Cecil Beaton's *The Glass of Fashion*. As if to justify himself, Dior goes on to refer to Beaton's story of Violet, Duchess of Rutland, the mother of Lady Diana Cooper, who offered her daughters as a model the ravishing Italian diva Lina Cavalieri, who once worked in a tobacco factory but, as Beaton put it, "whose personal magnificence was a living proof of how great natural gifts of distinction can be found in those not born in the highest spheres."

Mitzah Bricard was a godsend. She was Dior's walking museum. If she had not existed, he would have invented her. There was something immortal about this face with the Cleopatra profile and incessant bravado, so much a part of her personality that no one dared openly take offense. There was no need for words between Dior and his muse. They were creatures of the same realm, of a past made all the more fabulous by not having to conform to the constraints of reality. Dior was free to reinvent bygone days by daring to create what Mitzah dared to *be* in flesh and blood.

"Do you have a favorite florist?" Stanley Marcus once inquired of this outrageous woman, wishing to thank her for some favor or other. "Certainly," came the reply. "Cartier."

For beings like Mitzah Bricard — people who have decided once and for all that their dream world is better than reality — everything is permitted. Christian Dior took similar liberties with life. The death of his mother, ambitious and distant as she was and more concerned with appearances than with feelings, allowed him to appropriate her image in the way one often does in life, reworking the past in terms of the present, to suit an existing rather than a previous reality. He was able to indulge in a vision of an idyllic childhood, a lost paradise where life was

---

* Lantelme and Gabi Deslys were "fast" women of the early 1900s, described in Cecil Beaton's *The Glass of Fashion*.

one big Carnival. The rest counted for nothing. It was gone, vanished and buried. All that remained was the garden wonderland, a Granville permanently on vacation, the smells of clean linen, and stolen moments of tenderness with his mother — regardless of how ungiving she really was.

Dutiful child that he was, he would never have envisaged being allowed to design dresses. His parents would have hated it and he would have hated to upset them. It would have been a great source of shame to have a dressmaker in the family tree. But with Madeleine gone, he was free of his guilt. By paying homage to his mother he was also seeking forgiveness for striking out on his own, for an act of independence of which she would never have approved. In his heart of hearts, in the depths of his soul, Madeleine Dior was present in every fold, in every yard of fabric unfurled by the designer in his yearning for *le temps perdu.* She was both his critic and his inspiration.

This fantasmatic link between his work and his own life caused Dior to entertain a very intimate relationship with his creations. And a very unusual one indeed! Only metaphorically, of course, a love story develops between the couturier and his dresses and goes through different stages, just like with human beings. At times he takes the role of "an anxious, proud, ruthless, passionate and tender father" as he agonized over his first *toiles,* wondering what "these dream-children of mine" would look like. This was the long-awaited realization of his adolescent fantasy: finally, he was the one in charge, dictating his conditions to those who had done the same to him for so many years. He was obsessed with his gowns: "dresses occupy me, they pre-occupy me . . . indeed they post-occupy me! Everything in my life revolves around dresses." Fascinating material for a psychoanalyst. It was like a love story in which his imagination had run riot and turned his creations into real people.

In Dior's mind, a couturier's creativity "could be likened to writing poetry." He confessed: "My life consists of preparing a collection, with all its joys, disappointments, and despair. There will be no more of it in the respite that follows and which, despite all the delights of a holiday, will seem interminably long. As the showrooms empty, my thoughts stray to my dresses. Who knows what tomorrow holds in store for them? In the meantime they are back hanging in their cupboards, as forgotten as an easy triumph. This is the moment when I would like to sit down in front of them, gaze at them all together, and thank them from the bottom of my heart."

Such fertile imaginings may have threatened to steer Dior off course, but he never lost his direction. All those suits and dresses were garments that "worked," never the gratuitous product of a raving mind. "For all its transiency, and without taking things out of proportion, couture may well be compared to architecture or painting as a form of artistic expression. But even if that is its prime aim, a collection can only be deemed a success if it is well cut and well stitched."

With that principle in mind, Dior put together a team to cover each of those functions: the idea (or ideal), the technical know-how, and the organizational capacity. Each of these very different roles fell to one of the three "fairy godmothers" on whom he relied so heavily. Once Mitzah had played her part, the workroom fairy Marguerite Carré would take over, juggling the tensions between artistic theory and professional practice. A perfectionist who was passionate about her craft, she knew all there was to know about cuts, biases, drapes, and folds. She was the one who allocated the various assignments among the workrooms according to their individual strengths. She was the miracle worker who could give a neckline all the fluid beauty of a waterfall, turn five tiers of flounces into a flight of swallows, and press a pleat back on itself as if a whip had been cracked over it.

As for the third one, the administrative fairy Raymonde Zehnacker, she was the cabinet leader, the head. Her task was to oversee production, order fabrics and other vital supplies and provisions, receive and pass on the boss's orders, make sure they were followed up, ensure communication between departments, and keep the whole machine running smoothly and on time. Without going into detail, the system she instituted was a model of reliability. She gave off an air of luxuriant strength, no doubt due to her Alsatian heritage and softened by the warmth in her blue eyes. There was also something quite enigmatic about her, but her kindly tone and friendly manner mirrored the courtesy and diplomacy of her employer, who referred to her either affectionately as "my little star" or reverentially as "my second self." She also shielded her master in his atelier from unwelcome intrusions but facilitated anything that might be considered useful or pleasurable. Like that of any powerful man — which was what Dior had become — Dior's schedule was a complex and delicate balance between the private and the public domain. This was where trust and savoir faire came into play. Madame Zehnacker could smooth out problems, keep secrets, and contrive the occasional tête-à-tête for Monsieur with an attractive young man or aspiring design talent, performing her task with all the delicious discretion of a go-between scuttling down hidden passages at the court of Versailles. She was also permitted to scold him for any excesses at the table, and it was she who sanctioned or forbade deliveries to the studio of the sweets Dior adored but for health reasons could not allow himself to enjoy. The ultimate cruelty of fate had placed the tempting windows of the famed Fouquet patisserie right below Dior's window on Rue François-Ier.

Unofficially, Raymonde Zehnacker was the "minister of the interior," privy to all the stories and snatches of information that were part of everyday life at Avenue Montaigne. It was up to her to decide which bits she passed on to *le patron*. The happy family atmosphere that prevailed over these years of rapid expansion was not without its conflicts, as the atmosphere of a couture house is particularly conducive to intrigue. Madame Linzeler, who was in charge of the fitting room, was perpetually at odds with Mademoiselle Marguerite, who was always complaining about Madame Minassian's habit of asking for things at the last moment. Madame Minassian (later better known as Yvonne de Peyerimhoff, a dazzlingly elegant blonde whom Dior chose to accompany him on his trips abroad, particularly to the United States because of her perfect mastery of English) could not stand the sight of Madame Levacher. Suzanne Luling was always most discreet except when it came to Mrs. Engel, but Mrs. Engel . . . and so on. Dior navigated his way adroitly among all these wonderfully impossible characters. In his divine wisdom Dior chose to treat them all equally by addressing them collectively as his darlings, "*mes chéries.*"

There was one particular day when all rivalry ceased and Christian Dior's supreme authority became overwhelmingly apparent — the day of the dress rehearsal. Surrounded by the solemn decor of the *Grand Salon,* beneath its crystal chandelier and gilt-edged mirrors, between its

Trianon gray walls, the couturier king gathered his cabinet for an event of such ritual it was reminiscent of a secret society. There were no invitations sent out for this preview; in fact the doors were draped with huge white curtains as an extra precaution against leaks, even within the establishment itself.

There was nothing quite like it. It was like the reverential hush of a chapel or the anticipation of a concert hall just before the curtain goes up. The silence was broken only by rustling, hushed whispers, and a gentle scraping of chairs. Two rows of chairs were set out, with Christian Dior's in the center, recognizable by its peculiar canvas pockets hanging over the sides. Next to the chair was a stool holding two long reels of paper and six dagger-sharp pencils with gray erasers on the ends — mere props when it came down to it, but if ever a camera were able to infiltrate the room without anyone knowing, it would have been irresistibly drawn to linger on that chair, forgetting for a minute the main attraction, the parade. For on that chair lay the most intriguing object of all, a pointer with a gold-ringed knob.

It had all the trappings of a throne room. Piously assembled to await the arrival of the monarch were his three most faithful companions: Marguerite Carré with her miraculously rosy complexion and brimming with buxom energy, Mitzah Bricard, in her element and poised to be even more daunting than usual, and Raymonde Zehnacker with her impenetrable gaze, armed with large sheaves of paper and notebooks. Knowing Dior's fascination with historical characters and given the formal ceremony of events like these, it would be tempting to liken the three women to Colbert, Madame de Pompadour and Mazarin — those powerful figures from the glorious days of Versailles. It was actually the musician Henri Sauguet who hinted at that comparison in describing his experience as a special guest at a dress rehearsal, both surprised and delighted to catch his old friend indulging in all the ritual of court.

Alongside this powerful trio came all the other members of the studio team. There were the fresh-faced assistants, the faces changing from year to year but including André Levasseur, Gaston Berthelot, and Frédéric Castet, all of whom were there from the beginning and some of whom went on to carve out glorious careers for themselves in the footsteps of their master — like Yves Saint Laurent, who came to Dior in June 1955, closely followed by Jean-Louis Scherrer — not to forget the apprentices, the *frontinettes* and *boutonnettes,* along with the handsome Claude Licard, who looked after all the fabrics, and the little Cinderella, Anne-Marie Mugnoz, in charge of folding materials at the back of the studio (Anne-Marie, Henri Sauguet's niece, made herself even smaller than usual but later, under Saint Laurent, would take Madame Raymonde's place as head of the studio). Finally Pierre Perrotino, Dior's chauffeur and erstwhile companion, appeared with his Leica. He was André Ostier or Willy Maywald for the day, the only photographer. It was also a holiday for certain senior members of staff like Suzanne Luling (minus her cigarettes) and Madame Linzeler, the Marquis de Maussabré, Hélène Levacher, and Jean-Claude Donati — the whole public relations department, in other words — plus Roger Vivier, the shoe designer, and the effervescent Michel Brodsky, a White Russian émigré. Last but not least came the two managing directors — Jacques Chastel, head of Dior Paris, and Jacques Rouët, globetrotter of the *griffe,* head of Christian Dior International.

There were as many people as chairs. Or rather "a place for everyone and everyone in his place." It was just like a seventeenth-century painting by a Dutch Old Master, with each character placed according to rank and profession and imbued with all the solemnity the situation demanded. It is an image of another era from which an onlooker today would feel quite excluded, but in the nobility of feeling emanating from it you can see on the faces that no one feels any more or less important than any other, all clearly identified by the roles they are called upon to play.

The *patron* arrives. There is something affectionate and unaffected about his entrance. He smiles, shakes a few hands, plants kisses on a couple of cheeks. He too has put a white overall over his day suit. He takes a seat, his gold-knobbed pointer in his hand. It is eight P.M. Let the show begin. No one knows precisely when it will end, late no doubt — one or two o'clock in the morning.

A voice announces: "*Monsieur, un modèle!*" The model appears, strides forward, makes a half turn, then comes to a standstill in front of the armchair. "The hat is wrong," says Christian Dior. "We need another . . . which one?"

Mitzah Bricard, seated on his right, does her best to provide an answer. And while Madame Carré waits her turn, Madame Zehnacker notes the details of the outfit on her large sheets of paper. André Levasseur quickly sketches the dress.

The next model appears, announced by the same figure in a white coat. *"Un modèle, monsieur!"* A second voice pipes up, " 'San Francisco.' " The model approaches the presidential chair. The stick waves about, pointing here, correcting there, reworking as it goes. "We need a bigger flower! . . . What is that little thing you've got in your hand? Let's try that. . . . Give it to me. No? Come on!"

Hands plunge into a heaped array of colors reminiscent of an oriental bazaar, plundering little trolleys piled high with accessories — feathers and flowers, belts and gloves, buttons, bijoux, and umbrellas. The atmosphere is at fever pitch but controlled, like some esoteric ritual worship at the altar of elegance and good taste.

There are some gowns that just do not work. Madame Bricard gets to her feet, joined by the supervisor of the workroom in charge of that particular gown. Handfuls of pins appear, one hand slides under the fabric, the shoulder is lifted slightly. . . . The petrified model turns into a waxwork, not daring to breathe until those darting hands are removed. Madame Bricard and the supervisor take a step backward to consider their handiwork and suddenly everyone is smiling again. Christian Dior approves but is still not quite satisfied. Something is not right. The model turns again. Dior stops her and gets up. It's the way the blouse is tied. He fiddles with the printed chiffon, his hands agile, abrupt, and sensual, hands that know exactly what they are after . . . like a gardener delving in his flowerbeds.

The stick begins describing its arcs again. Some outfits require only the slightest alteration, lifting the waist here a little, getting rid of that pleat . . . but others are sent packing amid floods of tears. Not even the magic scepter can save them, and so Dior picks up his pencil.

Marguerite Carré leans over him to watch. She has the solemn, complex task of translating the master's original sketches, nervous, flighty, bold things, sometimes so lively they are beyond imitation, into technical instructions to be passed on to the workrooms. Her sacred duty is to ensure that the original idea comes across.

"Have I expressed you correctly, sir?" she asks ritually, filled with apprehension, each time a particular model appears for its first fitting.

If the workroom has not succeeded in conveying the original idea, the answer is always the same: "Your dress does not express what I was after!"

Such intense moments unfold in total silence, and you can hear a pin drop. Everyone is concentrating to the utmost, as if trying to help Dior focus his attention on a solution. He consults his audience but no one replies. They know he is just thinking aloud. It is hot in the room but no one dares complain. "The word 'complain' was permanently removed from the Dior dictionary," Suzanne Luling writes. The orders keep coming, thick and fast. "Faster . . . Sit down. Don't worry, we'll give you a black umbrella." There are even moments of ecstasy, *oh*'s of enchantment, and cries of "That really *is* smart!"

"He was the oracle," as Henri Sauguet put it. "You don't succeed in a career like his by chance or imagination. And yet, dresses are the product of one's imagination. . . . He just happened to have the imagination of Leonardo da Vinci!"

Like the monarch who said, *"L'Etat, c'est moi,"* Dior *was* fashion, the world over. And Paris was good taste. That, certainly, was Dior's vision of haute couture, and why he couched the whole process in such mandatory, immutable ritual. It was also his way, in love as he was with the glorious past, of resurrecting the spirit of the Grand Siècle, the golden age of Louis XIV. This was the renaissance of the ethics and aesthetics of Versailles, of an epoch when the king of France held sway over the whole of Europe . . . only this time it was a couturier who would reaffirm the supremacy of French culture. To Cecil Beaton, the French are "past masters at the art of living" but their heritage is universal. That certainly was the sense of Beaton's declaration that "we are all Frenchmen." In France, he went on to state, even the humblest porter or concièrge has "a respect for beauty in its many forms. Possibly for this very reason fifty million Frenchmen have maintained the lead in the refinement and perfection of the minor arts and have developed them to a brilliant degree."

What is also clear is that the creative context, albeit outmoded, in which Christian Dior indulged himself was perfectly in keeping with the ambitious commercial strategy developed by Dior through the use of his label. The collections were the crowning glory of this empire.

Theirs was the mission of carrying its artistry to all four corners of the globe, *urbi et orbi* — spreading its gospel through the excitement and marvel of fashion shows and of models who made names like Victoire, Alla, France, and Renée as familiar in Sydney as in Montevideo — but also providing inspiration and motivation, through the Paris collections, for the hundreds of Dior buyers and licensees who regularly made the pilgrimage to Avenue Montaigne. The collections, therefore, were a means of communication, both external and internal, for the Dior concern. What was at work in the collections was Dior's own particular brand of magic, the magic of another era that permeated the studio at Avenue Montaigne and its creator, combined with the aura bestowed on him by the devotion and tireless efforts of his staff. Not one of these faithful workers would ever count the hours of toil required to achieve his "great work," calling on what seemed to be unlimited resources in the process, and allowing the designer to fulfill his commercial vision in perfect accord with his royal master plan. Authority combined with camaraderie and extravagance to create the perfect environment for Dior to pursue the absolute truth, or as Cecil Beaton says, a place where "fashion, the ephemeral, shares the last laugh with art, the eternal."

While Dior once said having taste meant having *his* taste, he was well aware that haute couture was a collective endeavor. For every dress that left the town house on Avenue Montaigne there were a dozen pairs of hands that could lay claim to a share in its production. Dior always showed the greatest respect and concern for his workrooms and apprentices and the spiritual importance of their craft. He wrote of "the fingers that fly across the fabric, pricking themselves with their needle or stopping to consider a seam . . . fingers that are working to create the fashion of tomorrow," or "priceless human hands. Everything they touch has something no machine could ever produce, the poetry of life." Those hands contained "the human element, the inimitable, the soul," with all the "uniqueness and originality of a work of art."

To think that all that art went into a mere twenty-five hundred pieces a year. Successful designs might sell sixty copies — one once sold 284 — and in all of Paris there were five hundred Dior clients at most.

Those figures come from Jacques Rouët, who points out that the average time spent on a dress was eighty hours.

The financial manager would never have dreamed of factoring in the hours spent by Christian Dior in creating a design. The couturier and his work were one and the same, like a king who never sets aside his crown or a priest who never really removes his vestments. In today's highly visual era, Dior when creating a collection could best be compared to a director making a film, in that he could never lose sight of the theoretical side of his work even while he was engaged in conceiving new designs.

Like the dress rehearsal, a series of rituals had to be followed for each collection, a process that occupied the couturier and his team over a full six months. The "production" of a garment was the result of a series of metamorphoses, from the period of reflection prior to inspiration up to the moment of interaction with the technical skills of the workrooms. The dress itself was the ultimate expression of fashion and its practitioners, in a schedule as precisely laid out as a church service. Each successive stage, described by Dior in minute detail, comes across as one more prescribed step in the designer's work and in the birth of the next fashion. There is one particularly solemn moment at halfway point — the period when the couturier would retire to the country for a fortnight to prepare his preliminary sketches.

It was like a retreat from the rest of the world, and only his closest colleagues were ever invited — people like Gaston Berthelot, André Levasseur, or Frédéric Castet. Raymonde Zehnacker was another member of the entourage. In the course of the first few days each person would sit in his own little corner and draw while Dior plunged himself into a "fury of scribbling," filling his sketch pads with "tiny etchings." At this stage they were nothing more than indecipherable hieroglyphics, a thousand tiny lines with no apparent shape to them, a host of images in no seeming order. Gradually ideas began to take shape. Then came the decisive moment, the famous, familiar evening when the master would inform his disciples with ritual solemnity, "You won't be seeing me tomorrow. . . ."

For around three days Dior would not leave his room. His meals were sent up to him on a tray. He even stopped shaving. But as Frédéric Castet remembers, "We knew that in three or four days the collection would be hatched." When Dior had finished, he would emerge from his room, drowning in paper. In line with the ritual, Madame Zehnacker was the first to enter his room. The floor would be strewn with sketches, an indescribable confusion of drawings in various states of completion still sizzling with Dior's creative fury. While Madame Raymonde picked up each piece of paper and carefully sorted them, Dior would hurry down to see his assistants, suddenly ravenous after three days in which food had been forgotten and anxious to see what they had "hatched" in his absence.

The point of this frenzied state of seclusion was, to quote Dior, to wait until the moment when "suddenly I would get a flash. One of the sketches would set off a spark." Gripped with excitement, he could finally visualize a dress emerging from his doodles and lines. "There it was, there was no mistake about it. This was it." This was the shape of the new woman. All had been revealed. One idea would generate another, a more evocative sketch would inspire a whole series of new drawings, and he would start to see just what it was that had set the process in motion. Preoccupied as he was with "time," Dior concentrated on triggering the mechanisms of involuntary memory as a way of conjuring up the past. And although he looked to the past, he was not looking for a "retro style." His dresses, the "children" he was eventually to give birth to, were more than just a tribute to the fashions of yesteryear.

The next stage in the creative process went from the all-holy selection of sketches through to the nerve-racking ceremony at which the various workrooms presented their first preliminary *toiles* made up in a light canvas. Next came the serious production process. After the preliminary fitting sessions, each dress would be sent back up to the workrooms, bristling with pins and scored with red thread, completely unrecognizable. Eventually the day of the first rehearsal would come around, at which the opening themes of the next collection would be finalized after a handful of models presented the "signature outfits." During the next working phase, all the *toiles* considered worthy of inclusion in the collection were listed, filed, and given names — "Amoureuse," "Pompon," "Bal bleu," "Aventure." Selecting the 175 to 200 models for the final show was a process requiring great skill. The concern for harmony had to be balanced against a need for diversity, the tastes and requirements of different women in different parts of the world had to be taken into account, a fine line had to be drawn between dresses that were bound to sell as opposed to the ones Dior called the "Trafalgars," the showstoppers. There were the ones that were sure to be a hit and the "swallows," which might not take flight this time but might just "make a summer" in the following season. Every collection featured a red dress, Dior's lucky color, and lots of black "because its stark accent makes it the most elegant color."

Rehearsals followed fitting sessions, good days followed bad, until finally there was no going back and the day of the dress rehearsal rolled around. No more delays, regrets, or tears. Judgment day had dawned and the couturier steeled himself to act without mercy. "I am only satisfied if I have not bowed to any compromise," Dior explained.

Keeping an audience spellbound for close to two hours with a show in which there were no characters and no plot was quite a feat. This was pure spectacle, a feast for the eyes in a breathtaking succession of magnificent gowns, sparkling as if touched by some magic wand, transporting the audience into another realm, touching off a series of chords with its own vibrant, fragrant atmosphere. On the eve of the presentation of the collection, a select group of close friends would be invited to keep Dior company in his studio while he inspected the final gowns. He needed people around him, he needed their warmth and friendship as he prepared "for battle." Alexander Liberman remembers how important those collections were for Dior. "It was his big performance," he says. The same friends who had perched on stools and chairs carried into the studio for the purpose the night before, dining on sandwiches with a glass of red wine and witnessing the arrival of embroidered dresses still to be sewn together, a model on the verge of fainting, a workroom head with an attack of nerves, were now bowled over by the miracle that had taken place in just a few hours. As Cecil Beaton wrote, "To see a collection of Dior's dresses filing past gives one the pleasure of watching a romantic and spectacular pageant. With an impeccable taste, a highly civilized sensitivity and a respect for tradition that shows itself in a predilection for the half-forgotten, Dior creates a brilliant nostalgia."

Clothes do have a memory. Fashion looks at art and sees itself.

Entranced by the painter, the sculptor, or the musician, the couturier picks up where they left off. He is the sorcerer holding up a newly polished mirror to society and reflecting a host of images from the past for its perusal. That was why they were all there, crammed onto the staircase, all these people from the world of theater, literature, and music — from Denise Tual to Henri Sauguet, not to mention Jean Cocteau, all beloved friends squeezed into one corner of the room. It was not just because space was tight and places sought after (although Dior liked to bring back the atmosphere of his student days when he and his friends were quite content to huddle in the top gallery just to be able to see the show).

They would not miss it for the world. Not a Dior collection. Hélène Rochas certainly would not, for one. "Dior's collection was a long-awaited moment, on the same scale as the first night at the opera or a performance by some fantastic orchestra. . . . It was terribly irritating for the other designers," she added (she had succeeded her husband Marcel, who died in 1953), "because they were compelled to match the same level of luxury offered by Dior." Liliane de Rothschild was another who would not have dreamed of giving up her invitation card. "We were all quite enchanted." The debutante Jacqueline de Ribes likened the experience to "a journey through time with all those dresses and their magical names."

Paris is like a theater where the aristocrats of today can mingle with their latter-day counterparts. It is as if the Countess Greffulhe — the model for Proust's Oriane — were still alive, congratulating "young Christian" on a job well done. Dior's clothes are like poetic metaphors, living temptations for modern Odettes to dream just a little and, in slipping them on, to slip into the past.

There were moments, in fact, during rehearsals, when one particular dress would stop everyone short, so stunning that for a moment they would all be at a loss for words. Finally, "It's a picture!" someone would exclaim. Here was Proust's Madame Swann "swathed in her gown as if in the delicate, spiritual apparel of a whole civilization," Albertine in a dress reminiscent of "the seductive shade of that invisible Venice . . . overrun by Arab ornamentation," or Odette, the contemplation of whose evening gown was "like being invited to look upon a Renaissance painting." Dior himself summed it up when he said his one desire was to be a magician. "Couturiers have a wonderful part to play. Only they have the power to transform a woman, now that Cinderella's fairy godmother is no longer practicing her craft. But that power would lose considerable prestige if transformation simply occurred without a whole apparatus behind it and without all the anticipation. Sumptuous dresses and spectacular fashion shows with all the festive trimmings go some way toward satisfying the longing for extravagance that exists deep down in all of us. In this gray world of ours, couturiers can still work a little magic." The little boy from Granville had achieved his dream.

But the man peering out from behind the curtain and waiting to hear the applause was not dreaming. This was really happening. "*Numéro quatorze, 'Ecosse,'* number fourteen, 'Scotland' . . ."

"They like this one, Monsieur," a little voice whispers.

"It's going well."

"Is it going as well as last time?"

"Even better, I'd say."

A theater man from way back, Dior had his own special "applause meter" to assist him in judging how well a collection was being received. The only person who could give him a reliable assessment was Raymonde Zehnacker. After all, she "knew her salon inside out" and could judge audience reaction "with her eyes closed." But oohs and aahs were not all Dior was after as he tossed dresses with names like "Caprice," "Bolero," "Sauvage," "Impénitente" into the salon like confetti at one of his favored parties or masked balls. More than mere odes to the impermanence of beauty, the very names of the dresses were a key to his own secret world and his sources of inspiration. Then there were names like "House of Cards," "Crossword," "Lucky Star," "Horoscope," "Soothsayer," and "Success" — a clue to Christian Dior the gambler and risk taker, who even then could not make a move without consulting his astrologer. The brighter his star shone, the greater his need for assurance from the world of mysticism. The more he won from season to season, from triumph to triumph, the more he had to lose. Christian Dior was worth millions of dollars, and now that his label was a worldwide success, it could not afford to fail.

*　　　*　　　*

We all think we know our friends well enough to know what might hurt or offend them. Fashion editor Alice Chavane, who loved Dior like a brother, certainly thought so — until the day she told her dear friend what she thought of Balenciaga's collection.

"I was astounded," she said quite innocently. "It was absolutely wonderful."

Dior scowled. "Astounded, were you? Really?"

"I realized then that I had said something very silly," Chavane recalls. "Even though Dior had the greatest admiration for Balenciaga, he had to feel he was the greatest of all." She had always considered Dior so successful he could hardly begrudge others a little good fortune, and quite generous when it came to the talents of others. But to her surprise, he was no different from anyone else.

With a regal impulse Dior constantly felt the need to shine, to bedazzle. . . . He also displayed a pompous, rather heavy touch at times, particularly in his evening wear and ball gowns, the dream outfits designed to carry the wearer off into another realm. His role in dictating hemline lengths was another function of that desire to make his mark, and the seasonal game of widths, lengths, lines, and silhouettes always worked to spectacular effect. He refined and reworked the New Look, untiringly shaping the female figure in some new way, in keeping with his belief that "a dress is an ephemeral piece of architecture intended to pay tribute to the proportions of the female body." It was a marvelous metaphor. But there were those who suspected Dior was creating change for the sake of it, and now that he was on the treadmill, he could not get off. He even went so far as to introduce two different lines in one collection. In spring 1948 there was Zigzag, with all the nervy boldness of a line drawing, and Envol (Flight) with hemlines that gradually dropped at the back, making the wearer look as if she were flying as she walked; the following winter featured Ailée (Winged), accentuating youth and casual lines, plus Cyclone, adding new width to ball gowns. Once he set the precedent, he was forced to continue. Season after season it was line after line — Trompe l'Œil, Milieu du Siècle (Mid-Century), Verticale, Oblique, Enlacée, and Muguet (Lily of the Valley); Ovale, Longue, Profilée, and Tulipe.

The names were like little catchwords, just the sort of *coups de théâtre* the public had come to expect from Dior, and perfect material for the front page of the newspapers. His experience with the New Look had taught Dior that fashion could be news, just as much as sports, entertainment, or politics. And there was no way he planned to bow out of the limelight. He personally wrote the printed program notes, containing a summary of the new directions, that were placed on the journalists' seats as they took their places for the fashion shows. His press kits would point up not only the latest trend but even the accessories to go with it — hats, umbrellas, handbags, shoes, and . . . of course, every dress, in full detail. No gown would go out into the world without a name, a birth date (autumn–winter 1948), and a pedigree (Zigzag line). Buyers would receive a technical file on each garment, its own personal list of specifications with a full explanation of what fabric was to be used, which buttons, how it should be lined, and the like.

The couturier was quick to defend himself against accusations of manipulating the variation in hemlines. "The distance between the skirt and the ground is of no consequence in itself," he said. "It is simply a function of the general look of my line." But every change generated as much fuss as novelty value. That was certainly the view of the Hollywood producers, who, as we have seen, felt compelled to speculate on where dress lengths would be when a particular film came out. It was almost as if fashion had become its own victim, so desperate was it to take center stage. For the spring–summer collection in 1950, Dior spent more than four pages in his program notes trying to anticipate the analyses and criticism his latest designs would elicit from fashion journalists and international buyers alike. Dior sales made up half, if not more, of total export earnings for Paris couture. And once money starts talking, the designer himself is in the line of fire, targeted by the enormous machine he is part of. Thanks to the New Look, haute couture now set the tone at every level, including what would eventually end up being the look on the mass market. So Dior was in a double bind. He had to please not only his clients but also the public at large. This was the crux of the dilemma in which he had rather too rashly placed himself. Fashion needs to make a statement. And yet nothing dates it as quickly as making that statement.

He was the "poet" of dressmaking, a special events manager, the purist, the elitist, and the public relations whiz all in one, a masterful communicator in an industry of mass consumption and the creator of an incredible phenomenon — the status symbol, the idea of a piece of craftsmanship becoming a luxury item and having a commercial value.

Everyone knew where Dior's real interest lay. One of his favorite collections was Longue, for autumn–winter 1951, part of his ongoing attempt to purify "the line." In that particular collection he perfected the little gray flannel dress, which, along with the black wool dress, was one of his timeless essentials. It was molded to the figure like the chassis of a car, a "second skin" effect he carried over into evening wear. Christian Dior's most exciting outfits were by no means all complicated, dressy affairs and he introduced hundreds of clever new styles and ideas to delight his clients. There was the calf-length, off-the-shoulder five o'clock dress, the cocktail suit in tennis flannel worn over a low-necked top, and the multipurpose mink coat with a series of detachable layers.

Paris went wild for them all. "This terrible wonderful public" was his favorite; to him Paris was the city that "breathed fashion." Pleasing Parisians was the ultimate for Dior and none of his New York shows ever gave him the same pleasure. He had no cause to complain about attendance figures at his Fifth Avenue showrooms but sensed an unbridgeable gap in sensibilities between his native land and the United States, despite the fact that he owed his real fame to the latter and not the former.

The American press sang his praises to the skies but there was something missing in its adulation, a sense of nuance. Parisian audiences would murmur in admiration at the sheer prowess of a wide skirt with the slenderest of waists or the beautifully cut pleats in an underskirt. The famous Dior pleat, for example, was designed to eliminate the unseemly sight of a split skirt opening at the calf and completely ruining its line. Dior skirts were always fitted with a taffeta lining edged with a wide band of the same fabric as the skirt. This tiny piece of fine-tuning meant that the split would open onto another skirt. It was an expensive exercise, doubling the amount of work that went into the outfit, but that was what made Dior's designs so magnificent — the little, almost invisible things, the fine touches, the sheer artistry of it all!

But the man *Time* magazine called "the King Barnum of fashion" knew he needed to jump through rather more spectacular hoops to keep the American public on the edge of their seats. Everything was on a grander scale there. The collections were held in front of two thousand people, "megashows" taking up the whole mezzanine level of a department store, and orchestrated to coincide with the kind of press coverage that would reach 180 million people. The announcement of a hemline jump of just an inch or two had Seventh Avenue buzzing as intensely as a fall on the stock exchange. The trick for Dior was to present his collection both as the delicate flower of the refined and tightly hierarchical system that prevailed in France and, abroad, as a well-orchestrated, high-powered wheel of a finely tuned machine.

By pulling off a *coup de théâtre* every season, Dior became the first to make his own fashion go out of fashion. The day finally came when, after having succeeded so consummately in finding new variations within the parameters of the style that first made his name, his silhouettes progressively softened to the point where he did a complete about-face, producing the rounded Tulip line in 1953. He had done all he could with his Corolla line, the "whorl of petals" that was the New Look, and had exhausted it in the process. From well-executed copies down to bad approximations, it had been adulterated to the point of vulgarity, and as the first to be aware of it, he lived up to his reputation for the outrageous and the unexpected (although he undoubtedly had no choice in the matter) and ceremoniously buried his flower-woman without a backward glance.

"A stunned audience looked on as seven years of the New Look were wiped away in a mere three hours," wrote Françoise Giroud, "to be replaced by the string bean look. It was a change if there ever was one! And the time was certainly ripe." As at the previous revolution, the so-called "French guard" Carmel Snow was witness to the event, which came with the 1954–55 collection. She immediately coined the term "the Flat Look," a less flattering epithet than her previous effort, and despite her arguments in its favor, did not have quite the impact she had in 1947. A flood of protest was unleashed in the United States. Marilyn Monroe announced that she was insulted (hardly surprising; the string bean look was not exactly her style). The H line, to give it its real name, flattened the bust, eliminated the shoulders and hips, and gave women a streamlined, adolescent figure that was both distinguished and smart. "It was farewell to the high-rounded bust, the slender waist and padded hips, and unpolished, unashamed man-pleasing techniques," Françoise Giroud continued. "Fashion had found more subtle ways of making women look desirable. The cards had been reshuffled in the eternal game of seduction." At Fath, Balmain, and the other couturiers, similar things were happening, but Dior still ruled the patch. In the golden age when haute couture reigned supreme, the king still held the keys to the gates of the Bastille.

He had not hit the jackpot this time, though. The New Look had come on the heels of the war and widespread shortages, while now the prevailing mood was more open to diversity. The tide would not turn in the dramatic way it had in 1947, heralded as it had been then by a wave of protest in the press. This new line was not scandalous; it just got people up in arms. But Dior was a good loser. "I would rather receive a pounding in three columns on the front page than get two lines of congratulation somewhere on the inside," he said. And sales certainly did not suffer. The A line that followed in 1955 topped the export charts.

The effect, however, had been to wipe clean the fashion slate. There was a general sigh of relief at seeing the last of the New Look (after all, fashion does not like to be dictated to for such an extended period), and Dior had come to acknowledge that women like to "be appropriately elegant from dawn to dusk without having to go home and change." The H line was followed by the A, the Y, the Arrow, and the Magnet — each continuing the theme of a longer, flatter silhouette.

The big event, of course, had been Chanel's reemergence a year earlier. Not that she had ever really left — her sense of style had become part of the social fabric. She was the complete opposite of Dior, never giving names to her dresses (even her perfumes were only ever known by their number) and flatly adopting a man's suit, adapting it definitively and accessorizing it ad infinitum with costume jewelry, to invent a look women could wear for both the office and a dinner out. As Chanel once peremptorily declared, "Women are either overdressed or not smart enough."

Although her first fashion show in 1953 was given a cool reception — the influence of Dior was still far too fresh — it is easy to understand why Hélène Lazareff, the powerful chief editor of *Elle*, leaped to snatch "Mademoiselle" from the jaws of fashion purgatory and, weary of being at Dior's beck and call, declared Chanel's next collection a triumph. She was just what all these voting, wage-earning, independent women were waiting for: a confident female role model with no time to waste — especially when it came to choosing her clothes — in a black sweater, costume jewelry, and a classic suit that was to weather the storms of time. Edmonde Charles-Roux of *Vogue* puts it this way. "For Hélène Lazareff, the migrant, the Parisian of the suburbs, Chanel was a way of getting even with the *grande bourgeoisie* represented by that cosmopolitan aristocrat Christian Dior." It was also a way for the press to visit revenge on the despot couturier.

The concept of different outfits for different times of day receded into the past like court etiquette. *Marie-Claire* magazine, which appeared for the first time in 1954, began its tradition of teaching women to question things and make their voices heard. "Women think they have to be what others want them to be," popular talk-show broadcaster Ménie Grégoire was to say not long afterward. The delicate, impossibly fragile woman who offered herself up to her husband's desires was crumpled forever like her own tissue paper wrapping. The woman of the next generation knew precisely what she wanted. She was unpolished like Sophia Loren, natural like Brigitte Bardot, or extraordinary like Marilyn Monroe, the ballerina type like Audrey Hepburn or a nineteen-year-old best-seller like Françoise Sagan, powerfully magnificent like Anna Magnani or a leader of a generation like Simone de Beauvoir. In her novel *Les Mandarins* de Beauvoir wrote of girls and boys roaming the night in search of a new reason for living — and it has to be said that if the existentialists from the Café de Flore had jumped onto the New Look bandwagon for a while, it had only been for want of anything better. They really came into their own with the New Wave.

The Dior woman was no longer alone in the world. Dior had single-handedly brought couture up to speed and set a tone of professionalism, but now he found his colleagues catching up with him. It was not long before Jacques Fath had left his glittering couturier image behind and adopted the look of a besuited businessman to embark in Dior's wake on the discovery of the American market, armed with the ambition of dressing other women besides the wealthy ones. With his Fath Université label, he launched a new, younger line in casual skirts, cocktail dresses, and evening wear, which retailed in department stores and boutiques. Two years later he was selling up to a hundred thousand copies of some of his designs. Prêt-à-porter had come into its own. Previously overshadowed by its much feted elder sibling, haute couture, ready-to-wear now found a parallel market and developed into a force to be reckoned with. It was still a considerable cut above mass-market garment manufacture, offering a young, dynamic image, synonymous with modern living. In the ten years between 1950 and 1960, prêt-à-porter became as much a part of everyday vocabulary as nylon, Bic pens, electric mixers, instant soups, permanent press fabrics, and plastic containers.

The legacy of the New Look, however, will always remain as a symbol of Paris and its spirit for perfection. And the story of Christian Dior will remain unique for achieving such astonishing success so quickly and over so much of the world. This is why his star still shines so brightly. Mrs. Kuniko Tsutsumi, from the powerful Seibu chain that introduced Dior to Japan, puts it this way: "If ever the stars were to die, Dior would be the last to go out."

What must not be forgotten is the way in which such immortality was obtained. It took a great toll on Dior and his health. Assuming the dual roles of creator and entrepreneur, he killed himself in the process. The anxiety associated with each new collection, the stress and exhaustion of so much travel, so many public appearances, and an ever-growing empire aged him by twenty years in just ten. For all the fame and glory this heroic figure had attained, there was a darker underside, like a pact with the devil, who would eventually appear to claim his due.

13

Racing for Time

Christian Dior was a combination of delusions of grandeur and shyness.

— Léonor Fini

"Just once more, please, Pierre."

"But this is the . . ."

"Please don't count, Pierre. Don't count."

It was the same every time. Whenever a new collection was about to be launched or sometimes for no apparent reason, like today, *le patron* would suddenly sit rigid instead of stepping out of the passenger seat. The man at the wheel, his chauffeur and friend and former lover, knew the ritual by heart. But this time he could not help feeling silently surprised. Once more would make it seven, and seven was an unlucky number for his employer. He never liked odd numbers, and seven, well . . . Over the years Pierre Perrotino had learned to recognize all the traps to be avoided by those who believe in astrology as a science and who live their lives by the stars. And if anyone fitted in that category, it was the man sitting beside him in the car.

He started the motor again. Rue François-Ier, Rue Bayard, Avenue Montaigne, Place de l'Alma, Rue Jean-Goujon — he could do it with his eyes shut. This time was once too many . . . but he complied.

Knowing too well the mind of his employer, to whom he had sworn eternal loyalty, Perrotino could only pray he would be asked to drive around yet another time. Eight was a much better number. But as he drew up at the curb, Christian Dior reached for the door handle and opened it, on the right side.

Observers would have been rather puzzled. Although the car had French license plates and the steering wheel on the left, it was patently a British make. But this unusual left-hand-drive modification was in fact carried out on all Monsieur Dior's English cars as a matter of routine. He did not like to walk around the machine to reach his destination. The path from the automobile to the door had to be short, discreet, and direct. That was all there was to it.

How, Perrotino asked himself, could he have left it at that? Seven times around the block . . .

Waiting for her client inside the couture house, as she often did, was "Madame Astrology," Madame Delahaye. Where once it was Dior who went to see her, now she came to him. Fortune-tellers were not fairy godmothers and, while those who had predicted the great couturier's fame and fortune had been right, they took care not to warn him that success has its price.

The founder of the House of Dior was in his fiftieth year when his *maison* celebrated its first seven years — seven years of success, seven times around the block. . . . It was a number that set Dior trembling. But what reason did such a successful man have to be so afraid? Success itself was the problem. To Dior it appeared increasingly elusive. The more the press sang his praises, the greater Dior's anxiety. The early collections had been just like a game. Now each one filled him with growing terror. It was a daunting challenge for someone who had always ranked himself above the others, as the one with all the aces, the only one who counted. He had become a hostage to his own success, dreaming of the quiet life but unable to resist throwing the dice just one more time. "The livelihood of nine hundred people is riding on my collection," he used to say in the early years. Now the Dior concern employed seventeen hundred people around the world and its chief executive was expected to be everywhere at once. His presence was demanded in all four corners of the globe, in New York and beyond, to launch a new license or visit a department store or open a new branch or make a speech or take part in a conference. . . .

Just as he could not escape his duty, he could not agree to relax his standards, insisting on "Dior" perfection at all times. Even when he was on another continent, he had to be in constant communication with Avenue Montaigne, by letter and phone, notes and messages. Jacques Rouët regularly received bulletins from his employer — like the one Dior sent all the way from America to discuss the manager of Dior Paris. "Don't let Chastel adopt that curt tone of his with the staff," Dior warned. "He is tending to do that a bit lately. Not only will he lose his credibility, he'll lose his position and his function. They must feel fond of him. And he mustn't take anything for granted. Nothing can ever be taken for granted."

There were plenty of men with the right constitution for this twenty-four-hour-a-day lifestyle but Christian Dior was not one of them. His mind might have been quick but his temperament was not. So much with Dior had to do with contradictions; his ongoing struggle was always with himself. Sadly, the merry-go-round he was now on was spinning too fast for him and the only thing that kept him going was the artificial high of overextending himself.

There were those eyewitnesses who could testify to what went on behind Dior's seemingly unruffled exterior. Madame Delahaye and Raymonde Zehnacker and Pierre his chauffeur could tell tales about the ways they buoyed him, coddled him, held his hand. They had been known to tuck him into bed at night and comfort him in the face of the anxieties that tormented him even in his sleep. Raymonde Zehnacker, for example, was on call around the clock, often being wakened in the middle of the night by her beloved employer sobbing like a child. But no one was to know any of this. All that was visible to an outside observer was Dior's expanding girth. The more his business grew, the more Christian Dior put on weight. But it was not merely a function of his age and hearty appetite.

Pierre Perrotino was privy to one piece of knowledge he would never share. He alone knew about Dior's two heart attacks. . . . The first occurred in 1947 in the gardens of the Jeu de Paume museum, the second in the Champs de Mars, where they were taking an extended stroll after a visit to the Rodin Museum. Perrotino would never forget the fright he got when Dior suddenly crumpled to the ground and had to be carried to the nearest bench.

Though he had been sworn to secrecy, Perrotino had often been tempted to say something. Fortunately, Dior's doctors had already issued their own warnings and forced Dior to set up a little room next to his office where he could retire for short spells. But as Perrotino knew only too well, his employer was incapable of resting. And there was no way of persuading him to eat a little less or to cut out all the rich and heavy things he loved. Dior was well aware that he had kidney problems and could not effectively eliminate fatty products. But Dr. Strumza might as well have been talking to the air. Perrotino could not help thinking all these admonitions were doing more harm than good, making Dior feel so guilty for not listening to his doctors' advice that his anxiety levels were actually increased. He might better have resigned himself to burning the candle at both ends and forgotten the warnings.

Everything was happening too quickly around him. That, at least, was the excuse made by those closest to him, who themselves had too little time to worry about these things. Besides, it was particularly endearing to have a boss like this, a great genius who was not ashamed to show his weaker side. It made them all feel protective toward him. It distressed them to see him disappear for a few hours into the little room off his office, stressed and worn out, and it was touching to see him standing by his window looking out wistfully at Fouquet's tempting displays.

He was so vulnerable, too, with all his superstitions and the collection of lucky charms and amulets he kept in his pocket at all times. It was common knowledge that he needed to touch a piece of wood to get through a collection showing or when signing a contract. It was Madame Delahaye's task to choose the most auspicious date for launching a new collection and it could never be an odd number. Everyone knew his phobias. You could never enter his office with an umbrella. Once an American buyer went in with his umbrella without anyone noticing. He was immediately asked to leave.

Dior was enough of a character to reveal his collection of lucky charms on American TV. The two hearts, a sprig of lily of the valley, a piece of engraved gold, a little piece of wood, a four-leafed clover, and the famous gilt star were all displayed for the inspection of the CBS audience in 1955. The rather rough five-pointed star — which he had reproduced, nonetheless, in gold — was his favorite charm, symbol of the fate that led him to found the House of Dior. The designer had chanced upon it as it lay where it had fallen from the hub of a carriage wheel, on the cobblestones of Saint-Honoré, right on the very spot where, three times in a row, he had bumped into his friend Vigouroux, the man Providence had sent to lead to the meeting with Marcel Boussac.

Several hundred copies had been made of the star and were used as a medal for model employees. And the House of Dior was the type of establishment where everyone vied for such an honor. Such an exceptional boss was worth giving one's all for, and the desire to emulate him was so universal, his perfectionism and devotion to his workers so infectious, it was impossible not to become fired up by it all. In their affection for Dior, his employees had fallen into a trap, observing a work ethic that totally bowed to Dior's ideal. That was the way things worked at Avenue Montaigne, where realizing the impossible was the norm and surpassing oneself was routine. This all-pervading heroism emanated from the designer's studio itself and no one escaped its thrall. The studio was considered a holy shrine where nothing but the most perfectly executed work would do. No one dared fall short of the ideal, an attitude learned from Marguerite Carré, who, when presenting a dress to Monsieur Dior, would respectfully inquire whether she had "expressed" her master's thoughts correctly.

He asked too much. But everyone loved him and was ready to do his every bidding. There were those who were still on the premises even in the evening. Jacques Rouët's daughter complains, "I never saw my father when I was growing up."

They indulged Dior to the hilt, even when he was moody, threw a little tantrum, or flew off the handle. Proof positive was the way rooms fell silent the minute *le patron* appeared. Whenever he crossed the salon or walked through a workroom, all idle chatter came to a halt. He was princely in his etiquette — like Louis XIV with a servant, he would always step back to allow even the lowliest apprentice to enter the elevator in front of him — but his ire could also be princely rage.

"I won't have it!" he would cry. "Not in my house. That sort of behavior is quite unacceptable. I want her out of here immediately."

"Her" might have been a model who criticized a dress or the irritated saleswoman who referred to a client as "that Arab!" (The particular Arab in question was Madame Cettaui, from an old Egyptian family and very much a Parisian.) Dior never let an offense go by without laying down the law. Manners in his *maison* had to be on a par with those at the finest royal court.

Entering the atelier was a ceremonious act and not performed lightly. Dior was always in collar and tie and, naturally, so too were his employees. Claude Licard, a young assistant in charge of fabrics, had been away on a trip when he dropped in at Avenue Montaigne still in his holiday clothes. Dior sent him straight home to change out of his polo shirt and into a suit. "Then we'll talk," he said.

"That man is a saint, I tell you. An absolute saint!" One young salesgirl was still worked up at the memory, ten years after the event. And a memorable moment it was too, unique, no doubt, in the history of the profession. Christian Dior had stood up for a salesgirl, against a client! And not just anyone. The client was no less a personage than Barbara Hutton. In a fit of gratitude for the trouble her salesgirl had taken to have a dress ready for her on time, even delivering it personally to her hotel, the heiress had spontaneously presented the girl with her earrings. Quite overcome by the generosity of the gift, the girl protested at first but, after her client insisted, she accepted. The poor girl had no idea that Miss Hutton was quite tiddly, in her customary fashion, and that she would wake up the next day completely unaware of her lavish gesture. It was not long before the phone rang at Avenue Montaigne. "My earrings have disappeared," la Hutton cried. "Question your salesgirl at once!" It could have been fatal but Dior, convinced of the honesty of his staff, took things in hand and telephoned the wealthy American in person. A little lesson in good breeding followed. "I am very sorry, Madame," he said, "but you gave her those earrings as a gift. The way we do it here in France is that gifts, once given (and even to hired help), cannot be taken back!"

Even on the occasions when Dior was in the wrong, he had a wonderful way of soliciting forgiveness. Imagine the astonishment of customers at the florist Dedeban's shop on Boulevard Haussmann on Christmas Day 1954. Standing at the till handing out change was none other than Christian Dior. The explanation for his presence had everyone in fits of laughter. Dior was paying a "forfeit," like a child attempting to get back into someone's good graces.

The incident had occurred the previous evening. Christian Dior was expecting guests for a Christmas Eve celebration, but the flowers had not arrived and Dior was livid. Without his flower arrangements — in this case a pyramid of fruit entwined with roses and a set of floral candelabra — the overall effect of his buffet was ruined, and if Madame Dedeban did not show up with the flowers before the guests arrived, he would not let anyone in the door and the whole evening would be ruined.

Madame Dedeban did arrive, at the very last minute, puffing and panting and blissfully unaware of what awaited her. The couturier launched into a series of invectives. The poor little woman leaped with shock, began trembling furiously, and fled in a fit of sobs. She was inconsolable for the rest of the evening. It took every ounce of rectitude and authority that Joseph the butler could muster to dare to admonish Dior once his guests had finally left. "I what?" exclaimed Dior, devastated. "I made my poor little Dedeban cry?"

And so the following morning there he was on Boulevard Haussmann with a case of champagne in his arms. As if that was not enough, he then dismissed the boy on the till, saying, "I'll do it. I have to earn my forgiveness."

The practical joker in Dior was always ready to strike. It was an aspect of his character that never left him. Using his privileged position of power, he would turn little events and announcements into special theatrical moments, for the sheer personal pleasure of it. He loved to see the look on people's faces and to hold them, just for a moment, in the palm of his hand.

One Christmas Eve, one of his young employees was summoned to the master's office. "*Le patron* wants to talk to you." Frédéric Castet, a fabric cutter in Madame Ida's workroom, was filled with foreboding. Why did the boss want him? Although he knew he had done nothing wrong, he rather wished it were someone else who had been called in. Slowly making his way up to the master's office, he knocked on the door with a shaking hand. Dior answered the door. "Follow me, my boy," he said without further explanation, his face inscrutable. He led the way to the fifth floor, relishing in anticipation the effect his surprise would have. They came to a halt in front of a closed door, on it a plaque bearing the words "Monsieur Frédéric." It was his Christmas present . . . his own workroom. The young man's face lit up with indescribable gratitude. Nothing could have been a better reward for his master than to see the open expression of love and adoration on Castet's face. "It was the best Christmas present I have ever had," he recalls.

There were Christmas presents for everyone at Dior. It was something of an institution and Dior would spend months organizing the right gift for each of his five hundred employees. He was assisted by Madame Dedeban the florist, his adviser in these matters, and made a point of finding something for every taste and interest. Sometimes he picked them out himself, at the flea markets, at antique shops, or around and about with his companion Jacques Homberg. Marguerite was especially fond of Murano glass, Jacques could not resist dogs, Raymonde loved anything blue. . . . On occasion he would ask the recipient outright. "What about you, *frontinette?* What would you like for Christmas?" "Oh sir, a mink coat!" She got a mink tie instead — no point getting everyone else jealous. No point upsetting anyone either, or forgetting anyone . . . the idea was to win their hearts.

Toward the end of December Dior would hold a series of parties at his home, transforming his dining room into a regular Ali Baba's treasure cave. Christmas Eve was reserved for the "family" from Avenue Montaigne. New Year's Day was for his "real" family, his oldest and dearest friends: Henri Sauguet and Jacques Dupont, Francis Poulenc, Victor Grandpierre, Georges Geffroy, Boris Kochno, Jean Bertrand, James de Coquet, Alice Chavane, Denise Tual, and Georges and Nora Auric.

In the school vacation between Christmas and the New Year came the little Colle girls' turn. Dior had "adopted" them when Pierre Colle died and was now a fully accredited great-uncle or even grandfather, receiving regular visits and as much a part of their life as Carmen Colle, running the first boutique, was of life at Dior. Dior would dress up as

Father Christmas and spend the whole week playing jokes and tag and other wonderful games with the girls. They would come with their friends to laugh and snack and play hide-and-seek, or simply to admire their presents. For those few days the walls were covered with a layer of paper to guard against any clumsy marks made during the heat of the game. It was a very happy time for Dior. Playing Father Christmas was definitely his favorite role.

They met in New York. He was handsome in a dark, mysterious way, with a farmer's tan and bright, hopeful eyes. He exuded good health, carried himself with the kind of poise found only in simple people, country folk who know what life is all about. He smiled like a kid who has not yet found out that the sun does not always shine, walked with the confidence of someone who knows who he is and where he is going . . . with all the arrogance and certainty of youth. It only took a moment and Dior was hooked, trapped once again by the unattainable, by the impossible.

His name was Jacques Tiffaut and he was from the Charente in central France. A tailor in his hometown, he had come to try his luck in the New World. It was a wise move. He showed promise.

But how to attract his attention? How to make him notice? How to make him fall for me? Long sleepless nights passed. Dior offered to give him drawing lessons, or perhaps a position in his couture house. Raymonde Zehnacker seemed to think it would be all right. But then, she was not the greatest judge of character. Jacques Tiffaut was the stubborn, proud, upstanding type . . . and he was determined to make it on his own or not at all.

The chief editor of *Vogue,* Diana Vreeland, had also noticed him and, as a neutral party, counted for more than Christian Dior. Still, there was a certain attraction between the two men. With all Dior's wit and charmingly foolish ways to offset his lack of physical charms, finally, it seemed, things might click.

But it did not last. It was always the same story. Dior wanted a lover and ended up with a friend. He cried out for love and got platonic loyalty instead. A trip to Egypt with Tiffaut and the Libermans did nothing to alter the situation. The Sphinx at sundown, the pyramids in all their majesty, the Nile and its silvery gleam . . . romantic as the

setting may have been, it did not sway Tiffaut's feelings. So it was on to
another round of presents — nothing excessive, one mustn't get carried
away by one's passions — and history lessons for this boy who had been
raised on a farm.

No, let's just be friends. Like all the others, Pierre Perrotino,
Jacques Homberg, André Levasseur, Gaston Berthelot. Just as that
gypsy fortune-teller way back in Granville had once predicted,
"Women will be your path to success." What was it about this man that
prevented any other man from making him happy while women would
do anything, even act as fairy godmothers? Besides those who worked
for him, who stitched and shaped his dresses, there was the silent army
who flocked to satisfy his every whim. And he, knowing that, loved and
cultivated them all, without exception, just as he cultivated his English
gardens. Suzanne and Carmen were his hostesses, Mitzah his model
and muse, Marguerite his seamstress. . . . Then there was Raymonde.
For years she had been one of them, the women of his dreams, who
shielded him, cossetted him, worked miracles for him, played her part
in the Dior orchestra, and contributed to the atmosphere of relative
harmony that prevailed. Then Dior started to miss a beat here and
there and she, Raymonde, came forward from the crowd to assist. She
was the woman of his sleepless nights and he needed her. The time
would come, however, when the woman he could not do without was
to feel supplanted in his affections.

They met on March 13, 1956. Thirteen again! How could Dior fail to
believe in the magic power of numbers? He was due to see his friend
André Ostier, the photographer, at the Monpensier Theater in Versailles. When they met during the intermission, Ostier was with a
friend. The newcomer was twenty years old, radiating youth, with the
classically pure features of a certain type of Mediterranean beauty. He
was also incredibly, touchingly shy. Even before shaking hands, Dior
and he knew they were meant for each other.

The young man's name was Jacques Benita. He had just arrived in
France from his native Morocco, where Ostier had made his acquaintance a few months earlier. Ostier was traveling in Morocco, and had
been at a show put on by the Air Force. Benita was one of the artists, a
singer of popular music. Now he had decided to try his luck in Paris.

Born into a Sephardic Jewish family in Oujda, on the border with Algeria, Benita had had a tough childhood and had been brought up without a father. Dior was to become a father figure to him. From the moment they met they became inseparable. Benita was to be Dior's last companion.

Raymonde, however, saw him as a threat to the established order. Benita had a set of keys to Dior's home and would frequently spend the night there, although he had kept his own lodgings on Rue de Saussure. During the day Dior would occasionally give him the car and his driver, saying, "Take the car today, I don't need it." Theirs was a delightful father-son relationship and — much to Raymonde Zehnacker's displeasure, as she was used to producing young men, some interested, others less so, to entice her employer — Jacques never tried to take advantage of the situation. Nor could he be manipulated. What's more, Dior was genuinely in love with him and included him in all his activities. When Dior threw dinner parties at home, Jacques would be seated at the end of the table opposite the host. They went to Barcelona together, where they dined with Salvador Dalí and his wife Gala. Dior hated to be without him but Jacques, who had an engagement at Suzy Solidor's Cabaret on Rue Balzac, would not let him see his performance, partly out of shyness, but perhaps out of coquetry too. Bowing to Benita's ban, Dior had to confine himself to sending notes and messages, delivered to Benita at the cabaret. There was one particular evening, though, when Dior was unable to contain himself. He was hosting a dinner party for twelve. But he so missed his friend that no sooner had the guests been seated than, turning his back on etiquette, Dior fled to find Jacques.

"*Patron,* you're overdoing it. Go and take a rest." Gently, diplomatically, with just the right note of soothing authority, she alone could lead him toward his little anteroom when he became flustered, breathless from raising his voice, exhausted after twenty-four hours of endless interruptions. She was the one who sanctioned or forbade the chocolates he adored. "*Patron,* they're bad for you." When he begged, she would use the unshakeable argument, "How will anyone find you attractive if you keep putting on weight?" He listened to her. When all his wiles had run out, she always had an answer for everything. She was the keeper of his secret appointment diary and played the go-between behind the scenes, lining up tête-à-têtes with any young man Dior might have his eye on. Hers was a subtle, delicate role. But she had one major fault, according to the others who aspired to be among the couturier's chosen few. She was indispensable. She was hardly to blame. It was Dior who was clinging to her harder than ever.

Everywhere Dior went, Raymonde Zehnacker went too. He would not have dreamed of being without her even at his house in Milly where he spent every weekend . . . with all his little family from Avenue Montaigne, in fact. They all had their own rooms. Raymonde had "Madame's" bedroom, with its swan-neck bed and white Swiss muslin hangings. She never used to arrive until Saturday morning. Previously married, Madame Zehnacker was involved with a doctor and tried as best she could to keep a little bit of private life despite Dior and his need to have all his people around him at all times. Mitzah Bricard would come with her husband and was never seen without her turban and high heels. They would arrive on Friday evenings. Pierre Perrotino would drive Dior down with his official companion Jacques Homberg, who had been with him when he found the house. "It's a ruin in a swamp," Homberg had exclaimed, none too convinced of the wisdom of such a purchase. Consisting of several little buildings and outhouses, a farmyard, a pond, a trout stream, and lichen-covered walls, the Moulin du Coudret was just minutes away from the village of Milly-la-Forêt, which Dior knew well from having often visited Cocteau there. The house had been his first major purchase, courtesy of the New Look.

He never did become an architect as he had once wished. His parents would have been forced to revise their opinions, however, had they seen how Christian worked to remodel each of his houses in their image, in homage to his parents, as a tribute to his childhood and to his native soil, defending it against all the bleakness of the modern infatuation with fake style and sham in the way his fiercely Norman forefathers had taught him. These were houses that would have fitted his mother like a glove; they were solid, sturdy, and deeply rooted in the real France, just as his father would have liked. He waited patiently until he could turn his new homes into replicas of his parents'. At Le Coudret the idea was to restore this country idyll, with its scent of hay and wildflowers, without spoiling its natural charms. He and Jacques Homberg combed the flea markets, burnished the original floortiles, protected the ceiling beams, filled the huge cupboards with lavender, and decorated in simple, light-colored fabrics, striped mattress ticking, whites and grays. The result had all the spartan, rustic charm of a house in a small country town.

Neighbors would drop by for lunch, like Jean Cocteau, who sometimes brought Marlene Dietrich. Every now and then the illustrator René Gruau would set himself up in a corner with his sketch pad. Dior would spend the morning in his garden, wearing rubber boots, a Russian peasant's hat, and a pullover if it was chilly. He and his Polish gardener Ivan would spend hours dreaming up some new layout. One spectacular idea was to plant dark red hollyhocks against the gray stone of the mill "with one heartbreaking pink rose blooming at their feet," as houseguest and *Vogue* editor Bettina Ballard recalls. It looked like an Impressionist painting.

This garden of "flower surprises" she goes on to describe as "a curious delight," which she discovered after a fine lunch of potatoes with caviar and the Martinican cook Madame Denise's famous pineapple dessert, followed by a sweet raspberry liqueur Dior made from his own berries. The garden reminded her of his finest gowns. When she remarked on this to the couturier, he smiled with pleasure.

Every afternoon, though, he would excuse himself and retire for a nap, shutting himself away in his room, in a cozy alcove where he felt safe and protected behind the hangings of his bed. This was where he usually dreamed up his next collection, roaming from one room to the other, from his bathtub to his chaise longue. In these periods of frenzied activity he found it vital to know that, somewhere on the other side of the door, Raymonde, Gaston, André, or some of the others were waiting to applaud the newest line and to cast an indispensable outsider's eye on the latest sketches.

Quite unintentionally his country refuge gradually became another creative workshop. Originally designed as somewhere to play truant from the world, where fellow artists and childhood friends could gather to laugh and play cards together, it no longer was a place to escape to. Instead he found himself thinking even more of the Paris *maison*. New surroundings were meant to clear his head, but the more he tried to get away from Avenue Montaigne, the more his mind pulled him back. Being away worried him. Not even the gentle rhythm of the river could soothe him as it lapped musically day and night outside his window. There were times when he wished someone could make it stop, the noise made it impossible for him to think.

Once, not so long ago, he had been able to shut his Parisian life away when he came to the mill. He would play a sonata on the piano, have a round of canasta, or take up his tapestry needle and absorb himself in watching it move in and out of the canvas. There was a time when he loved nothing more than to be in the thick of things. Nowadays he was happy just reviving old memories, like the time he went to the Greek islands with Roger Vivier and Michel Brodsky. "What a trip! What chaos! When you take off on the spur of the moment you have to be prepared for anything to happen . . . and it did. The minute we stepped off the boat there was an earthquake. And then they requisitioned the vessel as a hospital ship to take in all the people evacuating from the island. It was quite a sea journey. Do you remember, Christian? They took Mrs. Engel, in her little dress, for one of the nurses. It was hilarious."

There was a big crowd at the table that day. Everyone laughed.

If only he had known how to let go occasionally, instead of trying to instill perfection into every detail of his life. His white-gloved employees would brush their hands across every piece of furniture, stepping softly from one room to the next, checking for dust, buffing the silverware, making sure the lamps were working, that there was enough water in the vases . . . all with a view to preempting *le patron,* putting themselves in his shoes and walking around once more, making sure things were as they should be. Everything was ready. The candles were lit, the white damask cloth was set with crystal, the aperitifs were standing by, sherry, port, and vodka. The leg of lamb was resting in its juices. It was a solemn moment. This was not to be taken lightly. It was a regular ceremony. The only thing that ever varied was the guest list.

Christian Dior had moved to new premises. Looking out the window brought the past back to him, for destiny had yet again taken him full circle.

When he set out to find a new abode in Paris, this time to

purchase, not rent, pure coincidence led him to a dainty little residence in the fashionable Sixteenth Arrondissement that looked directly across to his grandparents' old apartment on Rue Albéric-Magnard. As an adolescent he had admired the columned balcony of the little town house, which used to belong to a theatrical lady from Saint Petersburg. As a child he had spent hours dreaming up novels around this mysterious and elegant figure and now here he was, in her home. You could not tell him this was not meant to be!

The first time he inspected the house he felt like an intruder, almost reluctant to step inside, like a thief in the home of a woman he had dreamed of night after night but whom he had never met or seen. Everything was just as he had imagined: arabesques, festoons, and astragals, like a cozy love nest. What really won him over was the winter garden, the perfect place to plant the kentia and phoenix palms of his Granville days.

Christian Dior's residences all followed the same mysterious pattern, reconstructing broken lives, picking up the threads of the past and retrieving even the most tenuous link with his childhood. One day he happened to find out that his old school, the Lycée Gerson, was about to be demolished, and he managed to buy the bells. In fact, he would have been tempted to leave the painted lady's home just as he had found it, like a picture album or a scrapbook. But the house was intended as an annex to Avenue Montaigne — a refuge but also a showcase.

To avoid offending anyone, he asked two decorator friends to take on the interior design. Georges Geffroy did the reception rooms, Victor Grandpierre the bedrooms and the study. It was neo–Louis XVI with a vengeance — potted palms, Aubusson rugs, a Delafosse console table, and, right in the middle of the drawing room, an Athenian plantholder in Paris porcelain to pay tribute to the glories of the eighteenth century. Upholstery and quilting abounded amid a riot of little frames, photographs, and ornaments, alcoves and velvet. Particularly indulgent was the bathroom, a delicious treat reserved exclusively for the master of the house. Here he would revel in bourgeois luxury as he took his bath in a tub speckled with silver, surrounded by an enormous mirror, and everything in faux marble. . . . The idea came from his friend Emilio Terry, whose own Empire-style bathroom at his home on Place du Palais-Bourbon was actually a copy of the bathroom of Madame

Tallien.* It was important to know how to indulge oneself, in secret, if nothing else.

Sometimes in the early morning silence when he first opened his eyes, curled up under his blankets, his breakfast tray and morning newspapers laid out on his bed, he would think with nostalgia of Rue Royale, his first apartment, his first four walls, after so many tough years. He had nurtured that place in the way one watches over one's first child. Everything about it was perfect, including its faults. He even liked the four flights of stairs he had to climb to get to his front door. What wonderful moments they had shared there, Dior and Jacques Homberg, in their hideaway. Those early years now seemed so serene and trouble free. In those days he could still afford to switch off occasionally, to not hear the telephone and rest as he wished.

But this was Boulevard Jules-Sandeau, where he lived alone in his little town house — alone if you did not count the six members of his domestic staff. Total silence reigned. He would not stand for any noise. Downstairs, of course, had been bustling since dawn. By now the butchers, greengrocers, and pastry chefs would have made their deliveries. But Dior had seen to it that no noise ever traveled upstairs, by asking every deliveryman to wear slippers in the house! He was well aware that such measures had many of his friends and acquaintances laughing at him behind his back, but let them laugh. Domestic staff had to be just as perfect as the lining of a Dior gown, unobtrusive but styled for maximum effect.

Once downstairs he would take up his position on a sofa opposite the portrait of his mother, sitting regal and dignified in black lace and a hat, like a Boldini painting. Every day he would greet her with respect. Generally he would partake of a second breakfast at this point, a little guiltily. What a sorry tribute to pay her, beautiful as she was . . . a misshapen figure like his. He would catch sight of himself in the mirror as he passed, "your old couturier growing fatter as he withers away," as he once described himself in a letter to Denise Tual. It had become

---

* Daughter of a wealthy Spanish banker, Teresa Tallien was the wife of Jean Tallien, founder of the Club of Jacobins. She was well respected in Paris and inspired a fashion of returning to antiquity.

increasingly true. He would have liked another slice of buttered toast but resisted the temptation. He wanted to be attractive but how could he when he was so fat and ugly? It wasn't fair!

The telephone had not rung so far this morning. Thank goodness. A few more minutes in peace. But why hadn't it rung yet? Incredible. No news from Avenue Montaigne, at this hour?

"Joseph, would you get me Avenue Montaigne on the line, please?"

And so another day would get under way. There was the present list to check one last time . . . and the menus. At least an hour with Madame Delahaye to go over the coming year. Try on the Father Christmas costume again and don't forget to congratulate the chef for that dessert the other evening. Tell him to keep the recipe. Definitely. And remind Joseph not to get too officious. He is only a butler, after all, he's not there to tell the guests what to do; if the ladies must smoke at table, it's fine. Be sure not to offend him, though. Liliane de Rothschild and Jean-Louis de Faucigny-Lucinge didn't touch their baked oysters with béchamel the other night. So don't serve them that dish again. Oh, and reorganize the seating plans. Vivien Leigh and Laurence Olivier will be in Paris next month. Make sure the guest list is different when they come. Perhaps they should meet my little Geneviève? Just the young leading lady they need. And find a date to see all my old friends . . . ah, there's never time for any fun!

Then again, things were different now, as Dior well knew. The extremely conventional and formal atmosphere that reigned at Boulevard Jules-Sandeau was hardly conducive to shouting, laughter, and impromptu charades. The old gang, gourmets and guzzlers the lot of them, had lost their disobedient ways when sitting around Dior's dinner table.

Even at home, it never let up for a moment. Dior was needed everywhere, to check everything. As he sat gazing at his mother's face he continued to run through the list of things to be done that day.

There are no secrets from a secretary, and bank balances never lie. They knew what was going on, Mademoiselle Vidmer and Mademoiselle Ramet and all the others to whom Dior was always passing instructions for a check to be made out to so-and-so, another for what's-his-name. . . . His public image was of an astute businessman with a head for figures, but the real Dior was a spendthrift. Nothing was ever quite right and he would rather have it done ten times over until it was. Then there were all the times he changed his mind. No one could figure out how he could earn what he did — his salary, his share of profits, his licensing royalties — and still keep asking for advances here and there. All his energy was invested in running the House of Dior and making it the success it was. His personal affairs were in a dreadful state. Every year he was late paying his taxes, and the warnings and fines and interest would pile up. No one but his secretaries knew the truth, which was that, by 1957, he had accumulated a tax debt of forty million francs.

It was easy to see that Dior wanted to make up for all the hardship of the bad years by living like a lord, albeit in a generous and totally unpretentious way. But why such frenzy, such excess, even in the way he organized his pleasures to the extent that they would devour him rather than give him the relief he really craved? It seemed he could not help it. Every time he took on a new house he would find himself prisoner of his desire for something more than perfect and the dictates of his overly fertile imagination. His infatuations caused him the same torment, usually ending disastrously. His strict morality did not help, either, never allowing him to give in to his desires. Even at home, in whatever one of his residences it might be, tranquillity evaded him. He was like a petulant child ever in search of his youth. His past became more and more remote, his forays more and more intense and impassioned.

The next stage on the journey was La Colle Noire.

"I want it to feel like a family home, one that has been passed down from generation to generation. I don't want anything new, it has to have a well-worn feel to it. It has to be old, rich in memories, bearing the mark of my ancestors and the weight of centuries. I want a five-pointed star set into the floor of the entrance hall, the little drawing room must be hung with the same fabric as Louise de Vilmorin's place at Verrières, but in red rather than blue. The front door has to be at the front of the house, not on the side, with two stone lions guarding the way. The first floor should not be too high, the pond has to be bigger than all the others, I need lots of water in case of drought and plenty of light at night. I want an antique statue, classical proportions, two towers instead of one and the garden has to be at least fifty hectares, full of flowers so that you can really smell their perfume . . . we need to call Madame Delahaye and Raymonde and . . ." And it would cost a fortune.

In 1951 Christian Dior discovered an old coach house not far from the family's former dwelling at Callian, in Provence, on the magnificent plateau that stretched from Draguignan to Grasse, empty save for a few lonely villages clinging to the hillsides covered with vineyards and orchards. It was not until 1954, however, that he was able to start renovations. He enlisted the services of the best-known architect in the area, André Svetchine, along with decorator Michel-Jacques Marsan. But he knew exactly what he wanted and all they had to do was follow his instructions.

He got his Olympic-length ornamental pond, which doubled as a swimming pool. It was like a magnificent mirror dominated by a majestic statue that was lit up at nightfall. He got his lions surveying the vast valley at their feet. He got his garden, after turning and returning the soil, ripping up old plants, putting in new. And he got the perfect symmetry he asked for. It was a huge job. Nothing was ever too beautiful, too big, or too complicated. Nothing was impossible.

He wanted to be the lord of the manor as the Diors once were in their native Granville. To get up in the morning and have the whole horizon, the sea, the world, and the universe to himself and himself alone. To see everything without being seen. To not have to go anywhere, except from one garden bed to the next, cultivating his shrubs and plants far from the noise and bustle of modern life. To stop still for a moment, hands in the earth, eyes turned to the sky.

Everyone remarked on how hard he seemed to find the stairs as he saw his friends to the door after lunch. The heat in mid-August 1956 was stifling. His guests that day included his old friends Alexander and Tatiana Liberman. There were five courses on the menu and Tania could only pick at it. Even Alex, who had more of an appetite, soon came to a standstill. The meal seemed interminable as they sat in their light cottons, longing for a little fresh air on their damp skin.

He had changed. During a farewell dinner he held Jacques's hand for all to see, melancholy with the thought that his companion was leaving him, forced by the war in Algeria to return home. For once Dior had forgotten his principles. So much for secrecy and discretion.

Everyone noticed the hand-holding — and commented on it. In fact, Marie-Laure de Noailles's musician friend Ned Rorem later recounted the episode in his memoirs, referring to Benita as "the Arab." The nickname, derived from Benita's Moroccan origins (although he was actually Jewish!), was bestowed on him by members of Dior's entourage like Pierre Perrotino and Jacques Tiffaut, who looked on jealously at the favors enjoyed by this latest arrival, or Raymonde Zehnacker, frustrated by her loss of absolute control over the situation.

Jacques left for Morocco . . . but managed to get himself discharged from military service and returned three weeks later.

Suddenly it was ten years. A hundred thousand dresses sold, a thousand miles of embroidered fabric, sixteen thousand sketches . . . and endless congratulations. Everyone was there to celebrate the event. Bravo, *patron,* we all love you. Countless photographs, interviews . . .

"Why have you never married?" asked one American television interviewer innocently. "Is it because you know women too well?"

"I have over a thousand women working for me in Paris, that's more than enough!" the couturier replied.

As he stood in that packed room loud with laughter, with everyone enjoying themselves, how could he tell them that all he wanted was to retreat into some huge empty garden somewhere?

There was Suzanne to see to his guests, Marguerite to cut his fabrics, Mitzah to amuse herself for him, Rouët to look after his accounts, and many others to design for him. The result was spectacular, unparalleled. All he had to be was the attentive onlooker, the father and founder, the mentor. It was a part he played well, nurturing up-and-coming talents at every opportunity, ever with an eye to the future. From the outset he and Jacques Rouët had worked to build up the business to last, as a training ground based on solid principles. The success of the House made their task all the easier. It was a natural magnet for the best and brightest, "like getting into the Polytechnique," as the young Jean-Louis Scherrer said. Scherrer did his apprenticeship at Dior and soon turned heads, going on eventually to his own label.

André Levasseur was another success story. His task was to do sketches of the patterns sold under license. But all he wanted to do was be a designer, a real one, and there were times when he could not resist giving the sketches a little personal touch here and there. His additions did not go unnoticed and, indeed, Dior was thrilled and unstinting in his praise, although unable to resist toying with the young man for just a moment. "I must tell you what I've done with your drawings, André," he said, putting on his sternest look. Levasseur stiffened. But Dior soon relented. "Two of them have been included in the New York collection. And one of them is without doubt the biggest seller this season." Dior burst out laughing at the expression on the young man's face. He would never win him as a lover; being a father figure would have to be second best.

Then there was Yves Saint Laurent, who came to Dior on the recommendation of *Vogue's* Michel de Brunhoff. Born in Oran, in the then French colony of Algeria, he was twenty years old in 1955. He had dreamed of Paris ever since childhood and at seventeen had won first prize in a competition, sponsored by the International Wool Secretariat, aimed at promoting new talents. At first Dior hardly seemed to notice the young prodigy, whom he sat at a little table in his studio. There was no immediate affinity. This shy boy with glasses, slender as a stem and stiff as a seminarian, was not the couturier's type. Henri Sauguet's niece, Anne-Marie Mugnoz, who tried to stay as invisible as possible while she tidied fabrics at the back of the room, was the first to make friends with him. She coaxed him out in the evening and, together with Karl Lagerfeld, they formed a little gang of three. But it was not long before the high priestesses discovered him, captivated by his fragile air, and brought him under their wing. Suzanne Luling, for one, took it upon herself to show him the Paris she knew, while Dior slowly began taking notice of his assistant's talent with a pencil. Finally, in 1957, he became convinced that he had found the one he would groom as his successor. "I want you to promote Yves Saint Laurent," he told Jacques Rouët. "All forty of his designs in the last collection were a hit and I want the papers to know about him."

This was no longer a game, and these young men were not just pawns to be manipulated at Dior's whim, to surprise for the sake of his own pleasure. He had other plans now and had begun to look beyond his own walls. His friend Alice Chavane introduced him to a young man by the name of Marc Bohan who was looking for a position after having had to abandon plans for going out on his own. Nothing came of the meeting, as the ever-present Raymonde vetoed the appointment. But Dior kept an eye on Marc Bohan at Patou and eventually asked Jacques Rouët to get in touch with him. He had the glimmerings of an idea. He had decided to ask Yves Saint Laurent to take on Paris with him, but he also needed someone to assist with the New York collections. He offered that role to Marc Bohan, swearing him to the utmost secrecy. It was not so much that he was planning to retire. What he did want was to feel reassured, to allay his anxieties and bring under control this enormous machine with its monstrous appetite for new designs. He wanted to be one step ahead, to provide for all contingencies. . . .

Next week he would call his attorney. He had to alter his will again. Seven years earlier, when it was first drafted, his estate was to be divided equally among Pierre Perrotino, Raymonde Zehnacker, Catherine Dior, and his old governess Marthe Lefebvre. Three more versions had followed, the list of beneficiaries growing progressively to include nephews and nieces, Jacques Homberg, his friends, his coworkers, the national museums . . . only to be pared back again. He did not forget the other Jacques either, his final source of happiness. He promised Benita he would buy him an apartment of his own, once the Moulin du Coudret was sold. For the boy with no family, this meant he would never have to want for anything again.

The final version of his will, however, dated August 30, 1957, was simple and to the point: "I Christian Dior hereby bequeath the sum of my worldly possessions to be shared equally by my sister Catherine Dior and Madame Raymonde Zehnacker. Furthermore I charge them with guaranteeing an appropriate living allowance to Mademoiselle Marthe Lefebvre." He devised his will as he designed his gowns — going from the most elaborate of concepts to end up with the most streamlined.

The allocation of his worldly goods was not, however, a final declaration of allegiances. He was both loyal and unfaithful, as fickle in his male infatuations as he was in favoring one *chérie* over the next. He was everyone's and no one's, and perhaps that is all that could ever be expected of him.

There was one woman, though, who truly believed she had won

his heart. She escaped most people's attention, being the shy, rather unapproachable type. Blond and delicate, fearfully sensitive and frightfully moody, the woman was Dior's florist, Paule Dedeban. Her rightful place, albeit discreet, is with the others who shared Dior's favors, although the relationship between two such tentative souls could only ever have been an unspoken one. Their liaison began in the early days of the Avenue Montaigne. Invited one evening to dine at the home of his friend Georges Geffroy, Dior was struck by a series of rustic flower arrangements, little masterpieces in their own right. Dandelions and tomatoes, what a fabulously daring idea and how delightfully amusing! He wheedled the name of their creator out of his friend. It was Madame Paule Dedeban.

But Dior was not the type to fall head over heels just like that. Besides, there was his regular florist, Lachaume, who did all the floral arrangements for the House of Dior and always to Dior's greatest satisfaction. The temptation was great, but how was he to decide?

The solution lay with Madame Delahaye. Dior devised a little ruse, with all his childlike cunning. The astrologer would get the florist to her house by ordering a bouquet of flowers. It would then be quite simple to find a way of reading Paule Dedeban's cards . . . and then phoning Dior to tell him what she had discovered. After all, he could not dismiss Lachaume before consulting his astrologer on the wisdom of such a move. The telephone rang and Dior seized the receiver. "Allô, Christian?" It was Madame Delahaye. "It's fine. Go ahead." The delighted Dior did not waste a moment in calling Georges Geffroy, brimming with excitement. "I have to meet this person who can work such marvels with next to nothing."

And so she was hired. Soon her pyramids of pineapples, tiny shrubs made of coral, and bouquets of butterflies fluttering around the mirrors at Avenue Montaigne had clients cooing with delight and amazement. Dior was entranced. This was an enchantress, a living treasure, a true craftswoman with all the passion for her art of the France of yesteryear. To Dior, she was part of his past, symbolic of the genuineness and good taste he was constantly tracing and recreating. She was the crowning glory, the past rediscovered.

There was the day when Madame Dedeban was summoned to see the comptroller at Avenue Montaigne, Jacques Chastel. Would she mind giving him a breakdown of the amounts listed on her accounts? It was a fair question. He could not believe how little she was charging. When she handed back the exact calculations he pointed out that she had forgotten to include her own expenses. "What does it matter?" she exclaimed. "I don't count those when it's for Dior."

As for Dior, he gave her a full description of his property at La Colle Noire, concentrating in particular on the garden, the local vegetation, and the horticultural projects he was planning. She listened with utter admiration. He had such good taste. She would so love to see the place. Christian Dior promised to take her there. "Just the two of us," she felt like adding, "like two lovers." But there was no need. The understanding was there. The pair of them were already at work on a secret plan, like two conspirators. It was a revolutionary idea, and one that would earn them a fortune. They would create "self-service" florist shops right across France, to be called (they already had the name) Dedeban-Dior. For the less imaginative customers, there would be a floral arrangement section attached to each shop. They were ready to get the ball rolling. Paule Dedeban had already signed the lease on the first premises, so sure was she of the plan and so convinced that it would not be long before Christian was ready to retire, to leave his troubles behind him and dedicate himself to his final career — flowers.

But when night fell it was dresses and more dresses that filled Christian Dior's dreams. The latest collection, the Spindle line, had been another success, but he could not seem to recover from his fatigue. In October 1957, before going on to the next collection, Dior decided he would have to take a break and undergo a cure for his liver, hoping as always that he might lose a little weight. If only he could feel attractive, *be* attractive, to Jacques waiting patiently for his master in the backseat of the Austin Princess parked outside the premises at 30 Avenue Montaigne.

He would get on to Raymonde, get her to organize a trip to Italy to take the waters at Montecatini. . . .

The weather was lovely in that September of 1957 but Madame Delahaye had seen bad omens in his cards. She was adamant that he abandon his plans to go to Montecatini. But Dior would not listen.

Nothing seemed to have any influence on him, and the clairvoyant found herself going to Jacques, asking him to try.

"He will listen to you," she urged. "Tell him not to go." Although Jacques did his best, Dior was determined to ignore all advice. Later it would be implied that Jacques was somehow to blame, that Dior wanted to lose weight in order to appear more attractive to him. Benita would always deny the accusation, saying, "I loved him as he was."

On the eve of Dior's departure, the pair had decided they would spend the evening together. Jacques, however, had to perform. So, for the first time ever, he agreed to allow Christian Dior to be in the audience while he sang. Dior was thrilled and immediately reserved a table at the Solidor Cabaret for himself and his entourage. His last evening in Paris was spent surrounded by his women — Suzanne Luling, Nadine Fayol, and Raymonde Zehnacker — and applauding his dearest Jacques for all he was worth. "When I get back from Italy," Dior promised, "I will help you with your career. Don't you worry anymore. You'll be famous, you'll see." As they stepped out into the street, Dior began dancing in the middle of the Champs-Elysées. The following morning he would take the train for Italy.

It was the last image of Dior on the streets of Paris.

14

Dressing the Angels

Caught up in the exhausting, constant process of renewal demanded by his profession, this cultivated man had virtually stopped reading, this musician no longer played or composed, this dilettante had become the narrowest of specialists. All his energies were suddenly swallowed up in his devotion to his talents.

— Françoise Giroud

*O*ctober 27, 1957. Like a shipwreck drowning in a sea of fragrant white flowers, Christian Dior's coffin lay in the nave of the church of Saint-Honoré d'Eylau. Even more monumental in reality than in the imagination, somehow, it lay beneath a profusion of hawthorn blossoms, garden pinks, camellias, tuberoses — and lily of the valley in flower, their tiny white spring bells nodding in the autumn breeze. Two thousand people sat in the church, heavy black hangings draped along its walls. At least half of them had faces you could put a name to. Outside, another five thousand onlookers lined the street.

It spelled death, this atmosphere of spring immersed in black. There was black everywhere, rippling, swaying, across the silent, close-packed crowd, their faces marked by the fear that only sudden death can arouse in the rich and powerful. There was sadness too, almost as much as fear. Tears trembled like brilliant pearls on black-clad chests. But if only it were so simple. More than a mere ceremony of mourning, this was eerie, like some strangely majestic Black Carnival. It was an apotheosis. Dior was dead, and his death, like some ghastly vampire, would drain the lifeblood of his mourners. . . . For all of those present, suddenly too elegant for life after Dior, something quite momentous and irreversible was under way, something they sensed deep in their souls, for all their wealth and privilege, and they felt afraid. This was no ordinary death, this was a suicide — a suicide in the name of beauty and all that it demanded. In his love for the young Jacques Benita, Dior's one desire was to be younger and slimmer. But you cannot shape the human body like a piece of expensive fabric. In the process his heart had given way, the blood vessels in his brain had burst, and by the time the doctor arrived it was quite clearly too late. Dior was dead, caught in the conflict between his instinct and his ethics, his wisdom and his desire for beauty.

It had happened four days ago. Dior had breathed his last silently, just before bed, still in the armchair where he had played a round of canasta with Raymonde, his goddaughter Marie-Pierre Colle, and Pierre Perrotino, who had come to join them. Within an instant the Hotel Pace at Montecatini was in chaos . . . by now just another story consigned to the annals of history. One of Marcel Boussac's private planes had been commandeered to fly the coffin back from Italy; too long for the plane, it was carried upright all the way to Paris.

The organ music swelled out into the street. Inside the church it was cold, despite the crush. With all the pride of those who "knew him best," each clung quietly, coolly, even jealously to a private memory of Dior, each laying a personal claim to the body lying in that coffin. Pierre Perrotino stood alone in the center of the church, his body stiff, almost mummified. He could not hear the silence. His ears were still full of that frightful, inhuman wailing, that almost animal cry that had raged around him for the last four days. How could anyone die like that, without warning, without having had enough of life? How could he be forgiven for that absurd desire to be attractive to someone who already loved him for what he was, who liked his generous roundness?

Jacques was there too. He had lost his companion . . . and with him a father, for the second time in his life. He thought back to that last evening, just a week ago, when Dior had come to hear him sing for the first time ever. He could still see Dior dancing with joy on the Champs-Elysées that night after the show, promising him he would never have to worry about anything again. "I will take care of you. You'll be famous." It seemed so long ago and yet it was only yesterday. The gossiping had already begun — blaming Benita for Dior's death, for forcing Dior to go to Italy, for making him want to lose weight. But Jacques Benita paid no attention to all that. Instead he decided to leave, to leave the "family" that had never really taken him in, in the first place. In a brief burst of affection, Catherine Dior had told him she had never seen her brother as happy as he had been since meeting Benita. He would go somewhere far away, rather than stay to claim his due. He went as far as America, only to return eventually with a new identity: Tony Sandro. He disappeared from the scene just as he had entered it, without a trace.

And how could those women make peace with themselves, the ones who had given in to his whims just one more time, proud to be part of his secrets, to share his infatuations. Dior's heart attack pointed the finger squarely at them. They had not been able to stop him, not even his cherished fortune-teller Madame Delahaye, who had told him that something dreadful would happen if he went away.

The organ continued its solemn lament. Christian Dior's spirit was everywhere. Row after row they sat, in order of rank — royalty first, princesses and begums, then the society "queens" of Paris . . . and of everywhere else besides. The survivors of a world that once sparkled with wit and elegance. And what a giddy whirl it had been — the "Ball of Kings and Queens," the "Proust Ball," the "Surrealist Ball" where women came astride camels or on sedan chairs, dressed as firebirds, Cleopatras, cherubim, Harlequins.

Today, however, they were in mourning — the Faucigny-Lucinges, Marie-Laure de Noailles, the Lopez-Willshaws, Marie-

Louise Bousquet . . . all the mythic personages who had hitched their star to that of the couturier and with him brought back the age of elegance, of balls and society parties. How many people could ever have said, as Dior did, that "the clientele I wanted was the one which answered my call"? Here they all were, one last time, gathered to grant his wish. This was Dior's world, but the world had changed around them. How many of them realized that life as they had known it was being buried that day alongside Dior?

Fashion tells us things about ourselves that codify or idealize our existence. The man who knew how to exalt fashion had gone and, with his passing, its aura faded too. Another government had fallen in France, standing on the sidelines as the old nobility went through its death throes, happy to leave it to bury its own. Only a few politicians had even troubled themselves to make an appearance today, sending underlings to represent them.

In their place, though, came the tributes from Hollywood, the spectacle of their wreaths lending a very special touch to a very special moment, turning "the end of a man's life" into "the end of an era." It was hard to say who was more grandiose, Olivia de Havilland or Marlene Dietrich. Certainly no one failed to notice their bouquets.

Also in the front rows were, of course, Marcel Boussac and his wife, the former singer Fanny Heldy. There was no mistaking him. One look at his drawn features was enough to identify him — Boussac the embodiment of industrial wealth, the symbol of the way forward (or so he saw himself). Behind his imperturbable gaze his mind was racing. While on the surface he was paying homage to the man to whom he had given everything and who had paid him back so richly, he was already pondering the future.

Should he close the House of Dior? His first instinct was to do so. Marcel Boussac was a great believer in people, and there was no one who could replace Christian Dior. No one else could emulate his talent. The great Dior adventure had come to a tragic end.

What Marcel Boussac did not realize, however, was that in the rows behind him, and outside in the street, were the Dior licensees, respectfully silent today but ready to protest tomorrow, ready to implore the great man not to close down the gold mine. What he also did not know, yet, was that his own vision was clouded. Too long the all-powerful magnate whose touch turned everything to gold, he could not foresee the supreme irony of fate that was to decree that the only one of his gold mines to survive would be the House of Dior, the only one always outside his control.

His mind flew back for a furtive moment to that satisfying moment on February 12, 1947, when the New Look was launched. What a genius he had been, after all, to discover Christian Dior!

The New Look was on other minds too. Behind him, *Harper's* editor Carmel Snow, with her homely, birdlike features and flat hat, pondered the phrase she herself had invented, her famous words ringing in her ears like the vibrations from the organ. Her pride at picking a winner was tempered by her profound grief at losing such a dear friend. Similar sentiments were being shared, another few rows back, by artists who had been Dior's lifelong friends: Michel de Brunhoff from Paris *Vogue*, one of the first to believe in Dior's ability, the decorator Georges Geffroy . . .

Throughout the congregation, they mourned him in their special ways. Over there were the ladies from the workrooms, the seamstresses from the House of Dior, the models who for just a moment had forgotten to look their immaculate best. But they all faded into the background behind the four "high priestesses" seated side by side, stronger than ever, haughty even in their grief, controlled and yet compassionate: Raymonde Zehnacker, Marguerite Carré, Mitzah Bricard, and Suzanne Luling.

Jacques Rouët had had four days to digest the news. Never one to let his heart rule his head, today he still had a huge lump in his throat. Preferring a more private display of grief, he tried to suppress his emotion by concentrating on the question of his master's successors. He knew Dior planned to put Yves Saint Laurent in charge of the Paris house and set Marc Bohan up in New York to oversee design there. Perhaps Dior had known that the end was coming. Surely not. He had been driven more by a desire to distance himself a little, to discover new talents to fill the breach. Jacques Rouët knew that he would have to keep his cards close to his chest. The two young men would not find it easy to work side by side. Both of them were far too gifted in their own right.

As it would turn out, Marc Bohan was to be Dior's heir, while Yves

Saint Laurent was undoubtedly his true successor, the one who would take Dior's place in every sense, carrying the torch into the coming decades with a quite different approach, the one who would change the rules to keep the spirit of haute couture intact.

Just a few feet away from Jacques Rouët, Yves Saint Laurent was also lost in his thoughts. He could still hear the *patron's* voice demanding that the press be informed of his, Saint Laurent's, own role in the most recent collections. The very memory of it made him itch with impatience: the future was in his hands. He would rise to the occasion, he would be another Dior, equal to the man who had showered him with praise and pushed him under the fashion spotlight. Christian Dior knew what he was doing. Yves Saint Laurent looked around at the famous faces on both sides of him without really seeing them, yet only too aware that he was surrounded by the world of haute couture, out in force, a world he already felt part of and in which he might one day have more than just a passing role. His friend Pierre Bergé certainly believed that, and believed in Saint Laurent too.

Pierre Balmain, Hubert de Givenchy, Pierre Cardin . . . even Balenciaga was there. By some sort of tacit accord, fired by a sense of respect only ever reserved for the most important occasions, every one of them had closed down his establishment for the day. Only Gabrielle Chanel with her famous angry pout had refused to join the cortège, sending instead a cross made of roses, her personal flowers, her perfume.

But what did it matter? Jean Cocteau, Romanesque, a work of art in his own right, stood out from the crowd, detached, seated in front of the main altar next to the Duchess of Windsor, who was kneeling on a prie-dieu. All eyes were on them, the totems of the two Parises, the capital of the cosmopolitan aristocracy and of the artistic world. This was a symbolic pair, standing for all that Dior had been, for his life caught between high society and bohemia, between good breeding and the affectations of a dandy.

The organ sounded a final chord. Slowly the giant doors opened, with a loud grating noise. A shaft of light poured in and the onlookers outside held their breath. From every packed observation point, people stood on their toes, craning their necks to see. Some had even climbed the lampposts for a better look, providing a running commentary for the others below. "I can see the coffin." Everyone started to push, even those far away, hoping to touch it. But it was all over in an instant. The huge box was quickly lifted into the waiting hearse and the driver in his cap and uniform repeated his instructions as he set off. It was not going to be easy to move forward with such a throng of people, and Avenue Raymond Poincaré was not laid out for processions.

At the sound of the motor, seeing all these people of such royal bearing streaming out of the church to form a cortège, the onlookers moved back to allow them to pass. Flowers continued to appear from everywhere, beribboned wreaths and baskets, each arranged more brilliantly than the next. It was as if all the gardens in the world had come together, as if every ray of sunshine that had ever shone in the streets of Granville had brought its light to Paris along with every one of the city's florists, their hearts heavy and generous and sad all at once. Such an abundance of blooms and blossoms was unprecedented. The House of Dior couldn't cope. Paris had been invaded by flowers, all in tribute to a man who, unknown only ten years earlier, had overnight given the French capital its first scent of feminine gaiety, its first graceful, lively silhouettes, after so many years of gloom and ashes. One parliamentarian, in a fit of demagogy, issued a protest at such a display of luxury — an insult to the working classes, he called it. But Dior had always had a response to counter that sort of argument. "I have always seen my profession as a kind of struggle against all that is mediocre and depressing about our age." On this extraordinary occasion, the City of Paris decided to give the House of Dior permission to display this amazing spectacle along the route to the Arc de Triomphe. The Place de l'Etoile was awash with color, brilliant with thousands and thousands of petals.

After proceeding slowly along Avenue Victor-Hugo (which had probably not seen anything like this since the funeral of its namesake) the hearse moved past the monumental arch down Avenue Marceau to Avenue Montaigne.

The town house at number 30 was deserted. Yesterday it had been a hive of activity, amid requests from around the globe for a little spot at the ceremony, hundreds and thousands of telegrams, the front page of the *New York Times*, headlines in all the international papers announcing the designer's death, to be clipped and, sadly, inserted in the *maison's* press files. Today, plunged in darkness, the House seemed to have lost its soul, like a relic of another era, a phantom from some glorious bygone age.

A long way ahead by now, the hearse was leaving the outskirts of the city and the crowd began to disperse. It was over. Only his closest friends and a few other privileged people would be part of the ensuing chapters of the Dior story. The convoy, meanwhile, had taken National Route 7, heading south. Christian Dior had chosen as his last resting place Callian, the village in Provence next to his country home at La Colle Noire. Behind the hearse with its curtained windows, a long line of vehicles followed the coffin with due pomp and ceremony, attracting curious stares as it passed. In low, muffled voices, they told stories about Dior, remembered images of him, of his dresses, the decor, his kindnesses, his fits of rage, his perfectionism, his savoir-vivre, his simple approach . . .

Oblivious to the changing landscape around them, the mourners were traveling quite a different path, back through their own memories. In the village of Montauroux, which served the parish of Callian, the local priest was only too aware of how his simple funeral mass would remain engraved in the minds of those present. He himself owed a great deal to Monsieur Dior, who had generously bequeathed him a little chapel on the hill above his church, prettily decorated with Renaissance frescoes and the perfect place to rehearse his little choir. His feelings toward Dior were a blend of gratitude and affection. In his long robes, a gift from the deceased, and with his strong local accent, the priest recognized one of his own when he saw him. That is why he insisted on the name Roses and Jasmine for his choir, his pride and joy, in homage to his benefactor who loved flowers so much. For that reason too he himself had supervised the arrangement of red roses, Monsieur Dior's favorite color, around the church choir.

But where to put all these visitors from Paris? According to Catherine Dior and her brother Raymond, there would be around fifty people for the funeral. The priest would have to conduct the whole ceremony outside, in front of the church. He felt intimidated at the thought of them all, not because of who they were — he had no idea — but because of their number. The idea of speaking in front of so many people set him pacing up and down inside his church as he awaited their arrival, his palms a little moist, repeating the phrases he had thought of saying as he went.

The path up to the village was steep, strewn with stones and crisscrossed as much by the wheels of carts as by tire marks. The convoy slowed to a snail's pace; bumper to bumper now, the Cadillacs found the climb heavy going. But they would see it through to the end, to the top of the hill as he had wished, to the final goal of a pilgrimage imposed on them all too soon.

Once they reached the top, the two groups stood apart studying each other, country folk and city folk . . . side by side, but members of two very different worlds. No one knew quite who the "invaders" were, other than that they came from Paris, that place none of the locals would dream of living in. As for the Parisians, they had no desire to find out about the locals.

The only feeling of harmony in the midst of such an improbable gathering came from the scent of pine needles and the throbbing song of the crickets. A rivulet of water trickled as it always did, oblivious of the occasion and the company, from the little well on the village square. The air was pure, the skies high and clear. Dior's friend Henri Sauguet had composed a *Pie Jesu* for the occasion, preceded by the Fauré *Requiem*. Suddenly, death asserted its sway over the bright, serene Provençal countryside, with all its abundance of life. "You feel sorrow, my dear brethren," the priest began. "But remember that if God called Dior to Him, it was because He needed him to dress the angels!"

The group listened in silence. Somehow, as they stood there surrounding Dior's family, the small gathering seemed more detached than it had been at Saint-Honoré d'Eylau. Was it the beauty of the location, the need for silence, the desire to be alone? There was no sense of united purpose, despite the fact that there had been thrown into close proximity people from such different walks of life as Henri Fayol, who represented the great Marcel Boussac, Raymonde and Mitzah and the others, Sauguet and his friends, Jacques Rouët and the timid, somewhat sickly Yves Saint Laurent. Once again it was to each his own and his "own" Christian Dior. And already they were moving on from his death, the event that had touched them so closely for the last few days, moving slowly on to the future, to the great unknown.

A few kilometers away, under the pine trees at the cemetery in

Callian, where Maurice Dior and their faithful Mademoiselle Marthe already lay in peace, at the foot of the family vault protected by its cypresses and crowned by a huge neo-romantic sculpture designed by Christian himself as a tribute to his father, violets in black crepe mingled with the peasants' kerchiefs while Pierre Balmain, who had shared those early years of apprenticeship with Dior at Lelong, read a prayer he had written in memory of his very special colleague.

The heavy coffin in Italian oak was slowly lowered into the grave, crushing the last few lilies of the valley on its way.

This is where I came to finish this story — where I, in turn, have come to collect my thoughts — by the tomb of Christian Dior. After all, he does belong to me too, just a little. I have followed his path all over, traced his steps, what was left, leafed through his photograph album. . . .

I would have liked to go beyond the words to the image, from the written lines to reality. I would like to have seen him just once before I left him, to find a little bit of him, something personal, a tiny souvenir just for me. It is no easy task in a part of the world now ruled by real estate agents and developers. I come across the local priest, the immortal Father Béal in his Christian Dior robes. He has christened the slope between his church and the chapel Christian Dior Hill. A few little houses are dotted up its steep sides. "I live on Christian Dior Hill" . . . would anyone say that? Then there is his grave, a marble slab covered with a floral cross, a little private garden for the man who loved plants so much. Reading the names engraved on the stone — Maurice, Marthe, Christian — I wonder what his father would think now, lover of the business world that he was, on opening his *Figaro* in the morning to check the status of his stocks and seeing a listing for Christian Dior holdings, there alongside some of the biggest names in the stock quotations, names like Michelin or Rhône Poulenc. . . .

Someone has left some fresh flowers there only recently. Their stalks are still damp despite the dry air. It is a simple little rustic bouquet. I don't dare touch it but I go closer and look at it, intrigued by this modest, delicate gesture. I wonder where it came from, what it means. Christian Dior is dead and my search ends here. Then again, standing next to me is Catherine Dior, and in her features I see so much of her brother. She too bears an unfathomable scar, protected by a gaze that gives away nothing of what might be going on in her mind, with the Norman dignity and courage assumed since her earliest childhood and honed by the years of her life. The Rocher des Anglais at Granville, a majestic piece of granite swept by the winds, solid in the face of the trials of time. This is the legacy of a mother whose willpower is traced in the features of her children, a woman who would rather have died than see the family name on a business sign, who would have considered it an embarrassment, a source of social shame. And yet, today the name Christian Dior is the only company on the stock market to bear the name of a couturier. History is thumbing its nose at the woman who drove him and held him back at the same time. Madeleine, lovely Madeleine, would you ever have thought it would come to this?

Callian, August 1994

Acknowledgments

I said at the outset that I wished to thank all those who contributed to this book: former colleagues, friends and relations of Dior, or experts in his field. I cannot list them all here, but their names appear in the "References" section at the end of this book. I would like them, along with the ADACD (AFCDE in English — Association of Former Christian Dior Employees), to know just how grateful I am to them all. I must, however, give very particular thanks to those who made this task possible: Jacques Rouët, whom I have already mentioned, and Catherine Dior, who granted me her trust and allowed me to visit her several times at Callian.

I wish to acknowledge Mr. Bernard Arnault for allowing me access to the archives of the House of Dior without hampering me in the freedom I needed to carry out my task. I would like to thank him here, as I would François Beaufumé, president of Christian Dior Ltd., and Marie-Christine de Sayn-Wittgenstein, head of research and development at Christian Dior Perfumes.

Marika Genty, conservator of the archives at Christian Dior, provided me not only with her knowledge but also with invaluable assistance in writing this book. I thank her for the enjoyable experience that it was to work with her. The same goes for Elisabeth Flory, curator of the Christian Dior exhibition at the Musée des Arts de la Mode in 1987. I must also thank Jean-Luc Dufresne, curator of the Christian Dior museum at Granville.

Among my own friends, I am particularly grateful to Bernard Minoret, who not only opened his library to me but, with it, all the arcana of Paris society and its literary world, of which he is the spiritual choirmaster. Many was the morning when my phone would ring with good news from Bernard, who had found a passage on Dior in whatever he happened to be reading. I must also thank everyone who allowed me to peruse unpublished diaries and correspondence: Brigitte Tortet for her aunt Suzanne Luling's diary, Geneviève Page, who should definitely have the diary of her father, Jacques Bonjean, published — a brilliant piece of writing — and Silvia Laurent Colle and Lina Lachgar for Max Jacob's correspondence.

I also relied on some well-loved resources in the fashion world: Didier Grumbach's *Histoires de la mode* was a great reference and our conversations gave me an insight into the way fashion ticks. I would also like to thank François Baudot, for similar reasons. His columns in *Elle* and his books on art do such a good job of cultivating the essence of things. And I cannot forget my spiritual mothers (in both senses of the expression) Marie-José Lepicart and Alice Morgaine for the part they played as I embarked on this venture.

In preparing my documentation I was assisted by Arnaud de Maurepas from the Sorbonne, who researched aspects of Dior's genealogy and family estate as well as company documents for Christian Dior Ltd. Xavier Narbaits, from *Connaissance des arts,* wrote a piece on the style of Dior's residences. And finally, there is Sonia Rachline from *Vogue* who, in the final phase of the book, was quite simply an indispensable little "star" (to use a Dior-ism).

I am also deeply indebted to Hervé du Périer de Larsan, Marc Bohan, Stanley Garfinkel, and Stanley Marcus.

I decided not to footnote the various sources so as not to disrupt the rhythm I felt necessary to the telling of the Dior story. The bibliography, however, lists all the authors and works cited. I am donating my archives and documentary sources, not all of which I was able to use, to the House of Christian Dior and to the Foundation of the School of Political Science, where he was once a student. I hope that my work might be used for further exploration, given the rich legacy left by Dior, especially with regard to our cultural heritage where he was the first to see commercial potential. For us, the French, that heritage is a past that is full of promise for the future.

Marie-France Pochna

References

Interviews

Alexandre
Bernard Arnault
François Baudot
The Reverend Father Béal
Michel Becquet
Gaston Berthelot
François Bertrand
Marc Bohan
Nicolas Bongard
Marcel Boussac (in 1981)
Michel Brodsky
Art Buchwald
Baron and Baroness Frédéric de Cabrol
Marguerite Carré
Frédéric Castet
Pierre Céleron
Edmonde Charles-Roux
Raphael Cluzel
Marie-Pierre Colle
Silvia Colle
Mr and Mme Jean-Paul Crespelle
Paule Dedeban

Rosine Delamare
Edouard Dermit
Catherine Dior
Mr and Mme Michel Dior
Mme Raymond Dior
Marc Doelnitz
Jean-Claude Donati
Maîtres Eclancher and Diot
Mihri Fenwick
Léonor Fini
Marinette Foy
Jean-Pierre Frère
"Frontinette" Benjamin
Jean-Louis Gaillemin
Odile Gaultier-Voituriez
Tan Giudicelli
Hubert de Givenchy
Gérard Grandval
Bettina Graziani
Jean-Pierre Grédy
René Gruau
Didier Grumbach
Valérie Guillaume
Jacqueline de Guitaut
The Honorable Pamela Harriman,
    the Ambassador of the United States in France
Olivia de Havilland
Pierre Jarry
Zizi Jeanmaire
Claude Joannis
Lina Lachgar
Eleanor Lambert
José Llopis Lamela
Armelle Lamy
Henri Lanfranca
Prince and Princess François de La Tour d'Auvergne
Colette Lebidois

Jeanette Legué
Marie-José Lepicart
André Levasseur
Alexander Liberman
Claude Licard
Patricia Lopez-Willshaw
Suzanne Luling (in 1981)
Jean Marais
Stanley Marcus
Her Royal Highness the Princess Margaret
Bernard Minoret
Alice Morgaine
Anne-Marie Mugnoz
André Ostier
Geneviève Page
Hervé du Périer de Larsan
Pierre Perrotino
Yvonne de Peyerimhoff
Bernard Picot
Mme Porthaut
Viscountess Jacqueline de Ribes
Hélène Rochas
Baroness Liliane de Rothschild
Jacques Rouët
Claude Saint-Cyr
Princess Marie-Christine de Sayn-Wittgenstein
Jean-Louis Scherrer
Marie-Hélène Serreules (de Ganay)
Brigitte Tortet
Denise Tual
Susan Train
Kuniko Tsutsumi
Anne-Marie Vacher
Andrée de Vilmorin
Roger Vivier
Stéphane Wargnier
Micheline Ziegler

I also drew upon interviews made available to me by the House of Christian Dior, conducted by Stanley Garfinkel of the museum at Kent State University in Ohio for his film Completely Dior *in 1989.*

Institutions Consulted for Research

Fashion Institute of Technology, New York
Institut National de l'Audiovisuel, Paris
Library of the Union Française des Arts du Costume, Paris
Musée Christian Dior, Granville
Musée de l'Arsenal, Paris
Musée de la Mode et du Costume, Palais Galliera, Paris
New York Public Library
School of Political Science, Paris

Bibliography

I. By Christian Dior

Je suis couturier. Edited by Elie Rabourdin and Alice Chavane. Paris: Conquistador, 1951. English version: *Talking about fashion.* London: Hutchinson, 1954.

"Voici pourquoi j'ai fait la révolution." Interview by Simone Baron. *Paris-Presse,* August 4, 1953.

Interview. *L'Aurore,* August 1953.

Christian Dior et moi. Paris: Amiot Dumont, 1956. English Version: *Christian Dior and I.* Translated by Antonia Fraser. New York: Dutton, 1957.

Lecture on haute couture given at the Paris Fair, May 31, 1957.

"Les Révolutions dans la couture: Comment on fait la mode." *Le Figaro littéraire,* June 8, 1957.

Lecture given at the Sorbonne, August 5, 1957.

La Cuisine cousue main. Preface by Raymond Thuillier, illustrations by René Gruau, recipes collected by Jacques Rouët. Paris: Christian Dior, 1972.

II. On Christian Dior

de Marly, Diana. *Christian Dior.* New York: Holmes and Meier, 1990.
Dior Story, The. Series in *Women's Wear Daily,* July 1953.

Giroud, Françoise. *Dior.* Translated by Stewart Spence, photographs by Sacha van Dorssen. London: Thames and Hudson, 1987.

Keenan, Brigid. *Dior in Vogue.* Foreword by Margot Fonteyn. New York: Harmony Books, 1981.

Musée des Arts de la Mode. *Hommage à Christian Dior.* Exhibition catalogue. 1987.

Musée Richard Anacréon, Granville. *Christian Dior, l'autre lui-même.* Exhibition catalogue. Published jointly with Les Arts et Culture, Office Culturel de Granville, 1987.

Perreau, Geneviève, ed. *Christian Dior.* Paris: Christian Dior, 1953.

Powerhouse Museum, Sydney, Australia. *Christian Dior: The Magic of Fashion.* Exhibition catalogue. 1994.

III. On Fashion

Ballard, Bettina. *In My Fashion.* New York: David McKay, 1960. For Dior, see pp. 231–248.

Barthes, Roland. *Systèmes de mode.* Paris: Editions du Seuil, 1967.

Beaton, Cecil. *The Glass of Fashion.* London: Cassell, 1954. For Dior, see pp. 247–259: "King Pins and Needles."

Benhaim, Laurence. *Yves Saint Laurent.* Paris: Grasset, 1993.

Bony, Anne. *Les Années 30.* Paris: Editions du Regard, 1982.

——— . *Les Années 40.* Paris: Editions du Regard, 1985.

——— . *Les Années 50.* Paris: Editions du Regard, 1987.

Chapsal, Madeleine. *La Chair de la Robe.* Paris: Fayard, 1989.

Charles-Roux, Edmonde. *Chanel and Her World.* Translated by Dan Wheeler. New York: Vendome, 1981.

Christian Dior Museum, Granville. *Style des années 40.* Exhibition catalogue. June 18–September 24, 1994.

Danziger, James. *Cecil Beaton.* New York: Viking, 1980.

Delbourg-Delphis, Marylène. *Le Chic et le Look.* Paris: Hachette, 1981.

Demornez, Jacqueline. *Balenciaga.* Collection of illustrations by Marie Andrée Jouve. Paris: Editions du Regard, 1988.

François, Lucien. *Comment un nom devient une griffe.* Paris: Gallimard, 1952. For Dior, see pp. 221–229.

Giroud, Françoise. *Françoise Giroud vous présente le Tout-Paris*. Paris: Gallimard, 1952. For Dior, see pp. 71–76.

Grumbach, Didier. *Histoires de la mode*. Paris: Editions du Seuil, 1993.

Guerrand, Jean R. *Souvenirs cousus sellier, un demi-siècle avec Hermès*. Paris: Editions Olivier Orban, 1988.

Guillaume, Valérie. *Jacques Fath*. Paris: Editions Adam Biro, 1994.

Harrison, Martin. *Appearances: Fashion Photography since 1945*. London: Jonathan Cape, 1991.

Laver, James. *Modesty in Dress*. New York: Houghton Mifflin, 1969.

———. *Taste and Fashion*. New York: Dodd, Mead, 1938.

Levin, Phyllis Lee. *Wheels of Fashion*. New York: Doubleday, 1965.

Lipovetsky, Gilles. *The Empire of Fashion*. Translated by Catherine Porter, foreword by Richard Sennett. Princeton: Princeton University Press, 1994.

McDowell, Colin. *McDowell's Directory of Twentieth Century Fashion*. New York: Simon and Schuster, 1985.

Morand, Paul. *L'Allure de Chanel*. Paris: Editions Hermann, 1976.

Mulvagh, Jane. *Vogue History of Twentieth Century Fashion*. New York: Viking, 1988.

Musée de la Mode et du Costume (Galliera Palace), Paris. *Paris couture années 30*. 1987.

Provoyeur, Pierre. *Roger Vivier*. Photography and illustrations by Michel Brodsky. Paris: Editions du Regard, 1991.

Snow, Carmel, with Mary Louise Aswell. *The World of Carmel Snow*. New York: McGraw Hill, 1962.

Veillon, Dominique. *La Mode sous l'Occupation*. Paris: Payot, 1960.

Vreeland, Diana. *D./V.* New York: Alfred A. Knopf, 1984.

IV. On the World of Art and Literature

Alliance Française, New York. *André Ostier*. Exhibition catalogue. 1988.

Andreu, Pierre. *Vie et mort de Max Jacob*. Paris: La Table Ronde, 1982.

Bernier, Olivier. *Fireworks at Dusk: Paris in the Thirties*. Boston: Little, Brown, 1993.

Bonjean, Jacques. Diaries. Collection of Geneviève Page.

Calet, Henri. *Le Croquant indiscret.* Paris: Grasset, 1955.

Ciry, Michel. *Journal: Le Temps des promesses, 1942–1949.* Paris: Plon, 1979. For Dior, see p. 56.

Cocteau, Jean. *Le Passé défini.* Paris: Gallimard, 1985–89. For Dior, see vol. II, 11, 235, 248, 310, 377, and vol. III, 106, 157, 197, 303–304.

Colle, Carmen. *Instant de vie.* Foreword by Lina Lachgar. Paris: Editions du Saule, forthcoming.

Dalí, Salvador. *Diary of a Genius.* New York: Prentice Hall, 1986.

Doelnitz, Marc. *La Fête à Saint-Germain-des-Près.* Paris: Robert Laffont, 1979. For Dior, see pp. 84, 157, 1580.

Dubois, André-Louis. *Sous le signe de l'Amitié.* Paris: Plon, 1972. For Dior, see p. 126.

de Faucigny-Lucinge, Jean-Louis. *Legendary Parties.* Foreword by Brooke Astor. New York: Vendome, 1987.

——— . *Un Gentilhomme cosmopolite.* Paris: Perrin, 1990.

de Fouquières, André. *Mon Paris et ses Parisiens.* Vol. I. Paris: Editions Pierre Horay, 1953. For Dior, see p. 87.

Etherington-Smith, Meredith. *Dalí.* London: Sinclair-Stevenson, 1992.

Green, Julien. *Oeuvres.* "La Pléiade" edition. Vol. IV. Paris: Gallimard, 1975. For Dior, see pp. 83, 90–91.

Heymann, C. David. *Poor Little Rich Girl.* New York: Simon and Schuster, 1983.

Jacob, Max. *Lettres de Max Jacob à Pierre Colle.* Foreword by Silvia Colle, annotations by Lina Lachgar. Paris: Editions Rougerie, forthcoming. For Dior, see letters of December 20, 1935, and July 10, 1936.

Jullian, Philippe. *Dictionnaire du snobisme.* Paris: Plon, 1958. For Dior, see p. 119.

Kihm, Jean-Jacques, Elisabeth Sprigge, and Henri C. Behar. *Cocteau, l'homme et les miroirs.* Paris: La Table Ronde, 1968. For Dior, see p. 243.

Kochno, Boris. *Christian Bérard.* Paris: Herscher, 1987.

Luling, Suzanne. Diaries. Collection of Brigitte Tortet.

Maxwell, Elsa. *R.S.V.P.: Elsa Maxwell's Own Story.* Boston: Little, Brown, 1954.

Mitford, Nancy. *The Letters of Nancy Mitford.* Edited by Charlotte Mosley. London: Hodder and Stoughton, 1993. For Dior, see p. 217.

Oberlé, Jean. *La Vie d'artiste.* Paris: Denoël, 1956.

Raczymow, Henri. *Maurice Sachs.* Paris: Gallimard, 1988.

Radiguet, Raymond. *Count d'Orgel.* Translated by Violet Schiff. New York: Grove, 1953, 1969.

Riva, Maria. *Marlene Dietrich.* New York: Alfred A. Knopf, 1993.

Rorem, Ned. *Paris and New York Diaries, 1951–1961.* San Francisco: North Point Press, 1983.

Sachs, Maurice. *Witches' Sabbath.* Translated by Richard Howard. London: Jonathan Cape, 1964.

———. *Au temps du Boeuf-sur-le-Toit.* Paris: Grasset, 1987. For Dior, see pp. 207, 253, 365.

Sauguet, Henri. *La Musique, ma vie.* Paris: Librairie Séguier, 1990. For Dior, see pp. 207, 253, 365.

Stein, Gertrude. *The Autobiography of Alice B. Toklas.* New York: Random House, 1993.

Thomson, Virgil. *Virgil Thomson.* New York: Alfred A. Knopf, 1966. For Dior, see pp. 145, 285.

Tual, Denise. *Au coeur du temps.* Paris: Carrère, 1987. For Dior, see pp. 249–251, 287, 299, 310, 313, 316–317, 352, 364.

Tyler, Parker. *The Divine Comedy of Pavel Tchelitchev.* London: Weidenfeld and Nicolson, 1969. For Dior, see pp. 60, 62, 649.

Audiovisual Sources

Christian Dior. Franck Maubert. Canal Plus, 1994.

Christian Dior Story. 16 mm, 12 min. Lavorell, 1950.

Completely Dior. Stanley Garfinkel. 1989.

Person to Person. Interview with Dior by Edward R. Murrow. 16 mm, 10 min. CBS, 1955.

Portrait de Christian Dior 40ème anniversaire. Transatlantic Video (INA), 1987.

Index